ROD CALBRADE

1   British Flies
tied by Ron Broughton

Apple Green	Blue Dun	Grey Duster	Howe's Special	John Storey
Hare's Ear Gold Head*	Pheasant Tail Nymph	Sawyer's Killer Bug	Olive Shrimp	
Bradshaw's Fancy	Foster's Bumble	Grayling Steel Blue	Red Tag	Grayling Witch
Partridge & Orange	Partridge & Red	Snipe & Purple	Water-hen Boa	Woodcock & Hare's Lug
B.P. Fly	Fog Black	Griffith's Gnat	Jackson's Blue Midge	Stewart's Black Spider
Adjutant Blue	Brookes's Fancy	Grayling Black & Red	Gold-ribbed Hare's Ear	Jim Wynn's Winter Brown

* Malcolm Greenhalgh

2 Scandinavian Flies

Swedish
tied by Lars Olsson

Black Bibio	Gim River Fly	Olive Mallard Dun	Sedge Pupa
Green Caddis Worm	Copper-ribbed Hare's Ear	Squirrel Sedge	

Danish & Norwegian
tied by Hans van Klinken

Para-ant	Wet Ant	Crazy Sedge	Culard
Caseless Caddis	Hodal Emerger No.1	Hodal Emerger No.2	
Klinkhammer Special	Once & Away	Leadhead	

3   Austrian, French and Dutch Flies

Austrian
from Michael Hofmaier

Buck Caddis	Diptera	Dun	Humpy

French
tied by M. Bresson, M. Devaus & M. Guy Plas. Specimens given by Raymond Rocher

La Loue	La Favorite	Gloire de Neublans	Jean Marie de Devaux	Jeck Sedge de Devaux
Cul de Canard de Bresson	Tinsel de Bresson	Peute de Bresson	Bécasse de Devaux	Caenis
Tricolore	Guy Plas Incomparable (39H16)	Guy Plas Emergant (48H16)	Guy Plas Thyma Tag (109H18)	Guy Plas Caddis Nymph

Dutch
tied by F.H.J Von Der Assen

Frutsels:

Black	Coachman	Green	Iron Blue

ROD CALBRADE

4 Welsh, North American (Canadian) and Russian Flies

Welsh
tied by Ron Broughton

Colonel's Game Pie Nymph	Droitwich	Grizzly Bourne	William Rufus	Y Diawl Bach*

North American (Canadian)
tied by Patrick Michiel

Renegade   Tom Thumb

Polish
tied by S. Clios

Three woven nymphs

Russian
given by Rod Calbrade

Pheasant Tail Nymph	Klinkhammer Special	Olive Hare's Ear Gold Head	Goddard's Mating Shrimp

* Louis Noble

5   Jennifer Olsson fishing the Idsjöströmmen, Sweden, with her split cane rod – the 'Jennifer Olsson mayfly rod'

LARS OLSSON

6   The River Agger near Cologne, Germany

ROB THOMAS

RON BROUGHTON

7   The Upper Wharfe after a flood above Buckden

SYLVAIN DURAND

8   Arctic grayling (*Thymallus arcticus*) from the Russian far east

9   European grayling (*Thymallus thymallus*) from the
Idsjöströmmen, Sweden

LARS OLSSON

10   Primitive whitefish from Alberta, Canada, illustrating its striking similarity to a grayling

11   Reg Righyni trotting a float in the River Braan at its
entrance to the River Tay at Dunkeld

12   The Welsh Dee at Carrog

The Complete Book of the Grayling

The Complete Book
of the
Grayling

RONALD BROUGHTON

ROBERT HALE · LONDON

© *Ronald Broughton, 1989, 2000*
First published in Great Britain 1989 in an earlier
edition as Grayling: The Fourth Game Fish

ISBN 0 7090 6423 3

Robert Hale Limited
Clerkenwell House
Clerkenwell Green
London EC1R 0HT

2 4 6 8 10 9 7 5 3 1

Typeset in 11/13 Classical Garamond by
Derek Doyle & Associates, Liverpool.
Printed in China through
Bookbuilders , Hong Kong

This book is dedicated to The Grayling Society

The river walks in the valley singing
Letting her veils blow . . .

(Ted Hughes: 'Torridge')

Contents

Acknowledgements

I AM GRATEFUL to Eric Restall for his introduction to the publisher, John Hale. This came through a contribution that he requested from me for the revision of *The Encyclopaedia of Fly Fishing* by Conrad Voss Bark and himself, and he encouraged me to consider a revision of my own book.

I should like to thank the original authors for their revisions and advice, and the photographers whose works grace the earlier book, some of whom have supplied new photographs.

The original chapters, many of which have been revised, are still highly relevant, and I am grateful that they could be republished. With considerable sadness, I had to seek permission for the republication of Dr Michael Hofmaier's chapter from his widow.

The new chapters come from a group of distinguished writers and fishermen, who merit considerable gratitude for their excellent work and for the examples of and tying instructions for artificial flies relevant to the new areas. I thank them too for the up-to-date information on where anglers can find help in organizing fishing expeditions on the continent. My thanks to Rod Calbrade for the new photographs of artificial flies, and to Ross Gardiner for organizing the group photograph of several grayling, to Raymond Rocher and to Simon Brown for the jacket illustrations, and to all the suppliers of new photographs and to those whose original photographs still grace the new edition.

To Margaret for her unfailing help and encouragement, to my good friends who have contributed so effectively, to my publisher John Hale and his staff for their patience and good advice, my most grateful thanks.

Preface

A FURTHER TEN years on and my friends again have given generous help in revising and expanding the first edition of *Grayling, the Fourth Game Fish*. It might well be expected that those who are interested in the study of, preservation of and angling for grayling would belong to The Grayling Society, which internationally cares for this fish, and that they would provide the writers and photographers that create this book. Indeed, most of them do. Knowledge of the fish grows apace, and what has changed out of all recognition is the status of the grayling in anglers' eyes. This is mainly due to the work of The Grayling Society and its offspring, the Grayling Research Trust formed the better to attract funds and encourage scientific study. It is becoming evident that throughout Europe angling groups concerned with the conservation of this fish are finding attitudes of contempt towards grayling similar to those in Britain twenty years ago that caused the creation of an international conservation society that has been well placed to assist those eager to conserve, study and angle for this delightful game fish.

So it is a good time to review and republish this book. Happily, the present publishers, Robert Hale, have allowed me to recruit more experts so as to expand it to cover rivers and areas not previously touched, giving a better representation of the territory of the fish throughout the Northern Hemisphere.

Ronald Broughton

Introduction

IT WAS JUST as I was coming to the end of a series of reviews of books written solely on grayling, that it was suggested that I edit a definitive book on the grayling. Because I was full, or perhaps overfull, of the writings of seven authors who had studied the ways of this fish in great detail and who gave freely of their unique personal relationship with rivers and fishing, I was extremely doubtful that I had any original observations or thoughts that could be of any interest to my fellow anglers.

When I thought of these authors whom I had come to know so well – Pritt with his magnificent *Book of the Grayling* and Roberts with the most recent works; from the slight volume of Richard Lake and Richard Woolley to the compendium of Carter Platts, from the delightful, idiosyncratic Reg Righyni to Rolt's curiosity about southern stream grayling – one thing stood out like the proverbial sore thumb: that apart from Charles Ritz, they were all English authors talking of the British experience. Further, not only was each book a record of one man's considered opinion, but apart from John Roberts they wrote at a time when there was no organized body of anglers who were concerned to preserve, to gather and to disseminate knowledge about grayling. They were single voices crying out in a chorus of prejudices and ignorance about one of the world's great game fish, the grayling.

It was thus that the form of this book virtually decided itself. All that remained was to gather together from all my good friends a small group who would have knowledge of other methods and other places as well as of those already written about. Inevitably most would come from within the membership of The Grayling Society, and perhaps those who were not could be persuaded to give the weight of their erudition and interest to a book that would be dedicated to that society. My food friends did not fail me, and I feel myself honoured to have been the cause of their coming together to form the original book and this present one.

There is a growing interest in the grayling as a worthy quarry in its own right, and there is little that has been written in its disfavour. Indeed, all literature, at least up to 1930, equates with zest the capture of both trout and grayling within the same book. It was probably the first Freshwater Act of 1878 that separated the two species, for, as the grayling spawned at the other side of the coldest months from the rest of the Salmonidae, it was ignorantly classified with the coarse-fish group of freshwater fish. Halford considered it an enhancement to any trout stream, even prolonging the season of fly-fishing. Skues, though he boasted of his larger fish, was not so sure.

There is no doubt in the minds of anglers in the south-west or in the north, from the Welsh Borders to the Yorkshire and Derbyshire Dales, and an increasing number who fish the chalk streams, as to the true worth of this noble fish. From somewhere about late July, right through the autumn, well into the winter and early spring when the dark Olive appears again, the grayling is a fish fit to be hunted and taken. I have known it to be taken on fly whatever the season, and on one cold February day Reg Righyni and I had a dozen fish from the top of the River Hodder, mainly on small dark flies.

It is this ability for specific feeding and quick rejection of the artificial fly through the coldest weathers that makes it such a fascinating and admirable quarry. There is great skill too in 'trotting' the worm, requiring fine tackle and delicacy of touch. I have taken fish this way when the river was all but frozen right over, there being a clear line of water where the strongest current lay. Those grayling that escaped did so by diving under the ice and shedding the hook in one swift movement. Those that I captured slid over the ice and were deep frozen by the time I picked them up. I have even had grayling on large flies when sea trouting in the dark of a summer's night. I do not mind them coming thus any more than I resent a greedy trout in the same circumstance. They fight as hard as a sea trout of a similar size, and though during the day one can tell by their action what sort of fish one has on the hook, at night they seem not to use their large dorsal fin and it is often impossible to tell what fish one has on until it is safely in the net.

Devoted fly-fisher though I am, my curiosity of other methods leads me to try all forms of legitimate fishing, and I find on occasion considerable satisfaction in fishing with a small gilt-tail, a barbless size 16 hook and a 2-pound breaking-strain line, on a cold day with clear water and the Ariel quietly ticking away.

Some people fish the hard way. I have never had to sleep out with a rifle by my side in case a brown bear wanted to share my sleeping-bag, nor fished amongst the high mountains of Scandinavia or in the deep valleys of Yugoslavia. It is fascinating in how many places grayling are to be found throughout the Northern Hemisphere, and to what lengths the intrepid angler will go to find his quarry.

Who would not praise the Umber, the grey shadow that will live and feed in the fast streams in summer and that will descend to the deep pools in winter? Fattest and most active in early autumn, by the time the trout have sensibly gone to their spawning becks, the grayling feeds on in seasonable time, responsive to the shafts of sunlight and sporadic hatches of fly. That is the time, the time of still days and high cold skies, of dew-wet spiders' webs and bare trees. Even the days of blustery showers and swollen rivers give their sport, and the year is never entirely empty of willing fish.

These fish are not for those who would have 'instant' fish, the sorry gargantuan stockies fed in ponds and put into the river to be instantly removed. No river should be swept clean at the year's end so that innocents may be introduced for the opening day. Angling has to do with wild, crafty, difficult fish and with the pollution-free waters of goodly flow in which they can prosper. To catch a grayling you must serve an apprenticeship and gain experience, meet disappointment, and discourse on your failures as well as your triumphs with your fellow anglers. Never will you regret the time spent in learning to capture this most magnificent of wild game fish, for it will be spent in the best school of all, the riverside.

It was the love of the grayling that led that most thoughtful angler, Reg Righyni, to consider a Society for its protection. He gathered around him a small group of his friends of like mind and, with an unending flow of enthusiasm and ideas, persuaded us to make his vision a reality.

A Chairman was chosen from amongst us and I was given the task of translating the idea into a complete and working entity. Norman Roose, who was to become our first President, was asked to provide a set of Rules and Regulations, and these have served us well, requiring very little modification as time has gone by. Later I was able to shed two large areas of responsibility when David Liversedge became Secretary, and when Barry Lloyd became the first of our long line of Editors. The committee was like any other fishing committee that I have ever chaired, dedicated, sensible and imbued with great enthusiasm. They were exciting days and culminated in the first meeting in the winter of 1977–8 in Eccles in Manchester.

The Society was formed from the beginning as the definitive international society on grayling. Its aims are to gather and disseminate knowledge of this fish, to protect it from the destructive effects of abstraction, pollution and extermination by netting, to share knowledge of old and new skills for its legitimate capture and, above all, to make known that we recognize it to be a game fish of the salmon family.

To this end the Society has been based on local branches, the central committee being concerned with general finances and the dissemination of information to the members, and communication with the branches outside the British Isles. An erudite and interesting journal is provided twice a year along with a bi-yearly newsletter, and a presence at all major Game Shows is being developed. The Annual General Meeting is held at a different place each year, and is accompanied by a day filled with speakers of note and topped with a dinner in the evening. The weekend would not be complete without the following day's fishing, arranged by the local group.

The Society is nearing its twenty-fifth anniversary and is steadily growing in numbers and influence. A few years ago it was thought necessary to form a separate Trust the better to attract funds from outside the Society to aid and further the scientific study of the fish and its surrounding. This in no way detracts from the recordings of the observations of the members and it is now becoming necessary to consider a safe place for the storing of the archives of the Society.

Despite the success of the original book, its restricted scope, the ever-changing world of angling techniques and equipment, and the advance of scientific knowledge, required a new approach. This new approach would not have been possible without the help of many members, and it is therefore only right that this volume should be dedicated to The Grayling Society.

The Origins and Present Distribution of Grayling

Ross Gardiner

GRAYLING ARE AN important group of salmonids. They are closely related to whitefish (the earliest branch of living salmonids) and, like them, have large scales. A key distinguishing feature of grayling is their large sail-like dorsal fin, not possessed by whitefish. The close relationship of grayling to whitefish is well-illustrated by their striking similarity in appearance (apart from the dorsal fin) and behaviour between a grayling and one of the most primitive whitefish – *Prosopium williamsoni*, the mountain whitefish – that still survives today in the Rocky Mountains of North America.

A number of species of grayling live in the rivers and lakes of Europe, Asia and North America between latitudes of about 40°N and 70°N. All are quite similar in appearance and are classified in a single genus, *Thymallus*. All are cool-water fish requiring average summer water temperatures less that 18°C and maximum water temperatures less than 24°C. Perhaps surprisingly, they are reasonably tolerant of low oxygen levels. As would be expected, the more southerly sites are at high altitudes. They are often locally abundant, but, because of their sensitivity to pollution, they are now rare or extinct in certain areas where they were once the dominant species. They do not occur in the Southern Hemisphere.

The classification of grayling into species is not yet totally agreed among scientists. The present consensus view is that there are two species with extensive ranges – the European grayling *Thymallus thymallus* and the Arctic grayling *Thymallus arcticus* – and one species, the Mongolian grayling *Thymallus brevirostris*, which is restricted to the Altai Mountains. Some of the other forms of 'Arctic grayling' occurring to the south of their range in Asia may also be sufficiently distinct to justify species status. The distribution of the various species is mapped in Fig. 1 (the map does not show areas where the range of grayling has been extended by stocking).

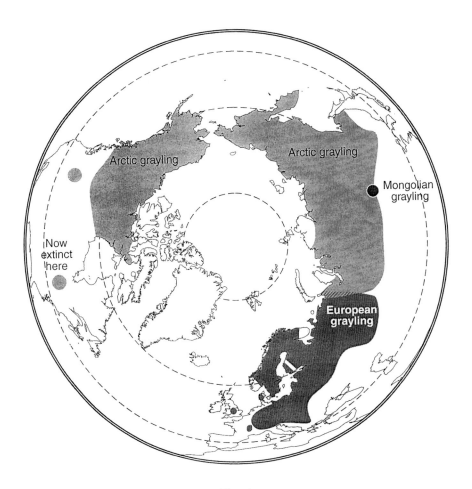

Fig. 1

European grayling *Thymallus thymallus*

This is a species of the central and northern countries of Europe, found mainly in rivers but also with populations in cold lakes. The lake populations often, but not always, depend on streams to provide spawning and nursery areas. Within the rivers where grayling are found such factors as current speed, the suitability of the bed for spawning and the depth and degree of pollution determine whether a particular stretch of stream is favourable for grayling. The slopes of rivers of different widths determine to a large extent current speed and bed type and are the best simple measures of likely suitability of riverine environments. For a small river of 20 metres wide, the most favourable gradient is two to six metres per kilometre. This gives moderate current speeds and many pools. Where grayling are present they are frequently the dominant species of fish in rivers of this sort.

In France, the grayling's native range is the Rhône, Rhine and Loire basins, and it is exclusively a river fish – a population which inhabited Lake Geneva having died out. Populations which occurred in Pyrenean streams are also now extinct. France lies at the edge of the grayling's range, and it has proved difficult to re-establish grayling in streams from which they have been lost or to establish them in new streams. The fish is not found in Spain, although there is a recent report of an attempt to introduce it. The species was introduced to lakes in the Atlas Mountains in North Africa, but failed to establish itself. Further east, it occurs in rivers in countries that include Germany, Switzerland, Austria, Northern Italy, Slovenia, Croatia, Poland and the Czech Republic. It is also present in a number of Alpine lakes.

The grayling has a toehold in Belgium, Luxembourg and Holland, while in Denmark it occurs naturally in four rivers in Western Jutland, and successful introductions have been made to other rivers. It is found in many rivers and lakes in Norway, Finland and Sweden. In Russia it is found east as far as the Urals and the upper catchment of the River Volga (where it has been adversely affected by the construction of man-made lakes); it is not found in the Dnieper catchment.

European grayling from the River Eden, England

LARS OLSSON

In Great Britain, the grayling's natural distribution is very localised – in the River Ouse, the River Trent, and their tributaries, and possibly the Hampshire Avon and the Rivers Severn, Wye, Thames, Ribble and Welsh Dee. The populations in many other British grayling rivers, such as the River Test and rivers in the south of Scotland, are the result of successful introductions, particularly last century. In Britain the species is found in only a few lakes, such as Llyn Tegid in Wales and Gouthwaite Reservoir in England. It does not occur in Ireland.

Arctic grayling *Thymallus arcticus*

This is a species closely similar to the European grayling, and is found in North America and Asia.

In North America, grayling are indigenous to northern Manitoba, Saskatchewan, Alberta, British Columbia, the Northwest Territories, the Yukon and most of Alaska. They occur in rivers, but many of the populations are associated with lakes, including the huge Great Bear and Great Slave Lakes. Isolated populations occurred in Michigan and, at a high altitude, in Montana, but the Michigan population is extinct and the Montana population is now limited to a few lakes and streams. Reasons given for the demise of grayling in these areas include unsympathetic management of timber, grazing and irrigation (which allow muddying and warming of the water and silting of spawning beds), overfishing and the species' inability, at the edge of its range, to cope with exotic salmonids. All these factors may have been involved. The decline in Michigan was dramatic. From being abundant there last century, with a town named after them, grayling had become totally extinct in this area by the 1930s. Nonetheless, successful introductions have been made in Vermont, Colorado, Wyoming, Idaho, Utah and California; although introductions to the mountains of New Mexico were unsuccessful.

In Asia, Arctic grayling are found from the Urals east to Kamchatka and the Bering Strait. There are none in Japan.

Although for a time there was doubt as to whether the closely similar looking Arctic and European grayling should truly be considered separate species, more recent evidence appears to confirm the traditional view. Where their ranges overlap in the Urals, the genetic differences between the types are reportedly sufficient to prevent hybridisation, despite their closely similar ecology and willingness to pair.

18

Arctic grayling

Mongolian grayling *Thymallus brevirostris*

Although the grayling *Thymallus articus* occurs widely in Mongolia, except in the desert south, the name Mongolian grayling is reserved for those found only in a localised area of landlocked basins in the extreme west of Mongolia and, perhaps, the adjacent area of Russia. This particular fish has an unusually large mouth for a grayling, and well-developed teeth, and reaches a very large size (5 kg). It is sufficiently different to be universally accepted as an independent species.

Other possible grayling species

Various other grayling found towards the south of their range in Asia are also sufficiently different in appearance to be considered independent species by some workers. These include:

- The grayling found in Lake Baykal in Russia. These have smallish scales and a smallish dorsal fin. There are two types: the shallow-water,

19

strongly coloured Baykal black grayling, and the greyish-coloured, deep-water Baykal white grayling.

- The grayling of the Amur catchment on the borders of Russia and China. This is a brightly coloured river grayling with an unusually large dorsal fin. It is also found in North Korea in the River Yalu, which runs into the Yellow Sea.

- A small dark-coloured grayling, reaching a maximum length of only about 30 centimetres, found in Lake Hövsgöl in Mongolia.

So, how did these various graylings get to where we now find them? The present range must be a result of where grayling first evolved and how they spread from there. Fossils of grayling and their relatives the trout, salmon, charr and whitefish are rare because these fish have habitats that are not conducive to fossil formation. Nonetheless, there are some fossils and also many other clues – such as the habitat requirements of present-day grayling, the degrees of difference between grayling found in different areas, and the geological history of the areas where they are found.

The diverse types of grayling in central Asia suggest a long and complex history there. Whether the origins of the genus lie in that area or elsewhere, it must have spread from its ancestral roots to the present wide distribution. However, paradoxically, present-day grayling seem to be poor colonisers of new waters. Even minor rapids and falls have frequently prevented the further spread of populations of grayling introduced to new rivers in Britain in the last century and, despite the amply demonstrated ease with which grayling were successfully introduced into some new British rivers, natural colonisations of adjacent river systems have not occurred.

What then could have been the conditions to allow grayling to spread so widely? For the explanation we must look to the last 2½–3 million years, when, in a unique epoch in geological time known as the Pleistocene, average global temperatures cooled and great ice sheets repeatedly developed during cold periods (the glacials) and then receded during shorter periods of warmer climate (the interglacials). The cycles of ice advance and recession are taking place every 100,000 years. At times ice sheets developed to cover nearly one-third of the earth's land surface, including Canada, much of the northern USA, northern Europe, Britain (south to almost London) and north-west Siberia. At these times sea levels were more than 100 metres lower than in the present interglacial owing to the locking up of water as ice.

Such ice sheets eliminate all aquatic life from the areas they occupy and lead to isolated pockets of fish in so-called refuges. During periods of climate warming and recession of the ice, recolonisation of areas by grayling and rapid and extensive colonisation of new areas would have been aided by an abundance of meltwater and extensive river networks with changing drainage patterns. Temporary freshwater bridges could have formed between adjacent rivers, if channelled by pack ice or over lowlands exposed by the low sea levels. Coastal spread in cold water may also have been a mechanism – brackish water being tolerated by both present-day European and Arctic grayling in the far north.

The distribution pattern and the uniformity in the characteristics of the European grayling over much of Europe, along with the geological history of the area, is consistent with dispersal from a refuge in the Danube basin being of great importance. For a time the upper courses of what would later become the Rhine and Rhône flowed into the Danube. As climate was warming at the end of the last glacial, Britain was still joined to the continent, and rivers of the east coast of England could have been colonised then via a common mainstream shared with the Rhine.

Similarly, much of the present distribution pattern, and the patterns of variation in physical characteristics (such as scale counts and the size and colour of the dorsal fin) of Arctic grayling in North America and a large part of Asia, is consistent with dispersal from two refuges, one in the area of the Bering Land Bridge (which, until relatively recently, linked the two continents) and another in the Mississippi–Missouri basin. For much of the Pleistocene period what are now Asia and North America were joined by an extensive land bridge – at times 1,000 km wide, north to south – and rivers now isolated on the two continents were headwaters of common Beringian mainstems. The close similarities in fish of various species on either side suggest that the Bering Strait has caused few problems in the dispersal of fish. Further south, the isolated Montana and Michigan populations would have arisen as warmer conditions caused fish to be lost from low altitudes at the south of the range (consistent with this is the occurrence of fossil Arctic grayling in adjacent areas where they now no longer occur, such as south-east Illinois). However, several of the types of grayling found at the south of their range in Asia are sufficiently different to suggest that they have had a long period of isolation and were a result of earlier colonisations sufficiently south to have survived many or all of the colder periods.

New genetics techniques, particularly those based on analyses of DNA samples, are presently allowing rapid progress towards establishing how closely different animal and plant forms are related, and how they should best be classified, both within and between species. Suitable samples are easy to collect, although sophisticated methods of analysis are required.

The methods may also be used on stored specimens in museums. Comprehensive work has yet to be carried out on grayling, although there are now some studies in progress. In the next few years, the systematics and history of the various graylings should become much clearer. Watch this space!

Grayling in the Chalk Streams

Robin Mulholland

IT IS SURPRISING that, although the chalk streams of the south of England provide extremely good grayling fishing, there is no great tradition of angling for them, as there is in Yorkshire and elsewhere in the north of England. As a result, the literature of the chalk streams has dealt with the grayling in passing, rather than as a sporting fish in its own right. The exception to this is Rolt's book, *Grayling Fishing in South Country Streams*. Even Frank Sawyer, who has perhaps had a greater influence on grayling fishing in this area than anyone else, deals with them as incidental to the trout, and his expertise was developed from a perceived need to reduce the population in his river. The enjoyment which he clearly obtained from fishing for them was, partly at least, a result of the contrast they provided to the rather easy stocked trout.

The grayling is widely distributed throughout the chalk streams, and all those I know support healthy populations. The **Kennet**, one of the best mixed fisheries in the country, has grayling as far down as Thatcham. The upper Kennet, particularly the Hungerford area, is mentioned frequently in the literature and appears to have had a healthy population for as long as anyone can remember. Although the Piscatorial Society had the Chamberhouse Farm waters below Newbury for a very long time, there was no mention of grayling in their early minutes. Trout, perch, pike and barbel appear to have been their favourite quarries, and whether there were many grayling in the years from 1900 to 1970 is difficult to determine. There is now a very large and thriving population, however, including some very big fish. It has been suggested that this is largely or partly the result of the perch disease: the decline in perch numbers leading to an explosion in numbers of grayling and dace. This appears logical and could well be true. Chamberhouse Farm seems to be the lower limit for Kennet grayling; the water quality downstream deteriorates to the point where it no longer appears to be acceptable to the fish.

23

DERMOT WILSON

Dermot Wilson on the Piscatorial Society's waters on the Itchen

The Kennet's main tributary, the Lambourn, also has good grayling. My experience of this river is limited to one stretch immediately upstream of Newbury and I always felt that the ecology of that particular fishery was fragile. The trout were often lean, in spite of good mayfly, and the breeding success of the grayling seemed to be erratic. Frank Sawyer describes his attempts at grayling fishing on the Lambourn with Howard Marshall and other owners in *Nymphs and the Trout*. He writes of old male fish, in poor condition and with empty stomachs, which he could only catch with a snare.

The **Avon**, in its middle and upper reaches, supports a huge population of grayling which used to be seriously affected by electro-fishing but, in this more enlightened age, has been allowed to settle down and find its own level. The effect of the electro-fishing was twofold: it brought the pike population under control (which in turn probably helped the grayling population), but it also removed the majority of the larger grayling, and as a consequence the population was made up largely of fish 1+ years old, weighing 300–500 grammes. These fish escape the nets of the electro-fishers in October, at around five months old, and survive for another twelve months before being removed the following winter. In spite of what man has done to them in the past, it is apparent that the Avon is well suited to grayling as are its tributaries the Wylye, the Nadder and the Ebble.

The Wylye I know well, and, as there are virtually no pike in the middle and upper reaches, it has been possible to avoid electro-fishing in these areas. The result is that in the Piscatorial Society fisheries from Stockton up to Heytesbury there is a normal population which has only been exploited by angling in a very sympathetic manner. Spawning seems to be consistently successful, and, although the fish are more obvious than the trout (they lie out in the open), there are rather more trout than grayling. The two populations seem to strike a good balance which produces a most acceptable fishery. During the many dry years that have occurred between 1988 and 1998 it has been interesting to observe that the ratio of trout to grayling has become almost one to one. During these years there has been very little recruitment of trout from the main spawning winterbournes, and the absence of water crowfoot in some stretches has clearly been of benefit to the grayling, with its shoaling habit (heavy swan grazing of the water crowfoot has also helped the grayling rather than the trout).

In recent years I have fished the middle **Test** occasionally and the upper Test on a regular basis. On the middle Test many fisheries still remove grayling, and heavy stocking of large brown trout and rainbows precludes any development of balanced populations. However the grayling still survive, in spite of man's best efforts to get rid of them, and could provide some very high-quality fly fishing if treated with more sympathy. On the upper Test they stand a rather better chance of being left in peace, and certainly on the water which I fish are regarded as important.

To almost everyone's surprise the upper **Itchen** has received a population of grayling, and the species is now firmly established throughout that river. It would appear that there was an introduction of grayling to a lake in the top of the Itchen catchment, and the fish spread from the lake into the river and thence downstream to link up with existing populations in the middle and lower river. Where I fish at Abbotsworthy there are certainly more grayling than there were previously. In the previous edition of this book I wrote of a peculiar barrier which existed on the Itchen, above which there were no grayling. What has become apparent, following this introduction of the species to the upper river, is that the barrier was probably man-made and was almost certainly a hatch; grayling are known not to be very good at passing upstream over obstacles. (The likelihood of the Itchen barrier being a hatch or something similar is supported by the spread of grayling throughout the upper Wylye following the removal of many of the hatches during the 1960s.)

ROBIN MULHOLLAND

Nicky Mulholland waiting for a grayling rise on the River Test, Leckford

Moving further afield, the **Tees** – in the years up to 1967, when I fished it on a regular basis – had very few grayling above Whorlton, where there is a small waterfall and above which there are a number of other small falls. Having returned to the river in the 1990s I find grayling as far upstream as Newbiggin, probably introduced by man above the many small obstacles and able to spread downstream. The Wharfe also has a number of water-falls which become serious obstacles to the easy spread of the species. This inability to surmount comparatively small obstacles explains many of the peculiarities surrounding the distribution of grayling in this country.

The **Dorset** chalk streams also support good grayling populations. The Frome has some big fish, and I have seen them in the tiny river Fontmell, a tributary of the Dorset Stour.

On all of these streams the fish seem to reach a mature size of 700–900 grammes, and very few exceed this. Taking the natural population of the Wylye as my example (and from what I know of the Avon, Itchen and Test, they are similar), there are numbers of fish up to 900 grammes or 40 centimetres, but very few fish which reach one kilogram, or even two pounds. This mature weight is reached at about four years of age.

Dr Anton Ibbotson of the Institute of Freshwater Ecology is currently two years into a study, funded in part by The Grayling Research Trust, enti-tled 'Year Class Strengths and Recruitment in a Grayling Population'. This is already producing some interesting and useful data. The study is using the Piscatorial's fisheries on the Wylye, and the sampling and measuring carried out so far support the concept of fast-growing, short-lived populations in the chalk streams. Of 543 fish measured and scale-sampled in 1998, only 25 were 4+ years old, and of those only 6 were 5+. Judging by the list of large grayling caught over the years, the Frome may differ slightly. Sampling by electro-fishing on the other chalk streams supports this picture of age distribution, and it is apparent that record-breaking grayling are unlikely to be caught in a chalk stream (unless it be the Frome).

Certainly until 1939, and to a degree since, the majority of chalk-stream anglers fished only the cream of the season, May and June, after which they went off to fish for salmon or sea trout. There were exceptions (Skues and Howard Marshall spring to mind), keen and knowledgeable anglers who fished for the whole season, but I am convinced that the majority approach had a major effect upon attitudes to grayling and the lack of interest in them as a sporting fish. During the height of the trout season they are a nuisance, rising fairly freely to the heavy spring hatches of olives and iron blues and occasionally committing suicide during the mayfly. The larger fish are not at their best at this time, and as a result the general run of chalk-stream fisherman never saw the grayling in its winter glory.

It is from September onwards that they begin to show their real virtues, and the angler who pursues them quickly realises that he is fishing for truly wild fish. When they are rising to surface fly they are usually very specific, and an effective imitation is needed to deceive them. At that time of year small flies are needed. The naturals available are reed smuts, *caenis*, small olives and even smaller pale wateries. When the hatches of *Ephemeroptera* are heavy the grayling can be caught on the popular dry patterns, such as the Beacon Beige and the Tup's Indispensable. When they are concentrating on very small stuff, such as reed smuts and *caenis*, then deception is more difficult. Grey Dusters in the smallest size, Black Gnat patterns and the Janus (a fore-and-aft fly) with cocked up tails, which are probably seen as wings, are likely to be needed. A fine point is required with such small flies, and the recent developments in double-strength nylons, copolymers and fluorocarbons have something to offer. The use of a fine point is a feasible proposition because, unlike trout, grayling do not head for the weed when hooked, and it is possible to fish for them with points of one kilogram breaking strain or less. As the shoal often lies out in shallow water, the use of a long leader is also an advantage. The chalk streams are at their lowest levels in the autumn; frequently the sun is bright, and the fish are easily disturbed by line and cast flashing overhead.

DERMOT WILSON

Dermot Wilson and Frank Sawyer discussing flies

Herl-bodied flies are successful on the chalk streams, just as they are every-where else. Rolt developed his Witch on the Wylye as both a trout and a grayling fly, and it is still successful on all the chalk streams. The explanation for the success of such flies as Rolt's Witch, Red Tag, Treacle Parkin, Terry's Terror and the various Bumbles seems to lie in the combination of herl body and bright tag. My conclusion is that this combination (and many of these flies are just as attractive to trout as to grayling) is a good representation of a hatching nymph: the rough body produces the furry effect of occlusion, and the bright tag at the red/orange/yellow end of the spectrum creates the effect of the haemoglobin in the nymph's body. On the other hand, Rolt mentions his Witch as being particularly effective close to or under the bank and in rough weather, so it may be that fat herl bodies are fair representations of a wide range of miscellaneous insects – some water-borne, some land-borne – which fall on the water, particularly on a windy day.

I prefer the former explanation; it is more logical and has greater appeal than the latter, although it is probable that both theories are true on occasion. The hatching-nymph theory is also supported by the Gold-ribbed Hare's Ear as a grayling fly. This pattern is perhaps the most successful traditional all-round fly on the chalk streams for both trout and grayling and can be fished dry, as an emerging nymph, or just below the surface, as a nymph which has failed to emerge or is not yet ready. Again, the rough body creates the impression of a hatching nymph, and the selective grayling are much more likely to rise to that than they are to a dun imitation. Grayling lie on the bottom, even during a hatch of surface fly, presumably because they take the majority of their food from the bed of the river, and as a consequence they rise from what is often a considerable depth. I am sure that this influences their reaction to duns: it's a long way to go to something that might fly away before they arrive! When they are lying in very shallow water or on top of weed, as they do when weed covers most of the river, then they are lying much closer to the surface and their behaviour in the rise is much more like that of the trout.

Recent developments in dry-fly fishing have tended to centre on new patterns. The Klinkhammer, developed by Hans van Klinken from Holland, presents a body in and below the surface film, and it is hugely successful on the chalk streams and everywhere else. Whether it imitates a hatching insect or a wind-borne terrestrial is not clear (and does not really matter) – the

Ron Broughton playing a grayling on the Piscatorial Society's water on the Hampshire Avon

fly both rises and hooks large numbers of grayling. The various *cul de canard* patterns typified by the 'F' fly are almost as successful, particularly during a rise; again they tend to present the fly in or below the surface film and support my theory that the grayling is consistently attracted to hatching nymphs.

John Roberts has written in the *Journal of The Grayling Society* of the problems posed for the grayling by the protruding upper lip, and the difficulty which it faces in taking a high-floating dry fly as a consequence. He subscribes to the theory of a tiny pressure pad, moving ahead of that protruding lip and causing the fish to miss the fly. Other authoritative writers have described the problems resulting from the grayling hitting the cast in front of the fly, if the dry fly is presented upstream as it so often is on chalk streams. What is clear is that large numbers of grayling which are risen are not hooked if the conventional shoulder-hackled dry fly is presented upstream. A higher proportion are hooked if the fly is presented across, and even more are hooked if a downstream parachute cast is used.

John goes on to describe his paradun dressings, which present the body of the fly entirely on or in the surface film. Such patterns are anchored by the hook bend, and so are prevented from being pushed aside by the tiny pressure pad. These in fact provide a similar target to the Klinkhammer and the 'F' fly, in or below the meniscus. They are on occasion even more effective if twitched, to represent a cripple which has failed to hatch successfully. If the grayling is coming up a long way, cripples are much more likely to be attractive than healthy duns which are likely to take off. My own success with the paradun principle has tended to be with parachute Iron Blue dressings (these provide an Iron Blue which I can see) and parachute Tups, which provide an excellent general-purpose autumn fly. Did Austin really intend this excellent pattern as a general Olive spinner, or was it a compromise to take in the Pale Wateries as well?

For much of the time, though, grayling – in particular the larger ones – do not rise, and if they are to be caught on a fly, then it is necessary to get the fly down to them. Rolt recognised this and describes how he surprised the keepers on the waters he fished with his catches of grayling taken on the wet fly. The flies he used were traditional grayling patterns, but he used lead wire in order to get them down to the fish. He did, however, fish his flies downstream, presumably in a fairly traditional down-and-across manner. From my own observations, the grayling will take a fly or a shrimp imitation even when lying completely static and not feeding at all, provided that the offering is absolutely in line and at exactly their level. All that they need to do then is to open their mouth and take it in. In some parts of the Wylye it is possible to test this off farm bridges and observe exactly how the grayling react in clear water.

DERMOT WILSON

John Goddard on the Hampshire Avon

This need to get the offering down to the level of the fish was recognised by Sawyer and Oliver Kite and forms the basis of their method of
fishing the nymph and the bug. The use of a weighted 'fly' fished up or up
and across has proved very effective on all the chalk streams, and it
enables the angler to catch fish throughout the day, with the dry fly being
used during the comparatively short hatch of an autumn day, and the
weighted 'fly' for the rest of the time. Of course, on those days when the
weather is hostile and no fly hatches, the bug can be used throughout. In
spite of the wide range of bugs and shrimp patterns which have been
developed, Sawyer's Killer Bug remains my favourite and in my opinion is
the most consistent and dependable. The size and weight can be varied
according to the depth of water being fished, and often it does well in

large sizes. Stuart Ashworth's 'Shrug' dressing is on occasions very good, and a gold head in its various forms can also be very attractive. The red spot shrimp and its refinement the 'orange head shrimp' also have their moments. My main variation on a bug is a large orange shrimp pattern, usually dressed on an 8 or 10 hook using hot orange seal's fur; this seems to be an attractive alternative when the shoal has lost interest in the conventional Killer Bug. I am certain, though, that pattern is of little consequence provided that it is possible to get the shrimp down to the fish's level. The joy of this style of fishing is that it is possible to see a very great deal of what is happening. By care and stealth – or by patience, if they have been disturbed – it is possible to get very close to the grayling shoals, frequently to within two or three yards. Having got into a position where it is possible to see the fish clearly, my usual practice is to cast the bug in front of the shoal and allow it to drift, without drag, through the shoal. If the fish are feeding the grayling generally take the drifting bug readily, usually as it sinks, and often rise to take it. The older, larger fish are very often the first to be caught. They lie at the head of the shoal or in the best feeding position, and therefore have the best opportunity to take the bug. It is not usually easy to tackle the shoal from behind, as is sometimes recommended. The need to get the bug down means it is often necessary to cast well in front of the targeted fish, and if one is attacking them from the rear, the cast tends to be right on top of the largest fish in the shoal.

If the fish are not feeding, it becomes necessary to use an induced take. Much of the time only a twitch of the bug is required, just enough to attract the attention of the fish. But this is where proximity to the fish is important. If it is possible to see the fish clearly, and even the bug itself, it becomes possible to control the induced take and at the same time watch the reaction of the fish. If the bug is not visible it pays to watch the fish. Any reaction, a move forward or to the side, from any fish in the shoal should be followed by a strike (where a single fish is the target it is relatively easy to identify signs of a take: concentration is focused on one fish and not distracted by the shoal). When neither fish nor bug can be seen it becomes important to see the cast clearly, and here a greased butt or a strike indicator is a great help. When a fish is feeding boldly the take is often indicated by a good long draw, which is not difficult to detect; at other times, particularly when the take is induced, it can be no more than the checking of the line, and here concentration is important. Having watched many fish take my bug, I have come to the conclusion that the reason for the difficult-to-detect take – when the cast simply checks or 'bumps', without any sign of a draw – is that the fish, having moved some distance to take the bug, remains absolutely static once it has done so. It does not return to its original lie as one would expect, it simply takes the bug into its mouth and remains where it is.

Fish in shallow water are relatively easy; small bugs which are easy to cast can be used, and, unless the light is wrong, most of what goes on can be seen. If the approach is careful and quiet, the fish on many of the wide shallows of the chalk steams can be herded in front of the angler until a number of small shoals are brought together as one large shoal; even though they have clearly been disturbed they continue to feed. The fishing of a weighted bug, however, does present an opportunity to try for the large fish which live in the hatch pools. As the water levels drop in late summer and autumn, it becomes possible not only to see the fish in these pools but also to stand a chance of getting the bug down to their level. The bug needs to be heavy and hence difficult to cast, so it is wise to put away the carbon rod and take out an old cane favourite, which will not chip if hit by the bug. The problems of reaching the fish and detecting a take are so much greater in waters of this kind. The fish may be lying in an eddy or even facing downstream.

The first approach should be to use a long cast or leader and a strike indicator or greased butt. After casting the bug to a point where you think it will get the bug down to the fish, watch carefully for a draw as the cast sinks (it can be fascinating to watch the cast sinking slowly). Eventually, as

Reg Righyni fishing a hatch pool on the Avon

BARRIE LLOYD

the bug reaches bottom and the fish, there is a barely detectable draw as the grayling takes the bug into its mouth. On other occasions – particularly in a boiling hatch pool with a bug swinging around backwaters – the take becomes very difficult to detect, and an induced take can be used to good effect. The inducement in these cases should be a long draw. This not only puts the angler in close contact with his bug but also provokes a more vigorous take, which is more easily seen.

The Killer Bug does not work if it is dragged over the fish: a slow drag gives the fish too much time to examine the offering and produces lots of follows but few takes. Fishing the bug in a conventional wet-fly style, down and across, is largely a waste of time. The bug should be either without drag or moved in such a way as to provoke a reflex action in the fish. When the angler sets out to induce a take the inducement must be a sudden movement, preferably happening in front of the fish. (The induced take and the Killer Bug are not limited in their application to the chalk streams. They are also effective on spate rivers, and I have had success with them on a number of north-country streams.)

What does reduce the effectiveness of the bug is colour in the water. Once the autumn rains set in and some colour appears, bug fishing for grayling in the chalk streams is at an end. Surprisingly, it becomes difficult to catch even the odd fish once the water colours up. How soon this happens depends upon the season and the amount of greensand or clay in the river catchment. On the Avon, mid-December is the usual time for this to happen (the Avon has a lot of greensand in its headwaters, and the Wylye is similar). By contrast, the Test and the Itchen almost never carry any colour, and it is therefore possible to fish for grayling for much longer. When there is colour in the river the best chance of catching a grayling lies in the use of a dry fly or a wet fly fished on the surface. If there is a hatch of fly and the fish rise they will take a dry fly quite readily even in coloured water.

What of the future of the grayling in the chalk streams? It is apparent that, as long as water-quality standards are maintained and even improved, and in spite of the removal of grayling with electrodes, the grayling will thrive. The cessation of removal by electro-fishing would quickly allow grayling populations to recover, and within four or five years a normal age structure would develop. I wrote in the previous edition of this book that the trend would appear to be against this happening. However, there are now perhaps signs that an increasing number of people is beginning to realise that heavy stocking of chalk streams with large trout and their removal during corporate hospitality days is not perhaps a very good idea. Informed and keen anglers are increasingly

The Hampshire Avon: October grayling fishing

active in promoting the cause of the grayling, and they appreciate its qualities. The designation of nearly all the chalk streams as Sites of Special Scientific Interest, together with a reduction of abstraction, will be of great help in protecting, amongst other wild fish species, the grayling. The threat of abstraction will be reduced if not eliminated. The further designation of some areas as Special Areas of Conservation will provide additional support, and will help in particular to make funds available for restoration and maintenance work. It is important that all anglers recognise and accept the responsibility which these designations place upon them. Anglers are seen at the present time by other groups with an interest in the chalk streams as indifferent custodians of the environment, not sufficiently informed and not sufficiently balanced. It is important to the long-term future of the grayling that this image is improved.

Of Stillwaters and Welsh Rivers

Louis Noble

Stillwaters

FOR GENERATIONS, THE grayling has been romantically referred to as 'the lady of the stream', yet it is a fact, although not generally known, that they do inhabit stillwaters. (It would be interesting to seek the view of cock grayling regarding this traditional feminist label!) Before proceeding, it must be said that the term 'stillwater' is really a misnomer because, as we know, the effect of wind will cause a certain amount of movement in water of any size. In the case of the grayling, it seems to require a greater influence than merely wind if it is successfully to adopt a home other than a river. This will be evident as we discuss Britain's 'stillwaters'.

There are populations of grayling in lakes outside the British Isles. Great Bear Lake in Canada is of particular significance due to the density of the population and to the large size of these northern fish, with specimens of over five pounds being considered quite normal.

To the best of my knowledge there are four stillwaters in Britain where grayling can be found, all well spread out but with an important common characteristic, which will become clear. They are Lake Bala (Llyn Tegid) in Gwynedd, North Wales, Gouthwaite Reservoir in Yorkshire, Loudsmill Fishery in Dorset and Lymmvale Mere in Cheshire. They vary considerably in character but are united by the fact that each has a distinct and continuous inflow and outflow which gives various benefits. These include assistance in the maintenance of level, a regular through-flow, however subtle, an additional food supply and access to spawning grounds. Let us discuss them individually.

Lake Bala

The largest of the four, Lake Bala is Wales's biggest natural sheet of water, measuring approximately four and a half miles long, with a normal surface area of 1,084 acres. Situated near the delightful town of Bala, it has the River Dee flowing through it. This is created at the southern end where the River Lliw is joined by the Twrch to form, for a short distance, the Little Dee, which leaves the northern part of the lake to continue its way to the sea, via Chester. This beautiful winding river offers excellent grayling fishing for much of its length but it is Llyn Tegid (the Welsh translation of Lake Bala) with which we must concern ourselves.

The shore line is stony, and the depth in places awesome, reputed to exceed 150 feet, but the northern and southerly ends are the shallowest, and it is here that the best results can be expected for the fly-fisherman.

As a coarse fishery it excels, and its trout are huge, if you can tempt the largest from the depths. You may also be fortunate enough to catch the rare Gwyniad, but, unlike most waters, the trout season opens in January and it is between then and March that you have the best chance of catching grayling. Local knowledge is everything, and the favoured method is usually to fish wet trout patterns such as Red Spinner, Mallard and Claret and Black Gnats on sizes 12 or 14, together with an 'intermediate' line. It seems a strange time of year to be fly-fishing such a large water, but on a sunny day following early frost, providing it is calm (which is most important), then your luck may be in, as the grayling can often be seen rising amongst the roach. At this time of year the favoured area is at the northern end, near to the outflow.

This is no water for 'fancy' grayling flies, and I have a vivid, cherished memory of Reg Righyni, in the lake to the tops of his waders, fishing a team of three Yorkshire Spiders on a floating line. This was on the southeast side at Llangower, where the Nant Rhyd-wen flows in, and he took several good grayling, while sailing dinghies and sailboards passed not many yards away!

Of the four British stillwaters, scientific data is available only for Lake Bala, and this is based on research carried out by Dr J.V. Woolland, Scientific Officer for the Severn Trent Water Authority, during the period 1968–72 on both the lake and the main River Dee. This research covered distribution, movements, feeding, age and growth. For the purpose of this book, a summary only is practicable.

Grayling were found principally in the littoral (shore) zone at a depth of up to ten feet, with this area covering approximately fifteen per cent of the total lake area. Sites with a gently sloping bottom of fine gravel and silt were the most populated, with the deeper water apparently proving less suitable.

N. CLOSS-PARRY

Reg Righyni, the moving spirit behind the formation of the
Grayling Society

A tagging experiment took place to examine movements, and it showed that lake grayling are less likely to remain within a home area than river fish and move in an apparently random fashion from one location to any other suitable area. The pattern and frequency of movement varied markedly at different times of the year. The late spring, summer or autumn movement was extensive, yet the winter recaptures were virtually all close to the release point, which is probably associated with a general lack of activity at low temperatures. It would appear that the lake grayling adopt a more shoal-like behaviour pattern and roam in search of food. One individual tagged fish was recaught on five occasions, each time in a different lake location, and once in a feeder stream!

Summer netting operations suggest that many grayling migrate from the lake, as tagged fish were found in the main River Dee downstream of the lake and the feeder streams. All these recaptures were between July and September, and extensive netting in deeper water produced only one grayling. Those caught in the lake were in shallow water close to feeder-stream inlets. The reasons for this apparent migration may be related to

DERMOT WILSON

Conrad Voss Bark on a Tributary of the River Tamar, Devon

TED McCOY

Junction Pool at Llangar on the River Dee

high temperatures, reduced oxygen levels or possibly the large influx of perch and roach at this time into the shallows, but these are far from certain.

An autumnal return to the lake is strongly suggested by sharply rising catches in October from the shore line, with fish quickly spreading throughout the lake. Movements of tagged fish back into the lake from the River Dee and feeder streams were also recorded, which seems to support the theory.

Distinctive parasite infestations indicated that Lake Bale and River Dee grayling were entirely separate populations, and that mixing occurred only during the summer migration. Geological evidence also suggests that grayling entered the Dee system naturally and not as a result of stocking.

Studies on feeding showed that lake and river grayling fed actively throughout the year, although some reduction in feeding occurred at very high or low temperatures. The main food items for lake fish were crustacea, ephemeropteran nymphs and chironomid larvae, with bottom feeding being predominant, although mid-water and surface feeding did take place when food was available. Summer months saw consumption of terrestrial fly and chironomid pupae. A note of interest is that Gwyniad eggs were eaten in the winter by lake grayling. The study also shows that the older a fish gets, the more inclined it is to resort to bottom feeding on larger food items.

The oldest fish found in Lake Bala was six years plus, measured seventeen inches and weighed two pounds. This compares very favourably both with River Dee fish from the middle reaches and with the rest of Britain. As would be expected, faster growth rates are achieved in chalk streams, but the Dee-system fish are generally on a par with or better than other 'traditional area' grayling. The 'average' size fish that an angler may expect to catch is between nine and eleven inches and, say, five to ten ounces in weight, but I know that *much* larger fish are there.

A typical growth rate of a lake grayling is as follows:

Age (years)	1	2	3	4	5	6
Length (mm)	120	225	298	358	379	399
Weight (ounces)	¾	4¾	11	19¼	23	27

The lake is controlled by the Welsh Water Authority, and permission to fish is available from Bala Angling Association.

Gouthwaite Reservoir

Moving from North Wales to North Yorkshire we find this significant 'stillwater' nestling in delightful Nidderdale. Situated between Pateley Bridge and Ramsgill and described as 'a jewel in Yorkshire's crown', it is the only lake in England containing a natural grayling population. A relic of the Ice Age, the damming was completed in 1900 to form a two-mile-long reservoir, its level frequently varied to suit the needs of the Water Authority.

Containing only trout and grayling, its key feature is that the River Nidd flows both into and out of it, thereby providing a perfect spawning site for both species. It is said that at spawning time they are so dense in the incoming Nidd that to wade across means pushing them aside!

These grayling seem to share similar traits with those of Lake Bala, particularly in the way in which shoals move up and down the banks on feeding forays. Gouthwaite would seem to offer the best, yet most testing fishing as a shoal moves by quietly, perhaps only a rod's length out, deliberating sipping tiny black flies.

Here the fly-fisherman must be at his best, stalking them from behind suitable cover as if they were the most wary chalk-stream trout. His imitation must be good, and, here again, there is no place for the gaudy traditional patterns; it is the same offerings as for the trout that will succeed here. Known local experts favour, amongst others, Black and Peacock Spider, Silver Ribbed Black Gnat, Grey Duster, Blue Dun, and of course Fog Black. These are tied on either size 16 or 14 hooks and presented on the finest leader points possible – which are severely tested by grayling that average around the pound.

The fishing is reserved for a limited number of season-ticker holders, with no casual access possible

Following on from these two large waters with their indigenous populations, we now come to a different type altogether.

Loudsmill Fishery

If you were to categorise stillwaters, you could place Lake Bala at one end of the spectrum and Loudsmill at the other, for their characters are so totally different. We are comparing the acidic waters of Wales with the soft alkaline flow of Dorset; we compare one thousand acres with one acre, and a maximum depth of 150 feet with 10 feet. Yet Loudsmill has a place in angling history for yielding a record grayling. A close examination of the fishing reveals the origin of its noteworthy population.

Situated near Dorchester, it is privately owned and was created in 1983 as a trout fishery but later converted for coarse fishing. Approximately 120 yards by 50 yards, its depth varies from ten feet to four feet with an average of, say, six feet. The secret of the fishery's general success is high water quality, which it achieves by an inflow from the Loudsmill, a natural stream running from the Frome; the fishery itself is in fact only fifty yards from the main river. It has an outflow through the natural table and forms a second pool, also for coarse fishing, but there is no 'pull' to the water.

So how did the grayling get there? The Loudsmill stream supports a large variety of coarse fish of superb size, as indeed does the pool. We are talking of dace, tench, carp, pike and roach (with specimens of the last reaching three and a half pounds), but no natural grayling. They in fact found their way into the fishery as the result of a cull in 1987 in the nearby Frome, which is principally reserved as a 'dry fly' trout river.

Not wishing to see magnificent 'vermin' destroyed, Loudsmill's owner, a keen grayling anger, introduced fifty to his water, where they have positively thrived ever since. The view is held that they are in fact growing at a faster rate than those still in the main river, and it is estimated that all have probably been caught and returned at some time during their occupation. Fish over three pounds are regularly caught on sweetcorn and maggots. The present record is a four-pound-three-ounce grayling caught on the nearby River Frome in 1989 by Sean Lanigan.

Although not widely practised, there is scope for fly-fishing, and fish are known to take Sawyer's Bug with the usual enthusiasm. Two major differences exist in their behaviour when compared with Bala and Gouthwaite. These fish do not cruise around surface feeding, but instead lie in groups in the deepest water, and it is apparently possible to wade up to them without putting them to flight. Neither do they appear to breed, although the way into the feeder stream is barred intentionally to retain stocks. Some have been transferred from the pool into the stream, but the results are as yet unknown.

There was no definite strategy for future stocking; therefore, if the current stock is either unable or unwilling to breed, there can be only one outcome. Without doubt, this is an interesting experiment, but Loudsmill's present position as a stillwater grayling fishery must surely be considered as temporary.

I have been informed that there are a number of other stillwaters in this area with streams running in and out that have a *few* resident grayling, but, again, their status as authentic grayling fisheries could be questionable.

Lymmvale

Finally we come to the fourth water in our discussion. This Cheshire mere, situated near Winsford, was formed naturally by underground brine streams, from which salt used to be extracted as a local industry.

Again there are the features of a feeder stream and an outflow, and trout inhabit the feeder. Controlled by Lymm angling Club, Lymmvale is run as 'mixed' fishery, with trout being stocked regularly, and an interesting point is that a large population of orfe exists there.

Regarding the grayling, they were artificially introduced, and the stock is not high, but apparently, there are small specimens which might suggest that spawning occurs. Unfortunately, little information is available.

From our scant knowledge acquired so far there are perhaps only a few conclusions to be drawn. In those waters holding indigenous stocks, the study of their behaviour is absorbing, and there is obviously much more to learn, but it seems that a question-mark must be placed against the viability or desirability of artificial stocking. From the angling viewpoint, the natural waters certainly present a challenge, although to take full advantage of the best waters would entail much travel and expense.

Welsh Rivers

Despite the considerable challenge of Great Bear, Lake Bala and Gouthwaite, if running water courses through your spiritual veins and arteries, let me take you to the Principality. Here, the grayling fisher will truly find a piscatorial 'welcome in the hillside' as we say – 'Croeso-i-Gymru', or 'Welcome to Wales'!

Depending on your outlook, the fish may be called simply a grayling or scientifically, *Thymallus* or, lyrically, the 'lady of the stream', but in Wales it is crothell (pronounced – as nearly as I can say in print – 'crotheck'). So where can we catch crothell?

If my terms of reference were to deal strictly with Welsh rivers, we could undoubtedly look in depth at the mighty Dee, surely one of the most important rivers to the British grayling angler. Other smaller streams and rivers would also come under this umbrella, but it is worthwhile extending our vision a few miles, because we can then encompass the 'borders', which can also be said to possess waters of importance.

Our survey will predominantly cover three main rivers and their tributaries: the Dee, the Severn and the Wye. All are Welsh by birth but each one passes into England *en route* to the sea, which further endorses the 'border' theme. The Wye and the Severn start only yards apart, high up on Mount Plynlimon in Powys, and after many miles come together again in the Severn Estuary. The Severn is 220 miles long and the Wye 130 miles. These east/southerly rivers flow in a totally different direction from the eighty-mile-long Dee, which, after its birth in the Arenig Mountains of Gwynedd, discharges to the north after passing through Chester. The theory has been proposed that rivers with a predominantly easterly flow are more acceptable to grayling, regardless of their location in Britain, and an examination of Welsh rivers would certainly seem to bear this out. There are, however, always exceptions to the rule, and Wales is no different in this respect. The Usk of Gwent flows in the favoured direction and, despite being an exceptional trout fishery, to the best of my knowledge holds no grayling at all.

The only westerly flowing river with a proven population is the Teifi of Dyfed, which holds grayling in a length of approximately four miles. I have it on good authority that they have been here for at least twenty years and are caught from a mile below Lampeter bridge, down to Llanbyther. Fish up to two and three-quarter pounds have been caught with the most success on wet fly in March and April, at the start of trout-fishing activity. Normally the lunch-time period is best, but even on cold April evenings there has been success. Many local anglers catch a few in a season, mainly while pursuing sewin, but concentrated effort in the gravelly runs has regularly yielded catches of six, up to the pound mark, to an acquaintance of mine. The population is thriving, so more casts at 'splashy' rises, thought to be parr, may well yield surprises!

The assumption could possibly be made that the westerly and northerly flowing rivers have a differing water quality from the others, and, although they are generally notable sea trout and salmon fisheries, their trout fishing is poor. The fly life is not prolific in these waters, and we are becoming increasingly aware of their growing acidity due to acid rain and, perhaps more significantly, afforestation. Perhaps this is the clue, knowing as we do that grayling require a better quality of water than trout. We are also aware, of course, that a good food supply is not of prime importance to so called non-feeding migratory fish.

Grayling are believed to be indigenous to the Dee, the Severn and the Wye, and their access to each can perhaps only be surmised to be due to geological upheavals in the Ice Age, but available data as to which held them first is rare. Exist, however, they do, but it is a sad fact that their population is dwindling, although the degree appears not to be consistent between rivers. It is my opinion that the Severn and Wye are most affected, but could this be even more significant when we recall that their origins are similar? My observations are based on fishing observations and records,

River Dee at Carrog Bridge

not only of my own but also those of many friends, gathered over enough years to be meaningful. It must also be clearly understood that this apparent decline applies to trout as well.

I shall now look at the individual main rivers, plus those of their tributaries known to hold grayling. All is not doom and gloom for the angler, because there is a surprisingly high number of host waters in both Wales and the Borders, but their importance as fisheries obviously varies. Even if the chances of success are not high, each undoubtedly possesses its own charm either by virtue of its natural beauty, its history, its fly patterns, or whatever.

River Dee

This offers the knowledgeable angler the possibility of sport, certainly on a par with any of the rain-fed waters of England, and a whole lot better than many of the hitherto excellent Yorkshire streams, upon which much of our grayling literature was based. Rising in the mountains above Lake Bala, Gwynedd, the rivers Lliw and Twrch combine to create Dyfrdwy Foch, or Little Dee, which then, after a short distance, enters Lake Bala. Grayling are present in reasonable numbers in these small streams, but the prospects are best between Llanuwchllyn and the lake.

From the outflow at the northern end, the Dee resembles a fast-flowing canal until it reaches the sluice gates which control river levels downstream. Just above the sluice, it is joined by the Tryweryn, more famous now for its canoe slalom course than its fishing. However, it is still worth pursuing trout and grayling in the reaches above Bala town. This canalised stretch of the Dee can in fact produce exceptional grayling, with three pounders not uncommon and larger fish seen – the home of a future record, I feel. This stretch is good for trotting the worm and also for fly-fishing, although the more 'natural' water below the sluice gates may prove more attractive to the fly man. These large grayling are hard to tempt in the deep, cold waters of winter, but a local technique proved effective is to use large bugs in varied colours fished on fast-sinking lines so that the lure can be inched along the bottom, in the same manner as lake trouting.

The height of the River Dee is regulated by this sluice, with the result that it does not fall to very low levels in dry conditions. This regulation is not popular with salmon anglers, because the fish tend not to hold up in the pools in the ways of old, but the guaranteed flow is thought to be one of the chief reasons for the stability, if not increase, in grayling population. An increase in stock was noticeable after the completion of the Bala regulation works in 1956, and the reasons are thought to be: that the increased summer flow has a cooling effect which suits the grayling; that the more stable level reduces the scouring effect at flood time, thus protecting the eggs laid in under two inches of fine gravel; and that the chief food source of the grayling, the invertebrate animals, also survive better in the more stable conditions. It can also be surmised that the higher levels provide an increased territory for the fish. During the summer the level of the lake is raised to increase storage capacity, and this coincides with the time at which grayling fry enter the lake from the feeder streams. More areas of shallow water are then available for the fry, together with an increased food supply in the form of terrestrial organisms.

The Dee is not unsuitable for grayling along its whole length as its character changes considerably the 'older' it gets. The lower limit for seasonable catches is probably Bangor-on-Dee, with prospects increasing as you move upstream through Erbistock, Chirk, Trevor and then to Llangollen, where serious fishing begins. The magnificent Vale of Llangollen carries what is essentially a salmon river with many famous named pools, the run-ins to which yield excellent grayling, but fishing is not easy. The river bed varies from gravelly runs to slabs of rock between which lie deep channels, of which the wader must be aware. There is a good variety here, then, for both techniques of fly and trotting. The best of the fly fishing is probably over by the end of November, when trotting takes over until the season's end. I must say, however, that because the trout season opens on 3 March, in favourable conditions I have had great fun with grayling on the fly for the remaining fortnight of the season. It must be remembered by the long-trotter that, apart from isolated club stretches, the use of maggot is banned due to the presence of trout and salmon parr. This is certainly the case above Horseshoe Falls at Berwyn, but the grayling are certainly not averse to a well-presented 'garden fly', tripped along just off the bottom. As we move upstream, the grayling fishing simply gets better and better, with fish of two pounds and over causing no surprise. Before we mentally cast a fly onto the upper reaches we need briefly to examine why the quality of grayling fishing changes.

In 1959 a study related to fish management was carried out by M. Huet, in which he classified European rivers into four main biological zones, each characterised by a distinctive species of fish presence: trout, grayling, barbel and bream. In simple terms the zones related to the slope of the stream bed and its width. The trout zone is in the steep uplands where the water remains cool and well oxygenated all year, and the bed is usually rock, boulders or gravel. The grayling zone is lower down, where the river is larger, the water is still cool and well oxygenated, but the slope is less, with the ripples and rapids usually separated by pools and runs. These zones do, however, overlap to some extent.

TED McCOY

St David's Water, River Dee, Carrog

The longitudinal profile of the River Dee does not actually conform to these simple zones, although above Lake Bala it starts as a trout zone. Below the lake, the stretch from Bala to Glyndyfrdy conforms to grayling zone, but then due to increasing steepness, reverts to a trout zone. Below Llangollen, the pattern of the other zones becomes established, although the relevant species are not present (except for some bream in the very much lower Dee). This is why the grayling fishing is that much better between Glyndyfrdy – five miles above Llangollen – and Bala, with Corwen being particularly good. A drive along the A5 from Llangollen to Corwen, where the river can be seen, will clearly show the changing features.

Above Corwen, the river meanders through Llandderfel up to Bala, narrowing slightly as it goes but still retaining the width of a long cast from a fly-rod. One particularly good stretch is Llandderfel, where the size of grayling and the quantity is good, and there is another, slightly higher, at Llanfor. This is the final stretch from where the sluice gates can be reached after a reasonable walk, and the character of the riverside here will delight the angler, particularly on a calm autumn day. An easy flow over a regular depth of approximately three feet at normal height can be pleasurable when 'crothell' is rising.

Ease of access for the visiting angler is variable. Bala Angling Association issues day tickets which extend to below Llandderfel; Corwen is available only by club membership; at Glydyfrdy the Berwyn Arms issues day tickets, fly only, and the Llangollen Angling Association issues day tickets if the angler is accompanied by a member of the club, though this condition does not apply until 1 October.

Although the breath-taking scenery and quality of fishing would keep anyone constantly visiting the main Dee, one must not forget its tributaries. The Alwen, which enters between Cynwyd and Corwen, holds a good grayling population in its lower reaches and offers challenging fishing; the Alyn in its lower reaches near Rossett holds a few, and the delightful Ceiriog at Chirk has a population intent on pushing its way upstream. Some large specimens have fallen to a well-presented fly in the lower reaches, but access is only for those accompanied by a local association member.

In the section on stillwater grayling, mention was made of a survey carried out by Dr Woolland of the Severn and Trent Water Authority. This included the River Dee, and some interesting facts were revealed regarding growth, movement and feeding habits. Stomach analysis showed that caddis larvae accounted for fifty per cent of diet, and aerial insects for twenty-two per cent (including both terrestrial and aquatic), with the balance comprising nymphs and crustaceans.

TED McCOY

Lower River Alwen

Regarding competition between trout and grayling, the survey found that grayling lay closer to the bottom, feeding less on aerial insects, and trout fed from a mid-water position, taking more aerial food. Grayling also tended to occupy mid-stream positions in water of medium depth, while trout were located along the river edges, close to undercut banks and overhanging trees. If competition does occur, then it should be reflected in the growth rates of the competitors at different population densities. Stock comparison showed that trout were as dense at Bala as at Corwen, but grayling more dense at Bala. Grayling grew much faster at Corwen than at Bala, but trout grew only slightly faster at Corwen. This suggests that there is some competition between species, as reflected in growth rate, but that there is much greater competition within the grayling population than between trout and grayling. This shows that, although one species would do better in the absence of the other, the mixture of species more fully utilises the available resources, and a greater overall productivity results. Therefore, if grayling were absent from the Dee, the trout might grow slightly faster, but the total weight of fish produced in the river would decrease. (If other rivers showed the same results of analysis then we could perhaps sweep away the historical assertion that grayling inhibit trout when in the same water.)

Research also involved the movements of tagged grayling. Broadly speaking, it showed that fish occupied a home range, moving only slightly within it. A notable exception was one fish tagged at Llanfor and recaptured five months later at Llandrillo, over six miles downstream. Small mobile groups can also exist, and an example of this was a grayling released at Llandderfel in October 1969, recaptured almost two miles upstream at Llanfor in June 1970 and which was back again at Llandderfel in July 1970. Grayling removed and transferred to another site generally returned to their 'home', sometimes after two transfers; it is suggested that 'foreign' fish are often unable to establish a new home and are perhaps driven away as intruders. It is a point of extreme significance, I believe, that some of these grayling had to negotiate a five-foot-high gauging weir to return home. (I have heard it said that grayling have apparently disappeared from a stretch of another river, but this was thought impossible, as there was a weir at either end of it – what money on that theory now?)

With regard to fishing methods, I believe that more fly-fishing than long trotting is done, except perhaps in the harshest weather. Dry fly is popular, but deep-sunk flies are the order of the day when the weather is cold. Choice of fly is a tricky point; as on other rivers, many good anglers use the same patterns as they would for trout. This is especially so when naturals are still hatching in the late autumn. Many of the traditional 'flame-tails' are used to good effect – Red Tag, Priest, Red-Tailed Green Insect and the various Witches. My personal favourite is Powell's Orange Otter, fished dry; or, when wet flies are called for, I use a team of traditional tiny 'Clyde Style' patterns, scantily dressed and mainly black.

Undoubtedly there are some patterns created on the Dee system. One shining example is the Grey Duster, from the Alwen, the favourite of many. Another, from the Bala area is Y Diawl Bach, or Little Devil, a wet fly made public by that skilful angler and fly-dresser, Dewi Evans of Bala (*see* page 139) for the pattern). Another very effective pattern used by Dewi is a wet Red Spinner, Scottish pattern, which has a blue dun hen hackle in front of the usual red cock.

The Dee is a great black fly river, and the late, great Jack Hughes-Parry, of Fechan salmon-fishing fame, liked a cast of three, with a bit of red particularly on the tail fly and a very small Zulu on the top dropper. Perhaps we could do no better than to follow his example. Let us also not forget the other Welsh favourite, Parry's Black Spider, with its attractive silver tip.

Seemingly the most deadly method of luring the 'gig one' is to trot a natural caddis grub in the same way as worm. This is practised on the Dee as spring approaches and the weather warms slightly.

River Severn

This major river once had a fabulous reputation for its grayling, but sadly this is no more. The decline has been markedly increasing over the past few years, and the reasons are probably several. Conforming very much to the zoning theory, the Severn has a great reputation for its coarse fishing, particularly barbel, with salmon runs slowly improving. The real grayling zone starts between Llanidloes and Llandinam, this latter venue having been densely populated until quite recently. Trout were definitely in the minority here, but the flying fishing for grayling was superb.

It is a proven fact that acidity has increased to such a degree that scarcely any fish life exists from Llanidloes upstream, and the result of this must surely be reflected for miles downstream. I lived the first twenty years of my life in a village; I fished from its banks for many of these years, and the clarity of the water and the variety and density of the fish was superb. Today the water hardly clears there, and fishing for anything except barbel is poor. The water authority in recent years turned the Llandinam reaches into a 'put and take' trout fishery, heavily stocking them with fish of a size abnormal for the water. Was this a further cause of the grayling decline? Lower down, the water was opened up to maggot fishing after the close of the trout season – the result: apparent further decline. Ironically, due to falling attendance, the Water Authority has now dropped the lease, so that the fishing is in private hands again, and signs of a return to natural conditions are there, so let us hope that the grayling return.

Below Llandinam, Newtown has always held good stocks, although again over the past few seasons they seem more meagre. Local opinion has it that this may appear so only because of movement.

This section of the upper Severn is interesting because shoals seem to stay out in the shallower runs, even in hard winter conditions. Although they are caught in deeper water, such as that under the town suspension bridge, good sport can be had on the long sweeping bends below the town centre. I have an interesting anecdote to relate which illustrates this point and raises another. One raw winter's day some seasons ago, I enjoyed a day's fishing with a friend and local expert, Ken Glover. We fished fifty yards apart, with me trotting worms in deep water and Ken trotting maggots in less than eighteen inches of quite swift water. I fared badly, while my friend took several good grayling in a short space of time, so, probably feeling sorry for me, he invited me to share his swim. We stood only a few yards apart, trotting the same line of flow, but this time I also used maggot, and sure enough we both caught several good fish which took in approximately the same area. Now this area was only a few feet square over a rocky bottom, and we began to debate just how many fish there were here, when Ken hooked a good grayling, played it to his feet and, while trying to unhook it in the water, snapped off his hook. Well, I'm sure you can guess the rest! Sure enough, no more than ten minutes later, out came another to Ken's rod and, lo and behold, what was in its lip? Yes, Ken's hook – no doubt at all.

It was obvious to us that we were catching some fish more than once, which must surely go a long way to dispelling theories about panic-stricken fish feeling dreadful pain. It might just also pose a question about graylings' intelligence!

Before the decline, Welshpool was probably the lower limit for good grayling fishing, although the history books report grayling of five pounds at Shrewsbury. Anyone wishing for a change from the delightful gravelly runs of the upper Severn could tackle its tributaries, some of which were once noted for grayling, and are still worth a visit. Starting at the top, we find the Rhiw, where the lower reaches up to Berriew still hold grayling. Slightly lower, coming in from the other bank, is the Camlad, which has an excellent history, with five-pound fish well documented. The next tributary is a major one. The Vyrnwy, with similar physical characteristics to the upper Severn, still holds good stocks from Port Robert down to Llansantffraid. Tributaries of the Vyrnwy are of varying importance to the grayling angler. The Banwy has a small population in the lower stretch; the tiny Cain has good fish in the deep holes; but the Tanat is the major attraction – or, rather, used to be!

This delightful stream, with its long pools and runs, is well known to me, and up to the late 1970s could provide quite amazing sport to the dry fly in September and October. Successive years have seen a rapid decline to the point where it is difficult to catch more than a couple in a day; trickles of late olives float along untouched through stickles and pools that would have been 'boiling' not so long ago. The trout are as badly off, and the River Authority has two monitoring stations, but reports no pollution. What then is the reason? Despite this apparently disastrous state of affairs, autumn 1987 saw the capture of two grayling over three pounds to fly in the area above Llanyblodwel. These fish, however, were both from the same stretch, so the assumption must be that if a population remains, then it must be in isolated places. We must surely be thankful that these magnificent specimens were returned to the river alive.

We have now drifted our fly or trotted our float into Shropshire, and A.E. Housman reminds us in his *Shropshire Lad* that further pleasures await:

> In valleys of springs of rivers,
> By Onny and Teme and Clun,
> The country for easy livers,
> The quietest under the sun.

As a 'Shropshire lad' myself, I readily identify with his sentiment, and if we drop to the southern end of this beautiful border county, we meet the above-mentioned streams, plus the Corve (there are other minor tributaries, but we restrict ourselves to three known to hold grayling). What countryside they flow through, slipping quietly past hills, through gentle woodland and crossing lush meadows! What relaxing fishing they offer!

Of major consideration is the Teme, with its long history of grayling fishing. In the towns along its banks was written some of our most important angling literature, and it saw the creation of famous flies; but yet again it is in decline as a grayling fishery. This has happened particularly in 1987 and 1988, and the cause can only be guessed. The view was proposed that, due to the high level of dairy and crop farming in the area, run-offs of fertiliser from the land and chlorine washings from dairies may be responsible, but I leave this to better-informed authorities. Ludlow is probably the lowest point for good fishing, and the fame of the river was due chiefly to the magnificence of the sport at Leintwardine, the most productive area on the river. Above Ludlow, the Teme is joined by the Corve, Onny and Clun, which do have a population, but it needs to be looked for, chiefly in their lower reaches.

The low density of fish is more than compensated for by the sheer pleasure of casting a fly (for trotting is out of place here) onto the gentle mixture of pools and stickles. This border area is, of course, famous for the exploits of Canon Charles Eagles, the Reverend Edward Powell and their contemporaries. We owe them thanks for the creation of their patterns, but the Ludlow area itself had its share of creative fly-dressers, and some of their patterns are just as good today. Give a wetting to Coombe's Blue Variant, Moon's Butcher, Brookes's Fancy, Grant's Murderer, Bowlker's Owl Fly, Hancock's Pet, Sander's Special or the Silver Twist, in addition to the more standard 'flame-tails'. Remember, too, that the Teme is known as a 'white fly river'. Of grayling flies created specifically for the previously mentioned streams, it is worth considering Southam's Silver Twist, an apparently excellent pattern, whose birthplace was the Tanat. Most noteworthy, however, must surely be the Reverend Powell's Orange Otter, originally developed on the Corve, Onny and Teme, and now universally accepted.

River Wye

This is a magnificent river for many fish and also fits the zoning theory, although the grayling zone is more rocky than usual. Not normally thought of as a grayling river, it does yield, in certain areas, fish of a higher calibre than even the Dee. In common with the Dee and Severn, it also has several grayling-holding tributaries, although these vary in importance to the angler.

The upper reaches near Llangurig have very few grayling, and even as far down as Rhayader the fish are few and small. As the river widens and deepens between Rhayader and Builth, it is a different story – especially between Llanwrthwl and Doldowlod, near Newbridge. Admittedly, much of this water is private, but perhaps therein lies the secret. Over several years, whilst on holiday there I have consistently taken grayling around the one-and-a-half to two-pound mark, and one large fish actually had me stumbling downstream over the rocky bottom as if it were a salmon. Of course, the power of the water helps them.

Further down, reasonable stocks are to be found at Builth Wells, Hay and even as far as Ross, but much of these lengths are strictly preserved for salmon, so that access and information are limited. Recent studies on the upland Wye and Severn show a distinct advantage in favour of the Wye in terms of water quality, which may explain the better grayling and even trout growth.

The tributaries are better than the Severn's as far as grayling go. Working from the top, we have the Ithon, Irfon and Llynfi, which all have reasonable stocks in their lower reaches. (This 'lower-reach' syndrome seems common to practically all tributaries of major rivers, with few having populations all the way up.) The most famous tributary is the Lugg, although its average size for grayling is poor when compared with other waters, especially the Dee. Water quality is better in the Lugg, yet its fish are slightly smaller than those of the upper Dee, with its high and competitive population, and they are approximately fifteen to eighteen per cent smaller than Corwen fish.

The following table shows comparative growth rates for various waters:

	Age and length (mm)					
	1	2	3	4	5	6 (years)
Upper Dee	120	213	270	316	334	
R. Dee, Corwen	125	238	303	344		
Llyn Tegid (L. Bala)	120	225	298	358	379	399
R. Lugg (Hellawell 1969)	110	167	260	303		
R. Test (Hutton 1923)	159	286	335	387	413	432

The Lugg is a charming river to fish, with beautiful pools and stickles that twist and turn across the meadows and with much bushing along its banks. In many parts this makes for very testing fly-fishing, and the Presteigne area is particularly attractive. Apparently not a lot of grayling are to be found above this town, but from here downstream to the Wye below Hereford the population is good. Despite the smaller fish it is very popular, and in recent years has been the favourite of two influential angling authors. They are James Evans, whose book, *Small River Fly Fishing for Trout and Grayling* is surely both a classic and essential reading for the border man; and C.V. Hancock, whose *Rod in Hand* is simply a collection of the most delightful memories, chiefly of the Welsh Dee and border streams. Each has contributed a pattern of fly most useful on the Lugg: they are respectively, the William Rufus and the Droitwich, both wet flies.

Mr Hancock reveals that the word Lugg is an English adaptation of the

Welsh 'Llugwy' which means 'gleaming', so he refers to this area as 'The Land of Teme and Gleam' – quite lovely!

The Lugg has three useful tributaries, the Arrow near Leominster, the Hindwell by Presteigne and the Pinsley, again near Leominster, all three with grayling in them.

The Monnow was a favourite haunt of Canon Eagles and is excellent for trout as well as grayling, although strictly preserved. Bigger than the Lugg, it has a more even flow above Pontrilas, where I know it, and it is here that the much smaller Honddu joins it, again a good grayling stream. A minor tributary of the Monnow is the Dore, with fish in the lower reaches.

And so our flies drift into this final offshoot of the mighty Wye. The Troddi (Trothy) enters just below Monmouth and again has a lower-reaches grayling population.

What then remains to be said?

We have travelled from Gwynedd, through Clwyd and Powys into Shropshire and finally to Herefordshire in the quest for grayling. Many and varied are their habitats and long may it be so!

Yorkshire's Grayling

John S. Davison

My FIRST INTRODUCTION to grayling came not in Yorkshire but in fact on the Derbyshire Derwent as a student. I recall that I was taken as a guest to fish the Derbyshire County Council's water near Ambergate. There the river flowed over a weir, and many years ago the bed had been concreted, so that it was quite smooth. The concrete had been broken in parts by subsequent floods, and large shoals of grayling could be seen lying in about two or three feet of water as it flowed over the concrete and in and around the gaps. The fish responded well to dry fly, and large bags of thirty, forty or fifty fish were not uncommon, although a one-pound fish was a good one.

In due course I joined that club and enjoyed some wonderful years fishing on the Rivers Derwent, Manifold and Dove in Derbyshire until I moved to Wakefield in 1972. In 1978 I was fortunate enough to join a syndicate which had access to fishing on the middle Wharfe, and I have continued to fish the same water up to the present time, although I am now a member of the Huby angling club.

The River Wharfe is one of the main grayling rivers in Yorkshire. It rises in the high ground north-west of Pen-Y-Ghent at Calf Holes. The upper Wharfe consists of a bedrock of carboniferous limestone which is most prominent in Kilnsey Crag. The limestone is overlain by the Yoredale series of limestones, shales and sandstones. Downstream of Bolton Abbey the Wharfe flows across the Namurian Series of gritstone, and then, between Wetherby and Tadcaster, the river again crosses magnesium limestone before meandering across the drift deposits of the Vale of York. The character of the river therefore varies tremendously, with a fast-flowing upland section above Ilkley, the middle, slower-flowing, section down to about Boston Spa/Tadcaster, and the remainder, which is slow-flowing and tidal, down to the sea.

JANEY BROWN

Ron Broughton surveys the Upper Hodder at Knowlemere

The first grayling are found in the headwaters of the Wharfe and come in around Burnsall, although their numbers are very much diminished since 1968 when Reg Righyni wrote his famous book, *Grayling*. Historically, the Burnsall area appears to be the top limit for the species; Pritt notes in *Yorkshire Trout Flies* of 1885, 'the Kilnsey waters hold no grayling although this fish is plentiful below'. It is a matter for conjecture as to why grayling have diminished in numbers so much in the Burnsall area. Could it be because the river is now heavily stocked with large trout, and as a result the competition has become too intense? The matter certainly merits further investigation.

On the approach to Ilkley the grayling fishing continues to improve and is outstanding in this area down past Otley and Poole. The river goes in a series of runs, pools and glides, and much of it is superb fly water with fairly easy wading, although the river is wide, being thirty yards or more across in places.

As the river continues towards the sea it becomes larger, slower and deeper, and other species, especially chub and dace, become more plentiful. Bait-fishing methods tend to predominate over fly, but some good grayling catches can be taken in the Boston Spa area in winter on bait.

My favourite time to fish the Wharfe is September and October after a few cool nights. The weather often gives a few showers which bring the river off the low summer levels, although for fly-fishing I do prefer the

58

water clear, so that the fish can see my fly. When it is the colour of brown soup I have never had fish on fly, although maggot or worm can do well in the back eddies in such conditions.

The time of the year is also very significant on the water I fish. I have caught grayling out of season in cool weather in April and early May, and then they seem to disappear until September. I believe that this is caused by the fact that the fish may not feed in warmer months when they are all so busy spawning. The cool weather certainly seems to put them in a feeding mood, and indeed I have caught fish in February, when the margins have been iced up, as have the rod rings.

For anyone fly-fishing on the Wharfe may I suggest that they invest in a pair of chest-high waders. The banks are often steep and covered in nettles, and often the only way into the water is to slide down on one's backside into water which may be deeper than it looks. In many places the average depth of water is between two and four-and-a-half feet, but the bottom contains some holes which can mean a legful of water for the newcomer. Of course the fish always rise just out of casting range when you are at your wader tops and can go no further! 'Breast-highs' solve all these problems – although they should be combined with a stout wading-staff as a third leg for safety, and perhaps a buoyant waistcoat as well. It is certainly better to be safe than sorry.

I like a long rod for fishing the Wharfe, so that I can get the maximum control of the fly. My faithful companion for a number of years now is the Bruce and Walker Ten-Foot Light Line, with a Hardy's LRH reel which carries a number 5 line and an eight- to ten-foot-long knotted nylon leader going down to 2–3 pounds breaking strain to complete the outfit.

The golden rule of fishing is first to find your fish, and my usual method is to walk the water looking for fish activity and fly hatches. It never ceases to amaze me how one can fish away with no result; then a fly hatch starts, and very soon every fish in the area will be on feed. If one matches the hatch some good bags can be taken. The ideal weather is when we have a settled spell with cool nights, when the water is about 50°F and the air temperature about 58–60°F (14–16°C). Such conditions can produce good fly hatches.

Dry fly does well in the early autumn when the river is clear, and it can be fished either upstream or downstream. Timing the strike is the hardest part, as often the small fish rise very fast, whereas the larger fish has a much slower, more determined rise. Grayling are perhaps more obliging than trout and should give the angler plenty of practice until he gets the time to strike. Sometimes, however, one will get 'unhittable' fish. Small grayling often rise and splash at the fly without taking it: it can be sheer frustration.

SIMON BROWN

Ron Broughton into a good Hodder grayling

I believe, too, that light can affect how fish come at a fly. We have all had those days when fish come 'short' and splash at the fly. I have noticed in the fish-pond in my garden that my Koi carp take their floating feed boldly on some days, but on those days when the sky is a grey-blue and the water has that 'steely' look they seem to be extra wary and take their food in a very hesitant and cautious manner.

Apart from dry fly, two other methods of fishing can be employed on northern waters: the traditional downstream wet fly with 'a team of three', and the upstream nymph as used on chalk streams.

Some confusion exists in many anglers' minds about 'downstream' wet-fly fishing. Downstream refers not to the method of fishing at all but to the fact that the angler walks downstream as he covers the water. The flies used in such traditional fishing are the northern 'spider' patterns which have been evolved by dalesmen over the centuries and 'collected' by such angling writers as Walbran, Pritt, and Edmunds and Lee. Many of the classic patterns, such as the Waterhen Bloa, Partridge and Orange, Snipe and Purple, are still as good fish catchers today as they have been for hundreds of years. I for one can testify that they work as well on the grayling of the chalk streams as on northern waters. The flies are tied on hooks of between size 14 and 18, or even size 20, with size 16 being the most common. The fly consists of a slim (usually silk) body with a soft hackle from a bird such as a waterhen or a snipe. The flies are very sparsely dressed, the hackle being given only a couple of turns at the most. Another feature of the northern spider type of fly is that none of the traditional dressings have any tails, and the body length comes down only as far as the barb on the hook. Partridge's Captain Hamilton fly hooks are ideal for these flies. The idea of these patterns is, I believe, to imitate drowned duns or nymphs which have failed to hatch in the rough water. In both these cases the flies represent easy pickings for the fish!

It is the tradition of the north country to fish three flies on a cast, with two droppers and a point fly. My own preference is for a knotted leader about eight to ten feet in length. The first part of the leader is made of heavy nylon swiftly tapering down to a length of about four feet six inches of level nylon of about 2 or 3 pounds breaking strain. The droppers are spaced twelve to eighteen inches apart, with a dropper length of about three inches. This of course can be varied to some extent, but I consider that it is important that the flies are not spaced too closely together.

The downstream method of fishing using 'a team of three' is ideally suited to the rain-fed fast-flowing rivers of the north, as it enables the angler to search the whole of the river with his flies. Generally speaking, northern

JANEY BROWN

A good male Hodder grayling

grayling tend to lie in smaller shoals and over a larger area of river than their southern cousins, and it is for this reason that the water needs to be fully covered. In addition, it is of course impossible to see the fish here, unlike the chalk streams, and the only indication one can get of the presence of a grayling is by looking for a rise. The rest of the time one is fishing 'blind'. This is the second reason for a comprehensive coverage of the water.

In the downstream method, the flies are cast at about ten to twenty degrees upstream of the angler and allowed to swing around to about thirty degrees below the angler. The flies should come down the river 'dead drift' naturally in the current, and for this reason it may be necessary to mend the line to avoid drag, as in dry-fly fishing. A short cast is first made to cover the water near the angler, and then a longer cast to cover towards the far bank – but remember that, the longer the cast, the more difficult it will be to control the flies properly and to detect the takes. Having covered thoroughly the area of water in front of him, the angler then moves downstream a yard or so and casts again as before, thus ensuring that the whole of the water is covered by a fly. It is quite possible in a day to cover a mile or more of river by this method.

The great skill in the method is to judge the speed of the current, so that

Cromwell's Bridge over the Hodder, near Stonyhurst

CYRIL BEARDSWORTH

62

flies do not drag around. The other skilful part of the fishing comes in keeping in touch with the flies and hitting the take. It is a good idea to keep the rod point fairly high, to put a slight belly in the line, and to keep the fly line in one's hand. I watch very closely for the signs of any rise in the vicinity of my fly, any movement of the nylon leader or the point of the fly line, and I also feel for 'knocks' on the line. With a fairly soft-actioned rod it is quite possible to feel a leaf touch the line as well as a fish, and one should strike at anything that could be a fish. It is also possible to 'work' the flies by a figure-of-eight recovery, and by a gentle raising of the rod tip to imitate a nymph moving up in the water. As the fly comes down to the end of its swim, such a movement can be extremely deadly and encourages the fish to take a fly.

Traditional spider patterns are fished unweighted, as I doubt in those days lead wire had been invented. At times when there is no movement on the surface of the water the modern grayling fisherman may like to use weighted flies to get them further down in the water, particularly when the fish are lying deeper in the colder weather. These can be worked in the water as previously described.

The use of weighted flies brings me on to mention the third method of fishing in Yorkshire, which is the 'upstream' method. This, of course, is an extremely old way of fishing and is well documented by W.C. Stewart in *The Practical Angler* (first published in 1857). This is a more precise

Hooder Foot, the junction of the Hodder with the Ribble at Mitton

CYRIL BEARDSWORTH

method of fishing and can be used if the exact location of a shoal of grayling is known. One can use either a weighted fly on the point in the classic chalk-stream style or – as I prefer – a 'team of three' with a weighted fly on the point. Here a shortish line is cast upstream and allowed to come back 'dead drift' with an occasional lift of the fly. The angler should work upstream and either cast to rising fish or work in a fan pattern over the water. This will enable the whole shoal of fish to be properly covered.

Although it is possible to describe such methods in print there is really no substitute for the angler getting to the water and trying them out for himself. In fishing, as in so many other sports, what really matters is the person who has hold of the 'thick end' of the rod. There is really no substitute for experience, knowing the river well, and knowing where the shoals of fish are likely to be at the various times of the year. Of course, such experience can only be gained by actual practice at the waterside, and my advice to any beginner would be to select a length of river and to fish it regularly for two or three seasons, so that this valuable experience is built up. Much of the best fishing is either private or club water, of course, and again my advice to the enthusiastic grayling fisher is to get his name down for a good fishing club and join as soon as the waiting-list, if any, allows.

ARTHUR OGLESBY

Arthur Oglesby taking film of Reg Righyni fishing the Wharfe
at Wolfscar

64

*

It should not be thought that Yorkshire's only grayling fishing is in the Wharfe, although I must confess that that is where most of my own fishing takes place. The other main grayling fishing areas of Yorkshire are the Rivers Nidd, Ure, Swale and the rivers and becks running off the North Yorkshire moors, such as the Costa, the Pickering Beck, the Rye and the Derwent.

In complete contrast to the Wharfe is the River Nidd. Its original source is at Great Whernside in the high moors north of Skipton. It begins as a small, shallow river in the upper reaches and initially feeds into two reservoirs, Angram and Scar House (which, incidentally, offer some quite nice wild brown trout fishing, though the fish are not large). A few miles further on, the river flows through a third reservoir, namely Gouthwaite, lying in the ice age remnant of Upper Nidderdale. Gouthwaite fishing is privately owned and strictly controlled, but it does offer the chance of some superb stillwater grayling fishing. Again the fish, although numerous, are not large by some standards. The Nidderdale Angling Club controls some ten miles of river and offers day tickets, and to my mind this gives the visiting angler

ARTHUR OGLESBY

Reg Righyni fishing a quiet stretch of the Wharfe

one of the best chances of some day-ticket grayling fishing in Yorkshire – although it must be said that not all of the stretches are available to the day-ticket angler, and in addition there is no Sunday fishing. In the early season the fish respond extremely well to dry fly and are very free-rising, although later in the year maggot or worm can produce good bags.

The river is quite a contrast to the Wharfe, being much narrower, usually some ten yards across or less, and it is heavily treed. The visiting angler will find a short rod of some seven-and-a-half to eight feet particularly useful on this water. Casting can at times be difficult, as the trees can catch your fly. However, speaking from experience, although some stretches are wadable, wading should be exercised with great caution. There are some extremely deep holes in the river and large boulders and rocks which the unwary angler can easily slide down and take a nasty tumble into the river. A wading staff is particularly useful in this respect.

In complete contrast to the 'small-river fishing' of the Nidd, the River Ure offers perhaps some of the best grayling fishing in the whole of Yorkshire. It is a large river and, at over forty five miles in length, one of the longest in North Yorkshire. It stretches from Abbotside Common high up in the north-west corner of the county and meets the River Swale at Boroughbridge, and grayling are found in practically the whole length of it. It is a large and powerful river, similar in characteristics to the Wharfe, with fast runs and rocky pools where again, wading should be attempted with great care.

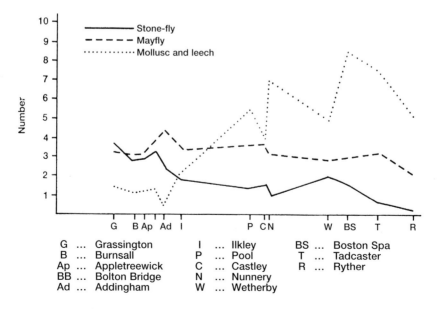

Fig. 2 Numbers of stone-fly, mayfly, mollusc and leech taxa in the Wharfe.

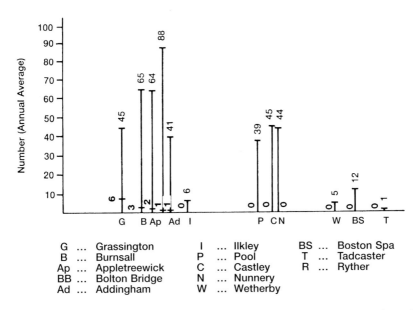

Fig. 3 Total Numbers of stone-fly nymphs and *perla bipunctata* in the Wharfe.

G ... Grassington	I ... Ilkley	BS ... Boston Spa
B ... Burnsall	P ... Pool	T ... Tadcaster
Ap ... Appletreewick	C ... Castley	R ... Ryther
BB ... Bolton Bridge	N ... Nunnery	
Ad ... Addingham	W ... Wetherby	

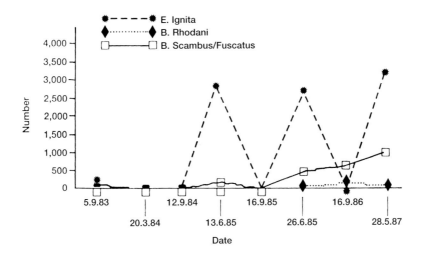

Fig. 4 Abundance of Ephemeroptera at Pool.

Some large grayling are present in the Ure, which has established its reputation as grayling water over the centuries. Pritt, in his *Yorkshire Trout Flies*, says that the Ure (or, to give it its older name, the Yore) is 'more of a grayling water than a trout fishery'. Most of the best stretches of the

67

ROD CALBRADE

Ron Broughton fishing the Upper Wharfe

river are, however, controlled by private clubs, and it is not easy to gain access to some of the best stretches. Nevertheless, when permission is given to the angler, whether solitary or a member of a group, he will find that the grayling are numerous and of a good size. In October 1988 my good friend Oliver Edwards in one day caught a total weight of five pounds twelve-and-a-half ounces.

The rivers draining the North Yorkshire moors, namely the Derwent, the Costa, Thornton Beck, Pickering Beck and the River Rye also offer grayling fishing in the north-east corner of the county. Again, most of this water is private or run by various clubs which control the fishing. The grayling fishing in these waters can be extremely good, and some quite large specimens of over two pounds are sometimes taken. Most of these waters are small, and dry fly or the upstream nymph are probably the most successful, since these rivers are usually very clear and the fish can be seen, as on the chalk streams of the south of England.

I understand that the river Swale also offers excellent grayling fishing in the higher reaches, although this remains a river to be 'collected' by me on some future occasion.

Bait Fishing for Grayling

Neil Sinclair

My bag
Sags with lures and hunter's medicine enough
For a year in the Pleistocene.

Ted Hughes: 'A Cormorant.'

T HE FIELD OF specialist grayling angling is primarily the province of
game fishermen. Many find the grayling co-resident with trout in their
regular waters, and that species provides a convenient means of extending
their angling year. Better still, existing tackle will often suffice, and no
fundamentally new techniques have to be mastered, as grayling, under
appropriate conditions, are ready takers of the fly.

The proviso 'under appropriate conditions' is well advised. In all but
the harshest winters, the angler in the south may find weather, water levels
and water temperatures sufficiently benign to allow fly fishing to be practised all the year round with reasonable prospects of success. His northern
counterpart, however, is in no such happy situation and may find that
after a few weeks, although the grayling themselves are in superb condition, the possibilities of taking them on fly tackle have receded to nought.

To many fly fishermen, the idea of bait fishing is quite foreign, conjur-
ing up images of sedentary, umbrella-shrouded figures spaced at intervals
of a few yards, periodically tossing in balls of groundbait. Only the most
ill-informed would be contemptuous of such anglers, though; a lot of
them pursue their art with a dedication and consummate skill that would
put many a casual fly fishermen to shame. Since the principal appeals of
fly fishing – mobility in pleasant surroundings, elegance and simplicity of
tackle, and the strongly visual aspect of the presentation and the take – are
so much at variance with the image of bait fishing, fly fishermen could be
forgiven for seeing themselves as 'horses for a different course'. However,
the methods of bait fishing for grayling which I shall advocate also
embody the same appeals and attributes, and I commend them as worthy
of the attention of all but the most hidebound purist.

River Clyde at Hazelbank, Lanark

Strategy

Make no mistake, the winter grayling is a bottom-feeding fish. Even a cursory examination of grayling anatomy makes it obvious that the species' penchant for a surface fly is a happy variation on the means of sustenance set out in Nature's original specification. As the season advances and the surface fly becomes scarce, so the grayling slips back into its more natural feeding pattern.

That is not to say that deep water must be sought out – rather that, irrespective of the depth of the pools or runs where they may be found, the grayling will be close to the river bed. And the less inclined they may be to feed at any given time, the more reluctant they will be to move any distance from it. This concept is critical to successful technique.

Overall strategy, then, will be to locate the fish and present an acceptable bait on or near the bed of the river. The angler must be mobile and not over-encumbered with equipment, and he will experience a visual feast.

Of the traditional angling methods, long-trotting with suitable float tackle suggests itself, and indeed is the primary technique I shall describe. This is not the only possibility, however, and at the end of this chapter I shall detail a more radical approach which, while it naturally has drawbacks of its own, nevertheless addresses some of the principal problems encountered in trotting – I refer to the use of the reel-less pole.

Long-trotting

Rods, Tackle and Bait

Rods

Just as carbon fibre has revolutionised the fly-fishing world, so it has brought the bait fisherman a new generation of sturdy, light-weight rods. Since the coarse-fishing market in the UK is colossal, there should be no difficulty in finding a suitable rod at an acceptable price.

The choice of rod is best based upon the likely venue. Match-fishing rods of fourteen feet or even longer are so light as to be perfectly practicable even for the roving grayling fisherman, and for a really big river, a rod of this length is to be recommended. For smaller waters, a twelve-foot instrument will be adequate and a delight to handle. For our purposes, certain qualities are highly desirable, and the following advice forms a check-list for the prospective buyer of a grayling trotter.

1. Most coarse-fishing rods are tip-actioned. Provided it is not taken to ridiculous extremes, this is a good characteristic in a trotting-rod, as it enables effective striking at a long range.
2. Be wary of very slim, light-weight 'canal' rods. A big grayling in fast water can be quite a handful, and although our outfit will be light and sporting, taking this principle too far will result in protracted encounters which do little credit to fish or fishermen.
3. A long handle, whether fully corked or not, is a boon. This is a standard fatigue-preventing device, and most coarse rods are suitably equipped as a consequence. With the reel in place, tuck the extreme butt end under the arm and ensure that you can stand comfortably and that the reel operates easily.
4. As with any good outfit, the winch fitting must hold the chosen reel securely. Look for a fitting which avoids contact between bare metal and the hand (the keen grayling angler will spend many hours in sub-zero temperatures).
5. High-stand-off rings are essential if trotting is to be practised in wet conditions. This may prove the major problem in obtaining an ideal rod, but it is imperative that the line is kept away from the rod blank. If the rings do not stand proud enough, a great many are required to achieve the desired end. I make my own rings for trotting rods from 29-gauge stainless steel

wire, but suitably furnished rods are obtainable over the counter.

6. For associated reasons, a high-gloss varnish finish is valuable, as it helps to shed water quickly from the blank; a sharp tap on the butt will quickly clear a well-finished blank. (Rod-flash is unlikely to be a problem in this type of fishing.)

Float rod

Great strides have been taken in recent years by manufacturers of carbon-fibre rods, in terms of both raw material and resin systems. As a result, float rods suitable for trotting are slimmer, lighter, stronger and, best of all, cheaper than ever. Rod fittings in general have also improved, and reel seats which avoid direct hand-to-metal contact are much easier to come by. Modern, high-stand-off, ceramic-lined rings make my home-made stainless-wire ones look like something from the Stone Age.

Crazy people, who still insist on making their own rods, despite the availability of perfectly suitable and inexpensive commercial products, might like to try something like the rod illustrated. This started life as a 10'3" AFTM 8/9 fly blank. The tip was cut, and extended using a medium-weight solid carbon section (known as a 'flick-tip'). The butt was extended to match by sleeving under the short forward handle. With the additional section inserted, a full-length skeletal handle is afforded, and an overall length of just under 12" is produced. The result is a marvellous trotting tool, light and super-responsive but well able to control large fish in the heaviest water.

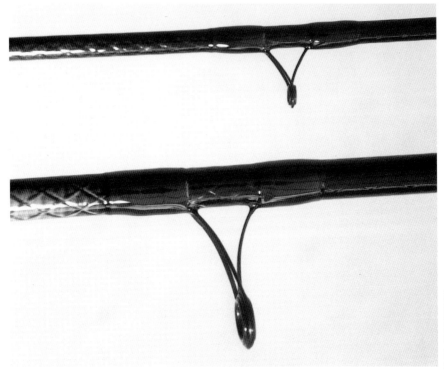

RAY GREENING

Stand-off rings

Long-trotting Reels

This is an area of controversy in which the centre-pin reel is pitted against its fixed-spool counterpart. I admit to unreasonable prejudice and detest the latter, having done all my bait fishing in recent years with the centre-pin. I will, however, attempt an objective comparison.

Long casting is rarely called for in long-trotting for grayling. Where it is required, the fixed-spool reel is the ideal tool. At long range, however, these reels do not feed line well, their performance becoming worse as amount of line left on the spool drops. This is a severe drawback. The centre-pin, on the other hand, feeds line better the more is put out.

A further consideration is line control when striking. With the centre-pin it is only necessary to drop a finger to arrest the spool. The fixed-spool reel must have its bale-arm engaged, and this leads to a nasty moment of non-contact. Modern fixed-spool design has gone some way to meet this objection, however, and to a skilled user this is no longer a problem.

Lastly, contact when playing a fish is generally accepted to be much more direct in a simple centre-pin layout than with even the latest generation of 'back-winding' fixed-spool equivalents.

Unless continuous long casting is envisaged, I must recommend the centre-pin. A good centre-pin is:

1. Free running. If the spool is flicked with the fingers, it should run for a long time before stopping. A good reel will tend to turn backwards slightly under its own spool weight when it does finally stop. Free running is imperative. A reel of this type cannot be too free.
2. Fitted with a line guard or full cage. A reel which regularly allows the light trotting line to find its way 'round the back' and across the rear of the saddle will drive you mad.
3. Fitted with an easily accessible check engagement lever. After striking, a simple single movement should engage the check, thus rendering over-running impossible. The same lever should disengage the check equally cleanly when it is not required.
4. Of a generous diameter, say 4½" minimum. This ensures good leverage at the point the line leaves the spool and an acceptable rate of retrieve.

There appears to have been a resurgence of interest in quality centre-pin reels. A number of small workshops offer superb examples, usually based on the old 'Aerial' designs, and at least two major manufacturers also offer precision trotting reels. With these products benefitting from modern materials and CNC machining techniques, the choice has never been better.

RAY GREENING

Centre-pin reel

There remains, however, no such animal as a good *cheap* centre-pin reel, but my advice is never to skimp on this item. Only a purpose-built, and therefore expensive, item is likely to fit the bill. Do not be tempted to 'cobble up' a trotting reel from, say, an old fly reel – disappointment and frustration will be the only results. Contrary to the situation with fly tackle, in trotting it is the reel, rather than the rod, which is critical to ulti- mate performance, and so this is the item then which is not to be skimped on. If you must use a fixed-spool reel, I suggest one of the 'closed-face' match reels; these perform better in the adverse weather conditions which are part of the winter angler's inevitable lot.

Lines

Nylon monofilament is readily available, inexpensive and quite suitable. Where a fixed-spool reel is used, it is of course standard equipment. For centre-pin trotting, however, an alternative exists in the form of fine terylene braid. For many years this material was unobtainable in the breaking strains appropriate to the method, but a supply in suitable sizes and of suitable quality has recently re-emerged upon the market, albeit at a cost.

Terylene braid used to have two major advantages over the monofils of some years ago, namely visibility to the angler (rather ironic, as monofils were designed to be the opposite) and lack of stretch. The former no longer applies, since yellow fluorescent nylon of high specification is now available and easily seen in all light conditions. Modern monofilament also now has better non-stretch properties than it used to, answering the latter objection to some degree. However, even specialised 'non-stretch' nylons still do not, in my opinion, compare favourably with terylene braid in this respect. With current advances in fibre and copolymer technology, this situation may well change in the near future, though. Minimal stretch is an undeniable asset in long-range striking.

A further consideration is buoyancy. A floating line can be picked up quickly and cleanly both when striking and at the completion of the trot. Nylon monofil takes the honours here, as its natural tendency is to lie on the surface. Terylene braid can be lightly greased to obtain similar behaviour, but it is imperative that this is not overdone, as the consequences for other aspects of tackle performance can be horrific.

The finer the line, the more satisfactorily it will serve our purpose insofar as tackle control is concerned. A small-diameter line does not tend to drag the float. It will feed easily from the reel and cut more cleanly through the wind. Against this must be set the necessity to land successfully the largest fish likely to be encountered. A balance has to be struck.

The late Reg Righyni, a master of grayling trotting with a centre-pin, regularly landed very large fish using a braided terylene line of 1½-lb breaking strain. Lesser mortals like myself are well-advised to be more cautious. Bear in mind that the hooklength must be slightly less strong, so that breakages as a result of snags (a few of which are inevitable when baits are being fished close to the bottom) will not result in the loss of long, continuous lengths of reel line being left to ensnare wildlife. A realistic reel line has a breaking strain in the 2–4-lb range; above 4-lbs the bulk of the line becomes an impediment.

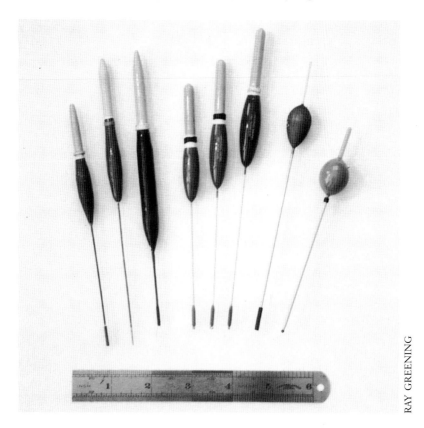

RAY GREENING

Floats: *from the left* the first three are Reg Righyni floats, the mid three are modified Wire Avon and the other a commercial and a hand-made pole float

Floats

The float is a joyous item of tackle. Like flies, floats come in endless shapes and colours, are fun to make, and are fun to fish with. And, as with flies, the opportunities for individual experiment and indulgence are legion. Floats are required to:

1. Support the shot necessary to take the bait quickly to the desired fishing depth.
2. Give accurate and sensitive bite indication.
3. Cock quickly and remain upright in the heaviest water in which they are to be used.
4. Cast well and without any tendency to tangle.

Long-trotting floats must also:
5. Be visible at long range.
6. Be able to be retrieved rapidly without undue resistance or fish-scaring disturbance.

Reg Righyni took account of these six criteria when he produced the grayling float which bears his name. The method for manufacturing these is given in his book *Grayling*, and those unfortunate enough not to possess a copy are referred to their local library.

The Righyni float is a balsa-bodied, wire-stem design and should be carried in two or three sizes according to the shot-carrying capacity required for the waters to be fished. I know of no commercial source of the exact Righyni pattern, the nearest equivalent being perhaps the wire-stemmed 'Avon' pattern. The design is particularly versatile in its tolerance of varying speeds of current – a major asset in a float which may begin its trot in a veritable torrent and complete it in a glassy calm. A typical size for a medium float would be $3\frac{1}{2}$" by $\frac{3}{8}$" maximum diameter, with a $4\frac{1}{2}$" stem.

Colours can be chosen to suit personal preference: say, a sombre dark green or brown for the immersed part, with a red, yellow or orange fluorescent top. In certain lights, black tops can prove the most visible, a fact which will be obvious to any dry-fly fisherman.

The original Righyni design was attached to the line by a rubber ring on the upper section and a monofilament loop at the base of the stem. To provide the resistance needed to prevent the float sliding up and down during casting and striking, Reg wrapped the line two or three times round the wire stem before taking it through the lower loop. This is a perfectly satisfactory expedient, but I prefer to use a PVC sleeve cut from electric cable and pushed over the lower end of the stem; if this is left long and projects beyond the end of the wire, a smooth and abrasion-free fixing results. I find this method facilitates depth adjustment, and offer it as a definite improvement over the original.

For the stem, piano wire of 20 gauge is specified by the inventor, but if stainless steel of similar diameter can be obtained, then there is no need to paint this part of the float to avoid corrosion.

To my knowledge, no floatmaker has yet taken it upon himself to include 'Righyni-style' trotting floats in a commercial range. This is lamentable, because this design remains supreme for the purpose. Latterly I have been modifying wire-stemmed Avon floats for grayling trotting by replacing the small existing tip with a much larger balsa equivalent. This gives a very pleasing result, but is difficult to achieve without extensive workshop facilities and not a little ingenuity. A recent contributor to the Grayling Society's journal suggesting gluing a quill tip over the wire Avon tip – a brilliantly simple method of obtaining a similar result. These wire-Avon floats have a moulded plastic sleeve at the bottom end of the stem which incorporates a tiny plastic ring to carry the line. This is superior in all respects to both Reg's monofil loop and my bit of PVC cable.

I am not sure for what type of fish the proprietary 'grayling bob' is intended, but it is certainly quite unsuitable for any trotting application.

Terminal Tackle

Good-quality eyed bait hooks should be obtained in sizes 14 and 12, and perhaps even in a 'small' 10. Look for a sturdy hook. When buying tackle from coarse-fishing suppliers, always bear in mind that the grayling trotter's requirements are relatively crude compared with those of many of their customers. Very fine wire hooks, for example, should be carefully avoided (a 1-lb grayling with back fin aloft in fast water on the Tay is a very different proposition from roach of similar size in a Surrey millpond). The smallest sizes of hooks sold for 'specimen hunting' are likely to be more appropriate to our purpose.

Premium fly hooks will do fair service, but I am convinced that purpose-made bait hooks are superior in all respects. Ring eyes are common on hooks of this type, and most game anglers will be happier with these than with the unfamiliar spade-end type. Barbs that are not too deep cut and short, sharp points are features shared with good fly hooks.

Where they coexist in the river, some trout and/or migratory fish will inevitably be caught when grayling fishing. Since the trotting method results in fish being hooked in the front of the mouth, returning them to the water in an undamaged condition is simply a matter of reasonably careful handling. Carry a disgorger, or a pair of very fine long-nosed pliers, and even the deep-hooked fish can be released unharmed. On most days, trout will not be encountered in large numbers, but occasionally, and for no apparent reason, they may indulge in a feeding frenzy which results in a trout in every trot. The conscientious angler may feel constrained in these circumstances to take special conservation measures.

Barbless hooks are one option. These hook and hold very well, provided that good technique is applied when playing fish. Even when loose line is inadvertently given to the fish, its loss is not nearly so likely as might be expected. (The reluctance on the part of many fishermen to use these hooks is primarily psychological, but the spectre of losing a specimen fish thereby is difficult to exorcise.) Experimentation will quickly build confidence. A more practical problem is that of obtaining barbless hooks of sufficient strength, as those on the market tend to be of the fine-wire variety.

The second option is to pinch down the barbs of regular hooks. This is easily accomplished with fine pliers, and gives the advantage of fishing barbless without the expense or difficulty of acquiring the purpose-made item.

Incidentally, if salmon are encountered, breakage in the delicate trotting tackle is a likely outcome, but provided that terminal tackle is designed along sensible lines, I have little doubt that these fish will not be badly compromised by the encounter. Whatever your choice of hook, if you are tempted to use those rejected for fly-tying purposes, on the grounds that 'anything will do' for bait fishing, then expect the results that you will deserve.

Lead shot enjoys a very bad reputation these days, and its use is proscribed in many places. Modern alternatives seem very good, being softer than some of the poorer-quality lead equivalents. Choose your sizes so that only two or three are required to cock the floats. In general, shot is concentrated close to the hook in grayling trotting applications, but occasionally it will be advantageous to spread it over a foot or two of cast. This has the effect of making the rig less depth-critical, which is useful when swims contain ledges or shallows, and 'holding back' is used as an expedient to extend the trot. Shot soft enough to allow some movement without damage to the line, then, is to be recommended.

Bait

Grayling are fish of fairly catholic taste. At one time or another they have been taken on everything from sweetcorn to 6-inch spinners. The choice however can be swiftly narrowed by a few pragmatic considerations.

1. Availability. Bait must be easily available in sufficient quantities.
2. Practicality. The chosen bait must remain on the hook through repeated casting and retrieving through heavy water.
3. Attraction independent of groundbaiting, if the needs of the roving angler are to be served.
4. Legality. Even where bait-fishing is allowed, restrictions may be in force.

This tends to leave worm and maggot (although, even on waters where general bait fishing is permitted, No. 4 may preclude use of the latter).

Any small (1–2") red worm will do the business for grayling fishing. Worm biology is a complex business, and local variation makes it difficult to discriminate between species. Brandlings are easily obtainable from smelly dung heaps, and, although some anglers may find them unpleasant to handle, they are very suitable for this fishing. Other varieties of red worm may be found in compost heaps or piles of rotting leaves, and these also make a very attractive bait. Some of these latter type may have a yellowish tail (the 'gilt-tails' advocated and popularised as the 'ultimate grayling worm' by Reg Righyni), though whether the 'gilt-tail' is a worm species in its own right is something I have never been able to find out. In any event, the gilt-tail is a fine bait, but not, in my opinion, endowed with supernatural grayling-attracting powers. Small red worms in the size range above (or even a little larger for big fish) will prove entirely adequate. For those unable to find their own supply, many tackle dealers now sell suitable worms alongside the traditional and ubiquitous maggot.

I have not used the maggot for many years (I prefer the worm), but its efficacy as a bait for grayling cannot be denied. In waters where it is regularly used as a bait, and particularly as a component of groundbait, the maggot will be familiar fare to the resident grayling and may prove superior to the worm. Where this is not the case, I fancy that worm, as the more natural bait, may have the edge. The maggot, however, bears a more than superficial resemblance to many waterborne larvae, and as such can claim to be truly imitative in the same sense as the artificial fly.

What is clear is that the effectiveness of the maggot as a bait is enhanced by loose feeding (i.e. throwing in a few in advance of the tackle). I have seen this done many times to good effect. While this could not be described as intensive groundbaiting, I nevertheless have reservations about it on ethical grounds. I leave it to the reader to make a decision based upon the dictates of his own conscience.

If maggot is chosen, one or more may be attached to the hook by nicking under the skin at the head; so attached, they are both lively and resilient. Worms can be impaled at a single point (in which case they will remain active for longer) or, alternatively, threaded into the hook – which reduces the chance of losing them. Newly dug worms are soft and benefit from the 'threaded' attachment. Use the former method when grayling are hard to come by, and the latter method when fishing is fast and furious.

Angling lore has it that storaging worms in sphagnum moss toughens them, and so improves their durability as a hookbait. The science of this assertion is dubious, but it does seem to work. I fancy that this toughening may be the result of malnutrition rather than the moss, but storing worms in this way certainly cleans them up and makes handling them more convenient. Most texts say that long-term storage in moss is practicable if a little 'top of the milk' is added by way of sustenance. 'Little' is surely the operative word, as the results of the milk turning sour before it has been consumed by the worms (and their consequent mortality) are unspeakable. The ideal method of long-term storage is to establish a 'wormery' in a small heap or plastic bucket, and to transfer worms to moss a couple of days before fishing; worms not used on the day can be returned to the main supply. Keeping the bait fresh in this way will pay dividends in effectiveness that will more than compensate for the trouble taken.

Fishing methods are the same for both worms and maggots, and subsequent remarks may be taken to refer to either.

As for other baits, those with the opportunity and dedication to collect caddis grubs, wasp grubs and large stone-fly larvae ('creepers') will find these highly attractive to the grayling.

Finding the Fish

Fish must be located before they can be caught. Where local knowledge is not available, this can be quite a problem, and guidance can be given in only the most general terms.

My experience is that, where they exist on a river, fast runs that end in long glides of fairly even depth are likely to find favour with grayling – and, by a happy coincidence, such stretches also represent ideal trotting territory. At the close of the trout season, grayling will be found in the fast waters at the heads of such pools, tending to oust the trout from the prime feeding stations. As winter progresses, a gradual dropping back takes place, its rate governed by the severity of the weather. I recommend making at least a few casts in the fastest water practicable, as even very late on in the winter the largest and fittest grayling may still be found there.

I stress again that this advice is of the most general nature. If grayling were as easily predictable as the above would suggest, much of the challenge of the sport would be lost. Once you have serviceable long-trotting tackle, you have at your disposal a very efficient device for fish-finding. Use it to investigate and explore; grayling may turn up in the unlikeliest places!

Handling the Tackle

Having set up rod and reel, thread the line through the rings and attach the float by your chosen method. Next, attach about 24" of suitable mono as a cast, and then knot the hook on. The half-blood knot will be the most appropriate for ring-eyed hooks, and, because a relatively large hook is being tied to a very fine line, the 'tucked' version of this knot is recommended for security.

Split shot should now be added. Where swim depth is expected to be fairly uniform, concentrate the shot about 10–12" from the hook. Otherwise, spread the shot out a little. In either case, place the smallest shot closest to the hook.

Now slide the float to its correct depth setting; this may be determined by a combination of knowledge of the water and trial and error. Note that the critical spacing is that between the float and the lowest shot. When set to optimum depth, slight contact with the stream bed will be detectable at various stages of the trot. If this is not the case, the tackle is set too shallow. Occasionally a shallower setting will be necessary where the bottom is particularly snag-ridden. Provided that grayling are well on the feed, fish will still be taken, but as their enthusiasm wanes, so depth must be added if continued sport is to be enjoyed.

The business of depth setting is one of the most fascinating and instructive aspects of this fishing. No matter how comprehensive your knowledge of a water may be, the use of the trotting tackle will reveal surprises, with holes and ledges being found where none was thought to exist. (A side benefit here is that the lessons learned can be usefully applied to fly fishing in its season, and this is especially so where a river contains migratory fish, for new lies can be located which are not generally fished. With the exception of the method which I will describe later, no angling technique develops the concept of a river in three dimensions more thoroughly than trotting with floating tackle.) Once an initial depth setting has been arrived at, the chosen bait can be impaled on the hook and a suitable position can be taken up to begin fishing.

Casting with fixed-spool outfits is easy and need not be described here. For a long cast using a centre-pin reel, a few pointers may be helpful. Initially the bait is allowed to trot out until its distance from the tip ring is about half the distance of the intended cast. (If a cast has just been completed, retrieval of the float can be stopped at this point.) Using the left hand, two or three loops of line are drawn from between each of the first few rings above the handle. Line is drawn simultaneously from the reel and from the length that was left outside the tip ring. This will leave an amount of line which can be comfortably swung behind the angler and to one side. A smooth swing forward is made, and the loops released *in order*, beginning with the one *furthest away from the reel*. Releasing in order is the secret of loose-loop casting. Fair proficiency can be gained with a little practice, but to become really accomplished takes a very long time. When carried out well, this casting technique is as elegant and satisfying as any of the classic fly casts.

Where the trot is being started at close quarters (which is very much the norm in smaller waters with the angler positioned at the head of the pool), the tackle can be overcast slightly and precisely positioned by drawing back to the spot desired. The trot itself can now be commenced. The object is to allow the bait, tracked by the float, to proceed down the pool at natural current speed. By adopting a high rod position, the line should be kept out of the water whenever possible, a straight line maintained between the float and rod tip, and the float checked as little as possible. Note that the speed of the float at the surface will normally tend to exceed that of the bait at the bottom, and the very slight checking induced by keeping the line straight helps to bring about the desired coincidence.

A skilled exponent with a suitable outfit can trot at long range and well out into the river, maintaining a tight line, with the line between float and rod tip out of the water, all without causing unnatural hindrance to the bait's progress. The beginner will find this impossible, but it is an indication of the potential of the tackle that practical fishing at 80–100 yards is achievable with good equipment.

An eagle eye must be kept on the float as it travels downstream. If it disappears, lift the rod in a gentle strike (if the tackle flies out of the swim to land at the angler's feet, the strike has been too violent). When the right 'touch' has been acquired, it should be possible to tighten enough to hook a fish if it has taken the bait, but to allow the trot to continue virtually as before if the desired contact is not felt. As already stated, some interference from fouling the bottom is to be expected from a correctly depthed rig, but, with some experience, the angler will often be able to distinguish this from the attentions of a grayling. Where he is satisfied that the bottom has been caught (not hooked, as in nine cases out of ten it will be the shot that has snagged), it will normally only be necessary to check the tackle momentarily to free it. The trot can then continue as before.

The grayling is often a bold biter, and a sharp dip of the float will frequently result in a well-hooked, hard-fighting winter grayling and a happy fisherman! In fast water, though, it must be said that the float can also dive very quickly if it snags. Where the bottom is very bad, some loss of tackle is inevitable and will have to be endured with equanimity. Breaks will generally result in loss of hook, shots or both. Loss of a float is fortunately rare, since one tends to develop an affection for this item which renders its loss a body-blow.

Occasionally, shy-biting fish may be encountered, and it may be necessary to strike a little earlier (i.e. before the float goes right under) to avoid being 'robbed' of the worm. A change to a smaller float may help if circumstances permit; otherwise, experimenting with timing may be necessary. Again, practice makes perfect, and as experience and confidence grow an instinct develops which will enable an acceptable percentage of bites to be struck successfully. Providing a fish has not been 'jagged', a further trot to the same spot will often result in the angler being given a second chance.

Weather

Let me say at the outset that I regard the winter grayling as the fish least affected by extremes of water level and temperature – although grayling lore has it that very cold days sharpen the appetite of the fish, and there may be something in this. What is certain, however, that very cold days have a very adverse effect on the fisherman, on his tackle and on his ability to handle it properly. The high winds encountered at this time of the year also cause problems. Be assured, though, that any conditions that you are able to endure will be perfectly agreeable to the grayling.

Obvious advice is to wrap up well, carry some sustenance by way of sandwiches and hot tea or soup, and avoid long periods of standing immobile. The last point is particularly important if the nature of the river involves wading in very cold water. The neoprene waders now appearing here from the US market are a complete answer to this problem, but few anglers would be prepared to make such an investment purely to further their winter grayling activities. Gloves are a thorough nuisance, but at times they make the difference between getting in some fishing and not being able to fish at all; fingerless mittens perhaps offer the best possibilities.

It has to be said that the primary object of the exercise is enjoyment, and that adverse weather conditions will arise in which even the hardiest and most determined grayling angler will be unable to enjoy his fishing. When this happens, go home!

As for tackle limitations, it is very difficult to trot successfully in high winds, because of line-handling problems, so seek out sheltered areas. In my opinion it is *impossible* to trot when the line is freezing in the rings, but see the following section for a solution.

Grayling on the Pole

Given suitable equipment and a little practice, long-trotting can be a highly effective and enjoyable method of winter grayling fishing. Few exponents would see any advantage to be gained by exploring other avenues. However, long-trotting is a very 'extensive' method, based upon ranging widely over the river seeking out the fish. I reasoned that an 'intensive' method, in which a smaller physical area would be more thoroughly fished, might offer a more viable alternative.

Origins

I had noted that anglers using unsuitable tackle, such as standard fly outfits, with float and worm often enjoyed relatively good results. In view of their drastically reduced fishing range, this could be attributed only to a very thorough coverage of the water available. I also noted that the reel was virtually redundant, being used only to play hooked fish. My idea, essentially, was to give up the long-range approach, dispense with the reel altogether, and to fish water close at hand in the most effective manner possible.

The advantages of being in close proximity to one's quarry are manifold in all forms of angling. Clearly, normal trotting tackle could be used more effectively at close quarters by simple application of will-power, so if an alternative technique was to have merit, real advantages over conventional outfits would have to be gained.

Tackle and Technique

A long rod for use without a reel presented no problem. Indeed, a huge array of such implements is available. Known as 'poles', these are much favoured by the coarse-fishing fraternity, primarily for use in match angling. I chose a glass-fibre example some twenty feet long, which cost

RAY GREENING

Pole rod with winder – 1999 version

around £16, as a happy medium between length and weight. As no reel is used, both hands are free to hold the rod and it is therefore not so ungainly as might at first be supposed. This choice has proved a reasonable one, but where price is no obstacle a better compromise could obviously be achieved with carbon fibre.

In match fishing, a very short link between pole tip and float is the norm, but in a grayling rig more versatility is required, and the overall spacing from pole tip to hook should be about one foot less than the length of the pole itself, with float position being determined by the depth of the water being fished. The smallest float that will carry the necessary shotting is used. Note that, as it will never be more than about thirty-five feet from the fisherman, visibility will not be a problem, and the small float will give a very good bite detection. Also, as the float is picked directly out of the water by the pole, and water disturbance on retrieval is no longer a problem, the bob-type float, with its inherent ability to ride rough water, now becomes a practicable proposition.

A hookline of about two feet of 2-lb BS monofilament is attached to a main line of 3-lbs BS monofilament, and a suitably sturdy hook as for trotting completes the rig. This tackle is swung out with the pole some way upstream of the angler, then tracked down with the pole tip, holding the line between tip and float high out of the water. In normal conditions, really accurate casting using both hands well spread on the butt is quickly mastered. With this tackle float control is superbly good. Inch accuracy

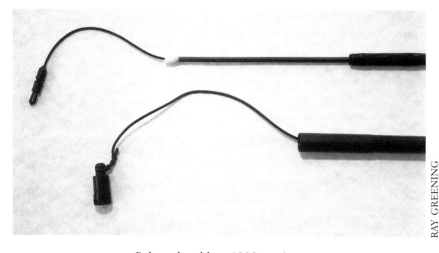

RAY GREENING

Pole rod tackle – 1999 version

can be obtained by overcasting and drawing back, and water can be searched out in a manner which would be quite unrealistic with conventional trotting tackle. Response to bites by raising the pole tip can be very positive and virtually instantaneous. Thus all likely water within range is covered. Waders are obviously an advantage, particularly to increase scope in bigger waters.

The matter of coping with large fish without a reel from which to give line must now be considered. The match fisherman who developed the pole technique to its present level of sophistication solved this problem by introducing an elastic link into the tackle to absorb shocks and to assist the pole's own limited springing to slow down a running fish. In my early experiments with the pole, I tried to achieve this by simply incorporating such a link into the main line. While this delivered the goods while playing large fish, it produced a most undesirable side-effect: chronic problems of tangling round the pole tip when casting.

I had almost given up hope of beating this, and was ready to abandon the pole as a bad job, when Kevin Ashurst's book *The Encyclopaedia of Pole Fishing* became available and presented the solution (Ashurst is a former world champion match angler, and the book is excellent, although much of its content is irrelevant to our application). The answer is to conceal the elastic within the top two joints of the pole, secured at the lower end by a bored plug and prevented by a stop from slipping through a smoothed-off orifice at the extreme tip. This is ingenious and totally effective, as the presence of the elastic is only apparent when a fish is being played. Note that this solution will involve some modification to the pole tip, unless a pole is purchased which already incorporates the feature in its design.

The elastic to use is available from coarse-fishing suppliers, and that designated 'strong' is most appropriate. While purchasing elastic, get some 'pole-winders' also. These are cast/float-carriers purpose-made of plastic to hold complete terminal tackles. Prepare tackles in advance, with floats attached and shotted, mount them on winders, and little else need be carried for a day's pole fishing.

You may harbour some doubt and suspicion about the ability of a long stick and an elastic band to keep an active fish under control in heavy water. So did I, but having since landed grayling of almost two pounds and (inadvertently) sea trout of over three pounds. I now know that – between the length and flex of the pole, the stretch of the elastic and the mobility of the fisherman – much larger fish could be played. (The sensation is weird and the excitement electric!) Small fish can be swung to hand, but use a landing-net for fish over half a pound, as beaching can be awkward when handling the pole.

The Pole

If trotting is made more pleasurable by the latest and lightest gear, then this applies doubly to the pole. Poles under about 7 metres length are known in match fishing circles as 'whips', being intended originally for high-speed fishing for tiny fish. I have discovered over the years that match anglers are notoriously fashion-conscious, and that last year's 'wonder whip' is wont to appear in the current sale lists of the big coarse-fishing suppliers at as little as a third of the original cost. This is excellent news for the aspiring grayling pole fisher.

I now possess two or three of these 'last year's Cinderellas', and at 6–6.5 metres (22' plus) they are light enough (and slim enough at the butt) to be held comfortably in one hand with the arm fully extended. Such an instrument is a revelation compared with my original outfit, and contributes enormously to the pleasure obtainable from this particular method of presenting a bait.

Other improvements to the pole rig are now readily available, from high-strength elastics to purpose-designed bungs, PTFE pole-tip bushes, and connectors. Finer elastic, in particular, means that less of the hollow tip-section has to be cut away to enable the elastic to pass through freely.

The number of commercial pole-float patterns is increasing exponentially. Most, although beautifully made, are much too delicate for our application, but sturdier bulbous-bodied river models in the 1–3 gram range are ideal for those who do not wish to produce their own.

One more thing about carbon poles (and the longer trotters and salmon fly-rods too): *LOOK OUT FOR OVERHEAD CABLES!* This advice is especially important for the roving angler. Survey your water before you start, and get used to carrying your pole/rod horizontally, with the tip behind you. Providing the favoured earth path with a few hundred kilovolts of electricity is one method of keeping warm in winter which I cannot recommend.

A Specialised Float

At a later stage of the development of the pole technique, I designed a float especially for this type of grayling fishing. The main criteria given for the trotting float still apply, but those relating to visibility at long range and retrieval without disturbance can be sacrificed to enhance the remainder. A float incorporating a more bulbous body than the Righyni type is less at the mercy of fluctuations in velocity in the immediate sub-surface layer of the water. However, I wished to retain the excellent cocking properties of Reg's design.

DERMOT WILSON

Late autumn pole fishing for grayling on the River Test

One of the primary techniques used with the pole method is to set the float over-depth and hold back, thus causing the bait to swing about just above the river bottom in a manner most attractive to the grayling; here the precision control over the tackle afforded by the pole really scores. The principle itself is nothing new, of course, and generations of coarse fishermen have used it in pursuit of other species, but much of their methodology is geared to the placid waters of the south, and is less applicable to swollen northern rivers like those where I do much of my grayling fishing. The float needs to maintain an upright and well-cocked attitude while being held back, so that sensitive and reliable bite indication is not lost. This is achieved by arranging for the floats upper point of attachment to the line to be in approximate alignment with its centre of buoyancy. A rubber ring, such as is used on slimmer profiles, is clearly out of place

91

here, and instead a 'side-eye' is incorporated, giving the desired attachment without sacrificing ease of depth adjustment. The final result of these deliberations is as illustrated.

Here is my method of manufacturing this float. It may be adapted to suit the equipment available and to produce individual floats of similar design. Float-making is great fun and can be addictive!

1. Cut lengths of balsa and hardwood dowels to suit the intended final dimensions. Round off one end of the hardwood tip. Dowel of around $\frac{1}{8}$" diameter will be found suitable for the upper sections of all sizes of float.
2. Drill the float body to half depth at a size to accept the hardwood tip.
3. Glue the unrounded end of the tip into the body with epoxy. This will give a little handle which will make succeeding steps easier.
4. Roughly shape the body by hand. Finish in a lathe or drill stand if available, chucking by the hardwood tip and finishing with fine sandpaper.
5. Cut a length of stainless steel wire (about 4" will suffice for a medium-sized float), and round the lower end to prevent damage to fine nylon. Push the other end into the float body; pull out, apply glue and push in again.

RON BROUGHTON

John Davison trotting for grayling on the River Ribble

6. Take a suitable-sized hook (preferably not one of your best Partridge's) and cut off the bend. Press into the side of the float body at such an angle that the eye finishes in a horizontal plane. Glue in as with the wire stem. This is a most convenient method of forming the side-eye.

7. To prevent abrasion of the nylon by the wire end, cut a sleeve from PVC electrical insulation. Leave it long, and in use do not push it fully on to the wire stem. (This is the same fixing as suggested to improve the Righyni float.)

8. Seal the balsa. Paint the body in your chosen camouflage colour and paint the tip white. When dry, apply fluorescent paint over this white base (this enhances the end result). I like to use orange or red, and to leave a little ring of white to separate tip from body, for cosmetic reasons. A finishing coat of epoxy varnish leaves the float sparkling and durable (without it, the fluorescent paints are inclined to flake off).

Summary

The above is a brief description of pole fishing for grayling. The method is much more versatile than it might appear at first sight, and, with the exceptions detailed below, I consider it applicable to all waters. Here are its advantages and disadvantages compared to long-trotting, so that you may evaluate the merit or otherwise of this heretical departure from the grayling tradition.

Advantages:
1. Superior float control.
2. Superior bite detection and hooking.
3. Intensive and accurate water coverage.
4. In very cold weather, line freezing in rings does not occur (no rings!).
5. Also in cold weather, there is no reel to fumble with, gloves can be worn without impairing tackle handling, and – if loops are incorporated in prepared tackles on winders, and a snap-link swivel is attached to the upper end of the elastic – no knots need tying with numb fingers.
6. Length of pole can reach over bankside obstacles, bushes and weed beds. This is useful in smaller, overgrown streams.
7. Inherent simplicity of tackle – not much to go wrong.

Disadvantages:
1. If you cannot get to within 35' of a favoured area, it cannot be fished.
2. The pole is somewhat unwieldy until you get accustomed to handling it, and still somewhat unwieldy when you have done.

3. Overhead bankside trees create real problems for the pole fisherman. In these circumstances, trot or go elsewhere.
4. Poling tempts the angler to wade in cold water. I have mentioned the inadvisability of this already.
5. Due to its thick section, the glass-fibre pole is quite unmanageable in high winds. High winds make trotting difficult but not unmanageable.

I have fished the pole alongside very experienced long-trotters on large rivers which might be expected to favour the traditional method, and the pole has more than held its own. As a technique, it has all the elements of developing skill, sportsmanship and personal fulfilment associated with more heavily trodden paths of angling. I commend it as worthy of the attention of the serious all-round grayling fisherman.

A Closing Observation

Fishing with natural bait is often presented as a method that, while pleasurable in its own right, should be resorted to only when fly fishing is not a productive option. Rightly or wrongly, many fly fishers who are looking to extend their season and for winter diversion do view bait fishing in this light. It is therefore relevant to consider whether any developments in fly fishing have occurred which might extend that method's effective season.

It is probably true that a reluctant and inactive fish is more likely to be tempted by a natural bait than an artificial, and is also probable that the single factor that is most detrimental to success in winter fly fishing is the difficulty of presenting a fly consistently at the feeding depth: i.e. on, or very close to, the bottom, often in deepish (4–6') water. Although the fast-sinking lines that are readily available ostensibly achieve this objective, unnatural movement of the artificial, and constant snagging, tend to lead to disappointing results.

It is now well-known that in 1990, at the World Fly-fishing Championships on the Welsh Dee, the Polish and Czech teams demonstrated a method of fishing very heavily weighted nymph patterns at close range with devastating effect, especially where grayling were the target species. In skilled hands, this method – known variously as the 'short nymph', 'rolled nymph', or 'bugging' – achieves effective deep presentation.

The method is difficult to master, exhausting in practice (due to constant extension of the rod arm), and is at best a somewhat distant cousin of the delicate dry fly – though, ironically but not coincidentally, it has more in common with my short pole tactics. But it can certainly produce results, particularly in the faster, medium-depth water which is beloved of the grayling and ideally suited to the method.

No further explanation is appropriate here, but, given suitable river conditions, short-line, heavyweight nymphing may well complement bait fishing as an alternative approach that can also produce good catches in the depths of winter. One of my colleagues, a dedicated fly fisherman, uses trotting gear initially to locate the grayling, but then reverts to these deep-nymph tactics (at which he is adept) to catch them on the fly rod.

Flies that Catch Grayling

Ron Broughton

Buds fur-gloved with frost. Everything has come to a standstill
In a brand new stillness.
The river-trees, in a blue haze,
Were fractured domes of spun ghost.

(Ted Hughes: 'The Morning before Christmas')

British Flies

Tied by Ron Broughton

IT IS MY BELIEF, as it will be of any angler who has considered the point, that there is no such thing as a 'grayling fly'. There are flies that will catch grayling, but these are precisely those which will bring their cousins, the brown trout, to the fisherman's basket.

There are fancy flies that were first created to take trout in low water summer conditions and were found to be very effective for grayling at the opposite end of the year. Such a one is the Red Tag. There are fancy flies that were tied specifically for grayling and were found to be great medicine for summer trout, such as Bradshaw's Fancy. There is a whole range of artificial flies that mimic the natural at a time of the year when trout are to be ignored or have sensibly gone to the spawning becks, and so they are used exclusively for grayling. And, of course, there is every artificial that was ever made for trout that will with equal facility deceive a grayling.

But for all that, the phrase 'grayling flies' is a convenient one, a sort of generic term, much as we use the label 'sea trout flies', as though there were some great difference, apart from size, separating them from salmon lures made from silk, fur and feathers.

The grayling, like the rest of this family of salmon, sea trout and brown trout, will seize any size of fly, from the smallest to the largest, when it takes his fancy. Many have been caught by sea-trout anglers, as many a Scottish or north-country fisherman will attest, but for all that, the cream of angling sport is to persuade a wild feeding fish that what one offers appears, in size, shape and motion, and in the proper position in the water, to be the very thing that he desires to eat. It is with this in mind that I have compiled this list of artificial flies that will take grayling.

The changes in fly-dressing have become more obvious since the first edition was written. It is not that in the last twelve years a mass of new material has suddenly appeared. Some has, but there has been an increased appreciation of man-made fibres among fly-tyers as some natural fibres and feathers have become scarce. Jim Wynn of Wharfedale was experimenting with artificial fibre and coloured tinsel in the late 1930s, and the history of gold head may go back four hundred years. It takes time for anglers to get used to new ideas!

But the use of polypropylene fibre and *cul de canard* – together with the study of subaquatic insects other than *ephemeropterae* in the diet of fish – have changed the whole structure of the artificial fly and emphasised anew the old form of fishing the artificial fly as 'the emerger'. And the cross-fertilisation between the theories of the artificial river fly and those of the stillwater has recreated Halfordian ideals of exact representation, as patterns from fly-tyers like Oliver Edwards testify – even to the representation of parasitic disease, as in the orange-spot shrimp. These new techniques and designs give anglers a wider range of artificial flies, but those first recorded almost 200 years ago are still prime deceivers of fish, and their use cannot be denied.

The original way of placing artificial flies in order was to describe them as they appeared, month by month. The modern alphabetical system is quite late, appearing only well into this century (Carter Platt's books on trout and grayling, published in the 1930s, are as early an example of the latter as I have found). This probably shows how divorced from natural life we have become; even though we aspire to an intimate knowledge of life in stream and stillwater, we approach it via methodical tabulation rather than as observant naturalists. However, I am but a product of my own age, so here is my alphabetical list of flies:

Adjutant Blue (*See* col. illus. 1) This was one of the often-used flies at the turn of the century for the autumn shade of the Iron Blue. It is still a very good fly.
Hook: Size 16.
Body: Originally a strand from the pinion of the Adjutant, a south-east

Asian stork. This was prepared by stripping the long flue from one edge and leaving the short flue on the other. Halford suggested as substitute a strip of quill from an old starling's pinion feather. Woolley advised the quill of a coot's wing feather. The illustration uses coot.
Hackles and Whisks: From a dark dun cock.

Apple Green (*See* col. illus. 1) This has been described as a fancy fly, but that is a term that is often loosely used to mean a general fly (Skues used much ink in his *Minor Tactics of the Chalk Stream*, in attempting to define the difference between the two terms). The Apple is to my mind a fly representing in a general way several of the smaller olive and pale watery duns found in rougher streams in the autumn, just as artificial flies such as Greenwell's Glory and the Red Spinner represent groups of flies in a general way.
Hooks: Sizes 16–14.
Body: Light green floss silk (*Soie Ovale* 2112, RSN).
Hackle: Ginger Cock.
Whisks: Three strands of the same.
Wings: Pale starling.

August Dun This has been tied in many forms, all very much the same. It is the same fly as Walbran's August Brown (he was very fond of using rabbit whiskers for the tails of his flies). It is in fact a wet form of the Autumn March Brown, which Ronalds advises is in season from the beginning of August to mid-September.
Hook: Sizes 14–12.
Body: Brown floss.
Rib: Yellow tying silk.
Hackle: Brown hen.
Whisks: Three fibres of the same.
Wings: Cock pheasant's wing feather.

Autumn Dun This is the pale blue dun seen during the autumn.
Hook: Sizes 16–14.
Body: Heron herl, or a dyed goose substitute.
Hackles and Whisks: Palest blue dun cock.
Wings: Snipe, under-wing feather.

Baby Sun Fly This famous pattern of the Reverend Edward Powell is one of those flies tied for early-season trout feeding on the black gnat, which has been equally of use for taking grayling at the opposite end of the season.

Hook: Sizes 16–12.
Tie silk: Brown.
Body: Dark rabbit fur taken from the area between eyes and nose.
Rib: Tie silk.
Hackle: Small Coch-y-bondhu cock, tied fairly thick.
Whisks: Black cock.

Badgers

There are so many flies using a badger hackle that it is difficult to know which should be placed in the category. The use of a white or cream hackle with a black centre is obvious for creating the illusion of a dark thorax and shining mobile wings, and it is so easily visible, especially to the wretched angler who is straining to see where his fly has drifted to.

Undoubtedly Badger Red Tag and Brunton's Fancy should be included, but being Badger variations on the Red and Orange Tags they have their separate places. Likewise the Priest, though it seems a more elegant fly than Woolley's Silver Badger. Woolley's list includes:

Badger Red Tag (*See* col. illus. 1)
Hook: Sizes 16–14.
Body: Bronze peacock.
Tag: Red silk.
Hackle: Badger cock.

Blue Badger
Hook Sizes 16–14.
Body: Blue floss: I cheer for Oxford rather than Cambridge.
Rib: Silver wire, using two turns to form a tip at the rear of the body.
Hackle: Badger cock, palmered in open turns from shoulder to tail.

Red Badger
Body: Red floss, and otherwise as Blue Badger.

Silver Badger
Body: Silver flat.
Tag: Red at head and tail.
Hackle: Badger hen.

Beetles

The Bracken Clock which Hofland tied in 1839 is not properly relevant to grayling fishing, as it appears in May to June, but for all that, the various representations of *Phyllopertha horticola* are useful as the season progresses into September. The most common, and one of the most ancient, equivalent to the Shorn Fly described by Best in 1787, is the Coch-y-bondhu. The following ties are of interest and have taken grayling:

Coch-y-bondhu
Hook: Sizes 14–12.
Body: Two or three strands of copper-coloured peacock herl, twisted together.
Tip: Gold flat.
Hackle: Coch-y-bondhu, which is a blood-red hackle with black centre and tips.

The Marlow Buzz Ronald's variant:
Body: Black ostrich herl, twisted with bronze peacock herl and black tie silk.
Hackle: Dark furnace cock tied palmer fashion. There were variations in this, some having silver ribbing and some gold.

Black Snipe Pritt says this is a very old Yorkshire fly and will kill all the year round, which is what we want of a good grayling fly.
Hook: Sizes 16–14.
Body: Dark green peacock herl.
Hackle: Jack-snipe feather from under the wing.

Blue Dun (*See* col. illus. 1) For use in the very early season.
Hook: Size 14.
Tie silk: Primrose.
Body: Pale mole's fur dubbed on the tie silk.
Hackle and Whisks: Pale blue dun.
Wings: Light snipe.

Bottle Imp
Body: Grey-blue wool. The procurement of the right colour of wool requires ingenuity. It is a matter of seeking permission to look among one's wife's darning wool. I was lucky enough to have a coat of what I

thought was the right shade, and was able to denude the seams of enough spare wool to create several flies.

Tag: Scarlet feather, dyed swan.

Hackle: Black cock.

In small sizes it is fished dry. Otherwise put on an underbody of lead and fish wet.

Black Gnat *See* 'Gnats and Midges'.

Bradshaw's

Bradshaw's little hairy monsters are famous and rightly so. They are without doubt the very essence of controlled Victorian exuberance and very well thought out. The creators of flies in the late nineteenth century may have produced the most curious-looking fancy flies, but they knew all about the powers of attraction of peacock and ostrich herl, a small red flash of colour, soft mobile hackles and a good 'entry'.

The three examples of Bradshaw's skill that concern grayling anglers are the ones illustrated and described in Pritt's *Book of the Grayling*, and are as follows:

Bradshaw's Adopted

Hook: Sizes 14–18.

Body: Bronze peacock herl.

Tag: Crimson floss.

Hackle: Cock starling neck feather.

Head: Crimson floss.

For a good 'entry', the floss at the head should be made with a couple of turns to form a head and not left loose like a revolutionary flag.

Bradshaw's Golden Crow

Hook: Sizes 15, long 16, or Captain Hamilton 16.

Body: Gold flat.

Hackle: Light neck feather of a Norwegian crow or of a young grouse.

Bradshaw's Fancy (*See* col. illus. 1) The doyen of them all.

Hook: Size 14.

Tie silk: It is most important to use a dark purple, not a black, gossamer silk.

Body: Copper-coloured peacock herl, two or three strands.

Tag: Crimson floss silk.

Hackle: As with the Golden Crow, a light, soft and mobile feather; the pale dun feather of a young grouse, or the palest of dun hen hackles, are usable as a substitute for the Norwegian crow.

Head: Crimson floss and peacock herl.

One way to do this is to carry the tag silk up the body and to cover it with the returning tie silk and the peacock herl. Tie in the herl at the shoulder, but leave one piece of herl and the tag silk extended over the eye to form the head later on. Tie in and take two turns of the hackle over these extensions. Tie in the hackle and cut off the waste. Take the single herl and floss which extend over the eye, twist together, take two turns in front of the hackle, tie in and whip finish. Do not worry too much about the slight increase in bulk in the body; it provides for what Reg Righyni used to call a 'meaty' fly.

Brookes' Fancy (*See* col. illus. 1) The invention of a Ludlow postman who fished the Teme. It is said by Michael Leighton to be particularly effective for grayling when fished 'semi-dry' during October. It is one of the several effective flies with dark bodies and light hackle. As Michael says, the use of peacock herl ribbing is as old as the European history of fly dressing, being in one of Dame Juliana's 'flyes' of the fifteenth century.

Hooks: Sizes 14–12.

RON BROUGHTON

Derek Bradley on the Chatsworth Estate water on the River Wye

Tie silk: Purple.
Body: Purple floss.
Rib: Peacock herl.
Hackle: White.

Michael Leighton's variant:
Body: Rear half – purple silk. Front half – peacock herl.
Hackle: White.
This is another fly that can be fished dry, or wet just under the surface.

Broughton's Point This originally had a blue floss body, and the hackle was an unrelieved black. With a claret body and black hackle it is the same as Pritt's Dark Bloa. It began life for use on Ullswater, the happy creation of a Penrith shoemaker about 150 years ago. It is not known who added the scarlet-red fibres, and whether this enhances its action in rivers as much as in lakes is a matter of opinion and debate.
Hook: Sizes 14–12.
Body: Dark claret floss.
Hackle: Black hen, with a few scarlet fibres of dyed white hen as a beard to mingle with the black.
Wing: Medium starling.

The B.P. Fly or Dr Broughton's Pupa (*See* col. illus. 1) One fine January day I spent a frustrating few hours trying to make out what the grayling were taking on the River Ure. What they were not taking were the small dark olive midges on the surface of the pools. I took a suicidal fish at last, and by stomach biopsy realised the truth: it was full of small midge pupae of a brownish olive colour. Some time later I returned armed with a simple concoction that seemed to solve the problem. Not only did this work in Wensleydale, but also in other limestone rivers in the winter months when there were midge pupae trapped by the surface tension, making them an easy picking for the grayling.

It is so simple a tie that it seems certain that it must have been used by others, but nowhere can I find it. I remember being puzzled by a fly on the Lune one spring many years ago and gave much thought to making an artificial copy of it (so absorbed in the problem did I become that the local pharmacist was finding and returning the most remarkable prescriptions that consisted of fur and feather instead of soothing medicines!). The great day dawned when the problem was solved – but doubts entered my mind. I had seen it before! I had rediscovered the Blue Dun! So, with trepidation, I announce the B.P. Fly or Dr Broughton's Pupa.

Hook: Sizes 14–22.

Tie silk: At head end only – yellow.

Abdomen: Nylon 2-lb breaking strain, taken down to right round the bend of the hook (a Limerick for choice) and back again in tight turns. This gives an irregular and segmented abdomen with the bronze of the hook showing through.

Thorax: A large wad of dark hare's ear from the base of the ear, left rough. When wet it becomes a dark olive colour.

A variation of the tie from Ken Smith of Durham (who has developed his own method of producing half-hitches from alternate sides of the hook shank, creating a more regular and translucent body): The two ends of nylon are bound down together behind the eye forming the basis for the wad of dark hare's ear. Small sizes of fly appear not to need side flashes or breathing filaments, the fish taking them quite happily as they are.

Brown Owl Pritt's tie, a *Perlidae* imitation, i.e. a willow fly.

Hook: Size 14.

Body: Orange silk. The illustration in Pritt's *North Country Flies* would suggest a hot orange (Pearsall's No. 19).

Hackle: The reddish feather from the outside of an owl's wing. A substitute might be found in a reddish-brown pheasant feather.

Head: Two turns of peacock herl.

Bumbles

Correctly classified, the Bumbles are one form of the group generally known as Palmers, being hackled from head to bend of the hook in open turns of either hen or cock hackle. The bodies in the original Foster Bumbles were of peacock herl and ribbed with floss silk and tinsel for, as he said, both use and ornament.

Previously Palmers had bodies formed of hog's fur, mohair or silk. The Derbyshire flies were peculiar in having the body formed of peacock herl and ribbed with floss silk. It remained for Halford, in his quest to make flies fit for dry fly work, to reverse the process and to return to silk for the body and relegate the herl to ribbing. It is in this form that we know them today, but it would seem a pity to lose the attractiveness, both to the fish and to ourselves, of the original Derbyshire Foster Bumbles.

With this in mind I have listed both forms in such a way as to show, I hope, the subtle variations of the many forms of this curious and effective fly.

David Foster's Derbyshire Bumbles

Furnace
Tie silk: Red-brown.
Body: Peacock herl.
Rib: Dark orange.
Hackle: Furnace cock.

Honey dun
Tie silk: Yellow.
Body: Peacock herl.
Rib: Orange floss (Pearsall's No. 6A).
Hackle: Honey dun hen.

Mulberry
Tie silk: Claret.
Body: Peacock herl.
Rib: Mulberry floss.
Hackle: Dun hen.

Ordinary
Tie silk: Brown.
Body: Peacock herl.
Rib: Orange and puce floss.
Hackle: Palest blue hen.

Red
Tie silk: Dark brown.
Body: Peacock herl.
Rib: Gold floss.
Hackle: Red cock stained red.

Frederick Halford's Bumbles
Hook: Captain Hamilton sizes 16–18.

Claret
Body: Claret floss.
Rib: Peacock sword, one strand.
Hackle: Medium blue dun cock.

Furnace
Body: Orange floss.

Rib: Peacock sword, fine flat gold.
Hackle: Coch-y-bondhu.

Orange This was known as the Priceless Bumble on the Test in the 1880s.
Body: Orange floss.
Rib: Peacock sword, fine flat gold.
Hackle: Honey dun cock.

Yellow
Body: Primrose floss.
Rib: Peacock sword.
Hackle: Pale blue dun cock.

Roger Woolley added the following stock, hook sizes 14–12.

Mulberry
Body: Mulberry floss.
Rib: Peacock bronze herl.
Hackle: Medium dun hen.

Rough
Body: Yellow floss.
Rib: Peacock herl, red silk.
Hackle: Medium dun hen.

Ruby
Body: Ruby floss.
Rib: Peacock from eye of feather.
Hackle: Pale blue dun hen.

Depending on the size of the fly, the floss silk is best divided. Usually it is in four strands, one or two of which will be adequate. The hackle is best tied in by its tip at the tail of the fly and follows behind the rib as closely as possible. Finish with two close turns at the head.

Cinnamon Fly This is representative of a sedge fly seen in August and early September. Ronalds considers it a creature able to withstand a blustery wet day, and so its artificial is then very useful. There are several ties, the one based on Ronald's tie being one of the most effective and the simplest.
Hook: Sizes 14–12.

Tie silk: Fawn: as such this is difficult to find, but 'Ash' (Pearsall's No. 10) will do very well.

Body: Fawn floss silk (Soie Ovale RSN 4534). Tie in at shoulder, wind down to the hook bend and back again and finish off at the shoulder.

Hackle: Ginger cock, not too much.

Wings: Yellow-brown hen's wing, tied to be flat over the body.

Cinnamon Quill This is one of the great dry flies for grayling, useful from August to October. It represents the small autumn and winter olive and pale watery spinners.

Hook: Captain Hamilton size 16.

Tie silk: Never quoted, to my knowledge, but Sherry Spinner (Pearsall's No. 6B) is satisfactory.

Body: Cinnamon peacock quill; this colour is found at the root of a herl quill from low down on the eye-feather stem.

Hackle and Whisks: Ginger cock.

Wings: Pale starling.

Cock Winged Dun David Foster's general wet fly to represent the small olives of October.

Hook: Sizes 14–16.

Tie silk: Yellow; a small portion of rabbit's blue underfur spun sparingly on the tie silk, so that the yellow shows through.

Hackle: Blue dun; this should be stained slightly by the use of a yellow felt pen, making it a pale dunnish green.

Corkscrew I have no first-hand knowledge of this, but Halford praised it as one of Marryat's best flies for use in coloured water. As this is all too common in autumn, it seems worth including.

Hook: Sizes 14–16.

Tie silk: Not given, but possibly dark brown (Pearsall's No. 17).

Body: The quill of a red-brown partridge's tail feather, the soft fibres having been cut away. This gives a segmented body.

Hackle: Brown ginger.

Crimson Tag This is one of Pritt's concoctions.

Hook: Sizes 14–16.

Body: Peacock sword feather, made full.

Tag: Crimson wool.

Hackle: Bronze feather from a golden plover's breast in full plumage. (Wings are easy to come by, but the body skins are usually discarded.)

Dark Bloa This is by Jackson for the very early season, being similar to Broughton's Point.
Body: Dark red-brown silk.
Hackle: Black cock.
Tail: Two strands of black cock.
Wings: Dark feather from side of water-hen's wing.

Dark Watchet (*See* col. illus. 1) This is a wet fly to imitate the Iron Blue. Pritt advises that it will kill on cold days through the season after the first swallows come. His tie is:
Hook: Size 16.
Tie silk: Orange.
Body: Orange and purple tie silk, twisted and lightly dubbed with blue fur from a water-rat.
Hackle: Soft dark feather from a jackdaw's neck (that from the scalp gives a smaller feather) or one from the outside of a coot's wing.
Head: Orange, formed by the finishing whip of the tie silk.

Dark Spanish Needle *See* 'Needle Flies'

Dazzler This is said by Carter Platt to be one of Rolt's concoctions, the acme of what a grayling fly ought to be.
Body: Tail half – flat gold. Head half – bronze peacock.
Tag: Scarlet ibis.
Hackle: Badger cock, dyed ruby.

Dotterel Dun Pritt says that it is effective on cold days from April to the end of the season, and it has been suggested that it is a pale watery imitation.
Hook: Size 14.
Body: Pritt gives two colours; straw and orange. As the season progresses, the colour becomes darker. The Cumbrian tie is formed from the fur from a hare's face dubbed on yellow silk.
Hackle: The original was the light golden-tipped fawnish feather from the marginal coverts of the male dotterel's wing. Halford suggested as a substitute the dun under-coverts that have pale tips from under a starling's wing. I have found, after much experimenting and help from the tackle trade, that lightly staining the tips of the starling feathers with a yellow felt pen produces the greatest likeness.

February Red or **Old Joan** This is an early-season *Perlidae*, and Ronalds says that it is present from mid-February until the season of the Blue Dun, or for modern-day purposes until the 15 March, and that it takes very large grayling. It is a useful fly outside the chalk streams. As a dressing it is certainly as old as the seventeenth century, having been described by Charles Cotton.

The simplest tie is the Partridge and Orange, but Ronalds' is a very good representation.

Hook: Size 14.

Tie silk: Brown.

Body: Dark red squirrel's fur mixed with an equal quantity of claret mohair, the most claret to show at the tail.

Hackle: Claret-dyed hackle.

Wings: Ginger dun covert feather from a mallard's wing or from a peahen.

Fog Black (*See* col. illus. 1) Another one of Pritt's, this is an excellent gnat representation.

Hook: Size 16.

Tie silk: Purple.

Body: Dark heron herl, one strand.

Wings: Bullfinch, or substitute from the feather of a jay where there is a dark root and a light tip.

Reg Righyni fishing the River Eamont for grayling

Gnats and Midges

This group of flies includes not only *Bibo johannis*, which is not a water-bred insect, but several other types of gnats and midges, some of which are waterborne. For all the wealth of definition over the years, anglers are a conservative lot and tend to designate any insect on the water that looks small and black as a 'black gnat', and anything that bites his ears and face of a summer's evening as a 'midge'.

The artificials created to represent the black gnat are so numerous that any section on them is bound to leave out somebody's 'fail-me-never'!

Black Gnat Pritt's tie, the simplest of them all.
Hook: Size 15.
Body: A little black ostrich herl.
No hackle or wings.

Griffith's Gnat (*See* col. iIllus. 1) This from the Wharfe, courtesy of Peter Nightingale of Kettlewell.
Hook: Sizes 14–22.
Tie silk: Black.
Body: Peacock herl.
Hackle: Grizzle cock, palmered in close turns.

Blue Gnat This is a fly for the months of September and October, as Bainbridge said.
Hook: Size 16.
Tie silk: Purple.
Body: Dubbed mole's fur.
Hackle: Blue dun.
Wings: Snipe, or not at all.

Charles Bowlker of Ludlow had a similar, simpler tie:
Body: Light blue fur mixed with a little yellow mohair.
Hackle: Small blue cock.

Jackson's Blue Midge (*See* col. illus. 1) Jackson used this right through into December.
Body: Lead-coloured floss.
Hackle: Grizzle.
Wings: From a water-hen's neck.

Green Midge
Hook: Sizes 16–22.
Tie silk: Yellow.
Body: Light green floss.
Hackle: Cuckoo cock.
Wings: Light woodcock put upright.

Knotted Midge
Hook: Captain Hamilton size 16.
Tie silk: Black.
Rib: Fine silver wire.
Hackle: Black cock, one at the tail and one at the head.

See the doyen of Black Gnats, the Reverend Powell's **Baby Sun Fly;** *also* the **Fog Black,** Rolt's **Imp,** the **B.P. Fly** and the **Saltoun.**

Gold-ribbed Hare's Ear (*See* col. illus. 1) The mark of a classic fly is to have so many versions based on its original effective self that it becomes almost unrecognisable. This is above all an olive nymph in eclosion, to be fished just under the surface so as to appear to be struggling to break free from both the surface water tension and its own shuck. It has been given wings and a hackle, elongated during its translation to a stillwater fly, and generally contorted into anything that relies on that most magnificent of all materials, the dark fur of a hare's ear nearest to the root.
Hook: Sizes 14–16.
Tie silk: Primrose or yellow, according to the season.
Body: Hare's ear dark fur, dubbed to make a thin abdomen, and a good
   wad to make the thorax, and well-picked out to make the legs.
Rib: Fine flat gold along the abdomen.
Whisks: Three short strands of dark dun cock, or ginger in the lightest
   versions.

Gold Tag
Body: Bright green peacock herl.
Tag: Broad gold tinsel.
Hackle: Blood-red cock.

Golden Crow *See* **Bradshaw's Golden Crow.**

Grayling Black and Red (*See* col. illus. 1) Harold Howarth, a fisherman and ingenious fly-tyer from Accrington near the River Ribble, produced a

little fancy fly that can be quite effective.
Hook: Captain Hamilton size 16.
Tie silk: Black.
Body: Red floss.
Butt and Rib: Yellow sewing cotton.
Hackle: Black hen.

Grayling Bugs

Sawyer's Killer Bug and Roberts's Dove Bug are two remarkable flies. They have the same reputation as did the Alexandra Fly in the 1800s of being extremely successful, and for the same reason are in danger of being used to the exclusion of any other artificial for grayling.

Sawyer's Killer Bug (*See* col. illus. 1) This was created to reduce the number of grayling in the Hampshire Avon and is usually considered as a shrimp when tied slim. I have seen some examples tied too fat, when they look for all the world like the biggest maggots in the world! I am reasonably sure that in the light-bedded chalk streams it looks to the fish like a crustacean attempting to copy local colour. Certainly they work less for me in limestone rivers, where I find a dark shrimp is better.
Hook: Sizes 14–12.
Underbody: A double layer of silver fuse wire to tie in the body wool.
Body: Fawnish-pink wool, originally Chadwick's 477 Darning Wool. At an auction of this rare material at the 1987 Grayling Society AGM, a final bid of £26 was made for a card of it! There is now a substitute on the market. Wind the wool so that it makes three layers on the hook. A curved hump in the middle of the hook is allowable.

John Roberts' Dove Bug This is a good dark variant. He originally put a red tag on it, but then found it to be more attractive to the rainbow trout. To make it so to the grayling he had to remove the tag! He told me that he found it equally of use in the chalk streams as in the northern rivers. To my mind it complements Sawyer's Killer Bug excellently.
Hook: Sizes 14–12.
Underbody: Three layers of copper wire.
Tie silk: Brown.
Abdomen: A mixture of orange and pink seal's fur dubbed on the silk.
Thorax: A mixture of orange and brown seal's fur. Rib both with copper wire.

Grayling Steel Blue (*See* col. illus. 1) This is Roger Woolley's tie.
Hook: Sizes 12–14.
Body: Peacock herl tied slim.
Rib: Gold wire.
Tag: Three turns of orange silk at the tail end.
Hackle: Grizzled light blue cock, palmered from shoulder to tail.

Grayling Witches *See* 'Witches'.

Green Insect This is the basis of Rolt's group of witches. There is considerable local variation. Halford translated it into a dry fly, and this is its usual form these days.
Tie silk: Black.
Body: Green peacock.
Tag: Red. Leighton finds the red-tagged version equally effective as a wet or as a dry fly.
Hackle: A pale cock. Carter Platt advises an 'almost white', while Halford gave it a pale blue dun. The wet version has a grey hen, palmered from tail to head.

Greenwell's Glory Canon Greenwell desired it, James Wright of Sprouston made the original tie, Mr Brown named it, and in 1854 it was christened on the Tweed.
Body: Yellow tie silk waxed with brown wax.
Rib: Gold wire.
Hackle: Coch-y-bondhu hackle.
Wings: Blackbird.
As is the way with classic flies, it has been translated into a nymph and a dry fly. There is considerable argument as to the redness or pale gingeriness of the hackle; and the wing has variously been from the starling, and blue feathers from teal, grouse and coot. It has been used as an imitation of dark olives, Iron Blues and BWOs. I have no doubt that it will take grayling in still waters just as it does in rivers.

Grey Duster (*See* col. illus. 1) This represents a remarkable number of flies, stone flies and *Perlidae*, early olives and olives of late summer and early autumn. I have used it successfully on Pennine limestone stillwater, and it will take grayling as readily as trout. It is particularly useful in a hatch of needle-flies.
Hook: Sizes 14–16.
Tie silk: Brown.

Body: Rabbit – a mixture of guard hairs from the back, and a little blue fur from under the white fur of the belly. Tie rough but slim.

Rib: Silver wire.

Hackle: Well-marked badger cock, often more successful with cream-coloured list than with pure white.

There are several variations. Coltman's Yellow-Tagged Grey Duster is the same dressing, but with a tag of bright yellow wool. Michael Leighton suggests that the body should have a pinch of hare's fur added to the rabbit and, unlike the original, it can be fished equally as a dry fly or as a wet just under the surface.

Grey Goose Frank Sawyer created many nymph- and shrimp-like artificials, reducing them to a minimum of materials – the best-known ones being the Grey Goose, the Pheasant's Tail, the Sawyer's Bug and the SS Nymph. Over the years, with the realisation that many nymphs propel themselves by their abdomen and hold their legs out of sight close under them, shapes and proportions became the greatest necessity in artificials, and hackles the least, until the absurd position of only a bare twist of copper wire at the head end of the hook was finally arrived at. Fortunately, both for our aesthetic tastes and for more practical reasons, the fish have rejected such logical foolishness. The Grey Goose is a nymphal representation of pale wateries and BWOs.

Hook: Sizes 14–15.

Tie silk: Fine copper wire to form an underbody with a humped thorax and a slim abdomen.

Body: Four pale grey goose-feather fibres or dyed swan; tie in and wind up the hook, together with the wire, to behind the eye of the hook.

Thorax: Lap feather fibres back and forward to make the thorax wing cases, hold in place and finally tie off with wire.

Tail: Tips of goose feathers.

Grey Palmer *See* 'Palmers'.

Grey Partridge *See* **Partridge and Yellow.**

Gold Head This artificial is far older than is currently realised. According to a private communication from Malcolm Greehalgh, the first British description (by him in *The Flytying and Fishing Magazine* in 1990) of the Austrian and Dutch flies, elicited from Japan news and a specimen of a small spider pattern – similar to a Partridge and Orange, on a gold hook with a small gold-ball head – used by Samurai 400 years ago. Later, in a fly wallet found at Eaves Hall in the Ribble Valley (once owned by the Brooke Bond family), was found a northern spider gold head on a late nineteenth-century hook tied to gut. This was examined by Malcolm. The presumption is that the tea business connection with the Far East resulted in the Gold Head being brought back to England and first used in Europe in Lancashire around a hundred years ago.

Malcolm's ties of the Gold Head are as follows, and an example tied by him is illustrated in col. illus. 4.

Hare's Ear Gold Head
Tie silk: Brown.
Head: Gold bead.
Body: Hare's ear dubbed loosely.
Rib: Fine round or oval gold twist.

Pheasant Tail Gold Head
Tie silk: Brown.
Head: Gold bead.
Body: Several strands of pheasant tail, the tips of which form the tails.
Thorax: Brown fur, with pheasant tail top cover.

B and P Spider Silver Head
Tie silk: Black.
Head: Silver bead.
Body: Peacock herl.
Rib: Fine silver wire.
Hackle: Soft black hen, two turns only.
Hook sizes on all three dressings: 16, 14, 12.
N.B. Always buy hooks and heads together, so that hooks fit heads.

Houghton Ruby This is the invention of W.J. Lunn to represent the spinner of the Iron Blue.
Hook: Size 16.
Tie silk: Crimson. Originally Pearsall's No. 13, but this is no longer made; one substitute is multi-fibre nylon thread.
Body: Rhode Island hackle stalk, dyed crimson. Cut the fibres away with scissors.
Tail: Three white cock fibres.
Hackle: Bright Rhode Island red.
Wings: Two light blue hen tips, from the breast or back, tied spent flat on either side of the body.

Howe's Special (*See* col. illus. 1) Tommy Howe, onetime Freeman of the Borough of Appleby, and a great fly tyer and fisherman on the Eden, was well known to Norman Roose, the first President of the Grayling Society, who recorded his patterns of north country flies. This is a representation of the pale wateries and medium olives, and is an excellent example of a fly with a mixed hackle of cock and soft feather.

Tie silk: Yellow gossamer, brown-waxed to an olive shade.

Body: The above.

Thorax: Hare's ear dubbed on the tying silk – two turns only, close up to the hackle.

Hackle: Rear, ginger cock; fore, small feather from the underside of a woodcock's wing.

Tail: Ginger cock.

Imp This is Rolt's dressing for an early autumn black gnat.

Tie silk: Purple.

Body: Light heron, two or three strands twisted.

Tag: Ibis or dyed swan, or a butt of flat gold tinsel.

Hackle: Black.

Imperial This is also known as Kite's Imperial, being the invention of Major Oliver Kite for the dark olive dun.

Hook: Sizes 14–16.

Tie silk: Purple gossamer.

Body: Heron, two or three fibres of primary feather.

Rib: Fine gold wire.

Thorax: Wind the herls back for three turns, and then forwards to finish close against the hackle.

Hackle and Whisks: Early and late season: dark honey dun, where the red is added to the dun background.

Infallible This is one of those remarkably useful flies for rough water that require a *cock*'s hackle for wet fly use, and the application of the 'flotant' bottle only for dry-fly work.

Hook: Sizes 14–16.

Tie silk: Claret.

Body: Dubbed with mole's fur.

Tail: Two or three turns of the body left free of fur.

Hackle and Whisks: Dark blue dun cock.

John Storey (*See* col. illus. 1) The original was given to Norman Roose by

Arthur Storey, a descendant of the originator (who had been a keeper on the Rye at Helmsley in the 1880s).

Hook: Size 16.

Tie silk: Black.

Body: Bronze peacock herl.

Hackle: Dark red cock.

Wings: The tip of a whole mallard breast feather. This is stripped to a likely length, doubled, and tied in an angle of 60° forward. The hackle is kept between the body and wing and the tie silk taken through it and finished with a whip finish in front of and in support of the wing.

Kill Devil Spider This is a group of flies tied for the Derbyshire rivers. The common factor is a peacock herl body with just two turns of a long-fibred cock hackle. Woolley's dressing:

Body: Peacock herl.

Tip: Gold or silver.

Hackle: Bright medium-blue dun.

The Red and the Black Spiders each substitute a hackle of the appropriate colour.

A cast and a take on the River Wye, Derbyshire

Knotted Midge *See* 'Gnats and Midges'.

Little Black This is one of Pritt's little dark flies for cold days, early or late in the season.
Hook: Size 16.
Tie silk: Purple.
Body: Dubbed sparingly with magpie herl. With such delicate herl, twisting it with the tie silk is the surer way of applying it.
Hackle: Black cock or starling's neck.

Little Chap This is a simple beetle-type fly for autumn use, being just peacock herl and a dun hackle on a size 16 hook. This southern version by Halford is a typical dry fly of the period, whereas the northern form, known as the **Smoke Fly**, uses just as typically a dun grouse hackle from under the wing to make a wet fly. The **Green Insect** is a third, lighter, form of the same fly. A further version has a body of magenta-dyed peacock herl tied with crimson silk.

Little Marryat This is a pale watery from that excellent fly-inventor, E.S. Marryat.
Hook: Size 16.
Tie silk: Straw.
Body: Australian opossum flank fur, a whitish tan colour.
Hackles: Two pale Cochin cock hackles; very pale ginger cock can be used.
Whisks: Pale Olive Gallina.

Little Pale Blue This is a fly of considerable antiquity, for use in the autumn at the same time as the Whirling Blue Dun. It is an autumn form of the pale watery.
Tie silk: Primrose.
Body: Dubbed with the pale blue fur of rabbit, mixed with a little yellow mohair.
Hackle: The palest blue hackle.
Wings: Pale blue sea swallow. Substitute feather from a herring-gull or the palest blue dun hen.

Little Red Sedge This is a Skues 'fail-me-never'.
Hook: Size 14.
Tie silk: Hot orange, brown-waxed.
Body: Darkest hare's ear.
Rib: Gold wire.

Hackle: 1 Long deep red cock, short in the fibre, palmered from shoulder to tail and then held in place by the wire rib which is taken in open turns from tail to shoulder.

2 A similar hackle but with a longer fibre, and given five turns in front of the wing.

Wings: The original was landrail, rolled and tied sloping over the back. Darkish red hen can be used as a substitute.

Lock's Fancy This is the Pale Watery imitation by John Lock of Andover.
Hook: Sizes 14–16.
Tie silk: Primrose.
Body: Primrose floss silk.
Hackle and Whisks: Pale honey dun cock.
Wings: Light starling.

March Brown The natural hatches too late for the early grayling, but there is an autumn form, which is smaller and very effective for grayling, known as the **August Dun**. The more normal tie for the March Brown is used throughout the season as a general fly, probably acting as a stone-fly nymph or shrimp, or just as a general dark olive nymph. One of James Ogden's ties is as good as anyone might wish.
Hook: Sizes 14–12.
Tie silk: Yellow.
Body: Hare's ear mixed with a little yellowish-olive mohair.
Rib: Fine flat gold or yellow silk.
Hackle: Brown hackle from a partridge back.
Whisks: Three strands of partridge tail feather.
It can be left thus and used as a nymph. Ogden advised wings of hen pheasant, a reddish brown, very upright and full.

Marlow Buzz *See* 'Beetles'.

Needle Flies

These are the smaller *Perlidae*, being thin, brown flies with long flat wings, inhabiting fast-flowing waters.

Needle Brown of Walbran. This is for the smaller *Perlidae* of September and October.
Hook: Captain Hamilton size 16.
Body: Orange tie silk.

Tag: A small piece of pale primrose floss to represent eggs.
Hackle: Honey dun cock.

Dark Spanish Needles

This is a description of their wings which have the same bluish-dun colour as Spanish Needles used to have. It is a fly serviceable until December.

T.K. Wilson's Yorkshire Tie
Hook: Captain Hamilton size 16.
Body: Well-waxed claret gossamer silk.
Hackle: Dark dun.
Head: Two turns of magpie herl.

Pritt's Tie
Hook: Captain Hamilton size 16.
Body: Orange silk.
Hackle: Darkest small feather from a brown owl's wing; substitute a dark brown hen, or the small dark hackle from the outside of a woodcock's wing.
Head: Two turns of peacock herl.

Light Spanish Needle Also Pritt's tie.
Hook: Captain Hamilton size 16.
Body: Crimson silk; use a strand of Soie d'Alger No. 945 from the Royal School of Needlework.
Hackle: Brownish dun-coloured feather from inside a jack snipe's wing or the breast of a young starling.

Olive Bloas

As we all know, representatives of olives in their various forms are almost without number. The ties known as Olive Bloas are as old as the hills, e.g. Water Hen Bloa (*see* page 130).

Small Olive Bloa This fly, by Jackson, is present throughout the winter.
Body: Yellow silk, brown-waxed.
Hackle and Whisks: Olive-stained hackle.
Wings: Starling primary stained to an olive shade with onion dye.

Olive Quill This is as good a dry fly as any.
Hook: Sizes 16–14.

Body: Peacock quill dyed olive.
Hackle and Whisks: Medium-dark olive cock.
Wings: Medium-dark starling.

Olive Sedge Sedge imitations are always useful in the late summer. I have never seen in print the olive sedge that I find so useful on limestone rivers and stillwaters. It is a development of Skues's Little Red Sedge, with the addition of a shuck at its tail. I first invented it some eighteen years ago, and so far, time has not diminished its effectiveness.
Hook: Sizes 14–12.
Tie silk: Yellow.
Body: Darkest hare's ear.
Rib: Gold wire.
Hackle: 1 Ginger cock, short-fibred, from shoulder to tail and held in place by the rib, wound from tail to shoulder.
2 A large-fibred ginger cock in five turns in front of the wing.
Tail: Tie in the smallest ginger hackle from the head of a cock of a length of that of the abdomen.
Wings: A bunch of hen pheasant tail spread out along the back, the top fibres of the body hackle being trimmed to allow the wing to lie flat.

Orange Dun This is Aldam's tie, effective from June to the end of the season.
Hook: Size 14.
Tie silk: A faded orange (Pearsall's No. 6A would do).
Body: Dubbed with brown squirrel's fur; this is a reddish brown, darker than a hare's poll. Mohair dyed a suitable reddish brown would do.
Hackle: Mid-dun hen hackle.

Orange Fly This, according to Ronalds, is the best fly for both trout and grayling.
Hook: Size 14.
Tie silk: Black.
Body: Orange floss.
Hackle: Dark Furnace.
Wings: Dark starling wing feather.

Orange Otter This was tied originally by the Reverend Edward Powell, Rector of Munslow in south Shropshire. Otter fur is now unobtainable, and Michael Leighton advises a seal's fur mix of three-quarters hot orange and one quarter claret. As seal's fur will become as rare as otter's, we shall have

to think in terms of sheep's wool, mohair and opossum, dyed in bright yellow dye (picric acid now also being rare) and red ink similar to the original.
Hook: Size 14.
Tie silk: Light brown.
Body: Dubbed with orange fur, tied full and no skimping at the tail.
Hackle: Bright red cock, tied in the middle of the body.
Tail: Red cock.

Orange Quill This is Skues's BWO Spinner.
Hook: Size 14.
Tie silk: Hot orange.
Body: Pale Condor quill, stripped and dyed hot orange.
Hackle and Whisks: Bright red cock.
Wings: Pale starling, somewhat long.

Orange Tag This is Halford's designation, otherwise known as the **Treacle Parkin**.
Hook: Sizes 16–18 as a dry fly; size 14 as a wet fly.
Tie silk: Black.
Body: Peacock sword feather.
Hackle: Bright red cock.
Tail: Originally from an Indian crow; nowadays a yellowy-orange wool is the substitute, and not a yellow tag as is often given to it.

Pale Autumn Dun This represents the autumn pale watery; Walbran's tie.
Hook: Size 14.
Tie silk: Pale yellow.
Body: Tie silk dubbed with the rusty-coloured fur from a red squirrel. These days dyed mohair or squirrel tail is the substitute.
Hackle: Pale honey dun.
Wings: Pale slaty-blue of a tern's wing; substitute lightest blue hen or from a herring-gull.

Palmers

There are about the most ancient of flies. The simplest and most constant dressing is as Bowlker describes it in the early nineteenth century.

Black Palmer
Body: Black ostrich herl.
Rib: Silver twist.
Hackle: Black cock, palmered from head to tail in open turns.

Golden Palmer This is virtually an early Bumble.
Body: Orange silk.
Rib: Peacock herl and gold twist.
Hackle: Red cock from head to tail.

Grey Palmer This was included by David Foster at the end of his list of Bumbles.
Tie silk: Black.
Rib: Fine round silver.
Hackle: Badger cock with whitish-grey list beyond the black centre, from
head to tail.

Partridge Variants

Amongst the 83 fly dressings by Jim Wynn of Addingham, Wharfedale,
gathered in a book (itself now rare) by Professor Tom Cross, there are nine
forms of patridge-hackled flies. The Red without doubt represents a stone-
fly mymph, with large thorax and side hackle fibres, and is useful at point,
with Partridge and Orange on the dropper, in coloured water after a spate.

Partridge and Orange (*See* col. illus. 1) This represents needle flies and
the February Red, and is a similar tie to Pritt's Brown Watchet and
Ronald's Turkey Brown. It is effective from early to late season.
Hook: Sizes 12–14.
Tie silk: Hot orange, which turns a mahogany colour when wet.
Hackle: The dappled feather from a partridge's back, not one with a broad
brown band across it. Note the set of the hackle.

Partridge and Yellow This is a pale watery from late spring on.
Body: Yellow tying silk.
Hackle: Light grey partridge feather.

Partridge and Red (*See* col. illus. 1)
Hook: Size 14.
Tie silk: Red.
Body: Flat red tinsel, ribbed with four turns of fine red tinsel.
Thorax: Bronze peacock herl.
Hackle: Grey-brown partridge palmered over the thorax. Clip the fibres
above and below, leaving side fibres only.
Head: Two turns of herl. Continue the flat red tinsel under the thorax to
give one turn to represent the eyes.
Wynn used this in preference to a dark red silk body ribbed with orange
tinsel in coloured water.

Poult Bloa This is a wet pattern to represent the nymphs of the pale watery and BWO flies.
Hook: Size 16.
Tie silk: Yellow.
Body: Dubbed with red squirrel fur; substitute a mix of dark claret seal and hare's poll, or mohair dyed a rusty brown.
Hackle: Slaty blue feather from under the wing of a young grouse.

Priest This is essentially a Silver Badger.
Body: Flat silver.
Rib: Fine oval.
Tag: Red ibis or swan.
Hackle: Badger cock.

Pheasant Tail Nymph (*See* col. illus. 1) This is one of Sawyer's generalized nymphs and now a 'classic' for deep fishing.
Hook: Sizes 12–18.
Underbody: Fine copper wire. Sawyer uses this as a tying thread and rib; it is used to build up the thorax, and then taken in close turns to the bend of the hook, where the pheasant fibres are locked in.
Tail: Tips of four strands of pheasant tail.
Body: The pheasant fibres and wire are twisted together and taken to behind the eye.
Wing covers: The remains of the tail fibres are lapped back and forth over the thorax, and the wire fastened down behind the eye.

Red Quill This is a general fly for use as Iron Blue Dun, Sherry Spinner or Olive Dun.
Hook: Sizes 14–16.
Body: Stripped, well-marked peacock herl from the eye feather.
Hackle and Whisks: Bright red game cock.
Wings: Pale starling primary, or as a hackle fly with a blue dun cock behind the red hackle.

Red Spinner The same as the last, with a red silk body ribbed with fine gold wire.

Red Spider *See* 'Stewart's Spiders'.

Red Tag (*See* col. illus. 1) This is probably the best-known fly for grayling. It was made first as a trout fly for low-water conditions in high

124

RON BROUGHTON

The Derbyshire Derwent below Chatsworth

summer, and known then as the Worcester Gem. It was brought to the Yorkshire Dales and used successfully for grayling by F.M. Walbran and rechristened.

Hook: Sizes 16–18 for dry fly; 14–16 for wet fly.

Tie silk: Black.

Body: Originally green peacock, it has gained a more sober hue now, often using bronze peacock, the brighter colour being reserved for its brother, the Orange Tag.

Tag: Scarlet wool or dyed swan.

Hackle: Bright red cock.

Rough Olive This is the large dark olive of spring, seen mainly by salmon and grayling anglers, before the first hatch of trout fishermen is seen.

Hook: Size 14.

Tie silk: Yellow.

Body: Three strands of heron secondary feather, dyed brown olive, or swan substitute that has been dyed a blue dun before the olive brown.

Rib: Fine gold.

Hackle: Dark brownish olive.

Wings: Dark starling.

Rusty Spinner Skues' fly, this is a magnificent animal that, according to size, will be taken for the spinners of Iron Blue, July Dun, Pale Wateries and, in the larger sizes, the BWOs.

Hook: Sizes 14–16.

Tie silk: Hot orange gossamer.

Body: Pig's wool or seal's fur, a red ant colour, which is a deep rich mahogany red.

Rib: Fine gold wire.

Hackle: A rusty dun cock, which is a darkish dun, shot through with red.

Whisk: Three fibres of honey dun.

Sage Fly This is Reg Righyni's salmon-approved Grayling Enticer, and described by him as 'some sort of pregnant spinner'. The sample for this was given by Righyni to Neville Gilder.

Hook: Captain Hamilton size L2A or a 16.

Body: Claret rabbit, claret polar bear, mixed well.

Rib: Gold twist.

Tag: Orange yellow, as with the Treacle Parkin.

Hackle: Hooded crow; substitute palest blue hen or herring-gull.

Saltoun Lord Saltoun of the Stockbridge Club created a little dark fly that uses well as a black midge.

Hook: Size 16.

Body: Black silk.

Rib: Silver wire.

Hackle and Whisks: Pale ginger cock.

Wings: Pale starling.

Carter Platt advises flat silver ribbing and a black hackle when fished wet.

Sanctuary Dr Tom Sanctuary made this for use on the Hampshire rivers, and it is one of those delightful flies that uses hare's ear.

Hook: Sizes 12–14.

Body: Dark hare's ear.

Rib: Flat gold.

Hackle: Coch-y-bondhu.

Sand Fly This is one of Bainbridge's favourite flies and is very similar to the Cinnamon Fly, but appears earlier in the season and lasts till the end of September.

Hook: Size 14.

Tie silk: Light reddish brown.

Body: Sand-coloured fur from the hare's neck mixed with a small quantity of orange mohair.
Rib: Same as the tie silk.
Hackle: Light ginger hen.
Wings: Sandy-coloured hen's wing as substitute for landrail, to be flat over the body.

Sawyer's Killer Bug *See* 'Grayling Bugs'.

Sea Swallow This is an old name for the tern. Substitute feathers of the lightest blue dun to be found in the herring-gull, or of the palest blue dun hen.
Hook: Sizes 14–16.
Tie silk: Yellow.
Body: Stripped peacock herl, dyed yellow.
Hackle: Substitute for the feather of a sea swallow.

Sedges There are innumerable dressings of these, some of which are included in this list of artificial flies. One of the best is **Skues's Little Red Sedge**. *See also* the **Cinnamon Fly, Olive Sedge, Sand Fly** and **Silver Horns**.

Shrimps

Olive Shrimp (*See* col. illus. 1) For use where there is a darker background than the chalk streams give. This mixture of the patterns made by Richard Walker, Brian Clarke and John Goddard I have found to be more to the liking of Yorkshire grayling.
Hook: Limerick size 12.
Underbody: A smooth hump of lead on the upper surface of the hook.
Tie silk: Brown.
Body: Mixture of hare's ear and olive seal's fur.
Rib: Fine gold wire from tail to head holding down the hackle.
Hackle: Dark ginger, palmered from head to tail.
Back: Clear polythene tied in at the tail and pulled tight over the back, the hackle fibres being allowed to splay out sideways and towards the bend of the hook.
See also **Sawyer's Killer Bug** and **John Roberts's Dove Bug.**

Silver Dun This is David Foster's winter dun, and it is illustrated, as is the Sea Swallow, in Pritt's *Book of the Grayling*.
Hook: Sizes 12–14.

Tie silk: Claret.
Body: Flat silver.
Hackle: Light blue hen.
Wings: Light part of quill feather of fieldfare, or substitute with medium starling.
Head: Formed from the tie silk.

Silver Horns These are small sedges about five-sixteenths of an inch long with curving antennae. Jackson thought that they were taken right through to October. Ronalds gives an effective tie for wet-fly use.
Tie silk: Black.
Body: Black ostrich herl.
Hackle: Small black cock.
Wings: Dark starling, tied flat over the body.
Horns: Fibres of a grey feather from a mallard.

Smoke Fly This is the same as the Little Chap, but tied for wet-fly use, with silver wire rib and the soft hackle from under the wing of a young grouse.

Snipe

There are several flies made with Snipe wing feathers, the most famous of which is the Snipe and Purple.

Snipe Bloa There are several variants; Pritt gives two.
Hook: Sizes 14–16.
Body: Straw-coloured silk, or yellow silk with a sparse dubbing of mole's fur, allowing the yellow to show through.
Hackle: The pale dun feather from under a jack-snipe's wing.

Snipe and Purple (*See* col. illus. 1) This is used often as a wet fly for the Iron Blue, and from spring to winter.
Hook: Sizes 14–16.
Body: Dark purple tie silk.
Hackle: The dark spoon-shaped feather from the outside of the snipe's wing at the 'elbow'.

Snipe and Yellow This is Pritt's Stone Bloa.
Hook: Sizes 14–16.
Body: Yellow silk.
Wings: From the feather under a jack-snipe's wing.

Spanish Needles *See* 'Needle Flies'.

Stewart's Spiders

These were described by him in his classic book in the 1850s, and one of them at least must have been well used at the time of the Battle of Trafalgar.

They are short-bodied Palmers, body and hackle extending at most to half-way along the hook from the eye. The hackles were strengthened by twisting stalk and tie silk together before palmering and whipping firmly behind the hackle. The name of the fly signifies the colour of the hackle, not of the silk.

Black Spider (*See* col. illus. 1) Tie of brown silk and hackle of black starling neck.

Dun Spider Tie of primrose or orange silk, and hackle of dun feather from under the wing of a starling. This is similar to a Dotterel Dun and was so tied originally.

Red Spider Tie of yellow silk and hackle of red hen.

Sturdy's Fancy This fly was first tied by Tom Sturdy and later by his nephew Jack Sturdy of Masham. This tie is from Sturdy's grandson, through Jim Nice, fly-tyer extraordinaire.
Tie silk: Purple gossamer.
Body: Bronze peacock – fat and round.
Tag: Red wool – very small.
Hackle: Cock off-white, called a 'mucky white': not exactly yellow, certainly not grey, but with an ochreish tinge.

Tommy's Favourite This is a curious drab fly, if one ignores the tag, but like Skues' Carrot Fly one that works.
Body: Quill from a yellow-blue macaw's tail feather; otherwise, separate fibres of blue and yellow dyed swan.
Tag: Red floss with small silver tip under it.
Hackle: Medium blue dun hen.

Tup's Indispensable This is another Devon fly of universal fame and many variants. The addition of ram's wool was to help it to float. Nowadays the mixture is too red. The only red, and that very little, should be mainly in the thorax. Wet or dry, it represents the pale watery.

DRY:
Tie silk: Yellow.
Body: Two or three turns of bare silk at tail, dubbed with a mixture of
tup's wool and seal's fur, and mohair of yellow, cream and crimson.
Hackle: Blue dun freckled with gold.
Tail: Honey dun.
WET:
Body: Dubbing almost to the tail; crimson present only at the thorax.
Hackle and tail: Short blue dun hen.

Water-hen Bloa (*See* col. illus. 1) This can represent the dark olive, the
medium olive and the iron blue, and so is used throughout the season as a
remarkable northern nymph-like fly.
Hook: Size 14.
Tie silk: Yellow or primrose, according to the season.
Body: Dubbed lightly with water-rat, the yellow to show through and the
body to be kept short, as in all northern-designed flies. Substitute rabbit
dark blue underfur for light-coloured flies, and mole fur for darker flies
in cold weather. The minimal touch of fur is to allow the yellow silk to
give an olive-blueish shade when wet.
Hackle: Water-hen wing; the glossy, spoon-shaped dun feather from under
the wing if you can count or guess it, from the second row from the leading edge.

Whirling Blue Dun To be used up to the last week in October.
Tie silk: Yellow.
Body: Squirrel's red-brown fur mixed with yellow mohair.
Hackle and tail: Pale ginger.
Wings: Medium starling.

Wickham's Fancy This is an old fly with all the marks of the late nine-
teenth century: a well-palmered hackle and plenty of tinsel. One of its
antecedents was a fly called the Cockerton.
Hook: Sizes 12–16.
Tie silk: Amber (Pearsall's No. 6).
Body: Flat gold.
Rib: Fine gold wire taken over the body hackle.
Hackle: Body, gingerish red cock; shoulder, one or two turns of the same.
Wings: Medium starling.

William's Favourite This is a descendant of all those ostrich-herled, black-bodied flies, usually palmered, that were probably old when Charles Cotton described his version. Useful in coloured waters, and, in small sizes, against bright skies.

Hook: Sizes 14–18.
Body: Black floss.
Rib: Fine silver wire.
Hackle and tail: Natural black hen. For dry fly, use a black cock hackle.

Willow Fly Found on the water in September and February, according to Ronalds.
Tie silk: Yellow.
Body: Mole's fur, dubbed thinly.
Hackle: Dark dun cock, strongly tinged with a coppery colour (i.e. a dark honey dun), tied palmer fashion.

Winter Brown

Pritt has two variations to represent the smaller *Perlidae*. One is:
The Winter Brown
Hook: Sizes 12 or 14.
Tie silk: A dull orange to form the body.
Hackle: A feather from the inside of a woodcock's wing.
Head: Peacock herl.

Jim Wynn's Winter Brown (*See* col. illus. 1)
Hook: Size 14.
Tie silk: Orange – not too bright.
Body: Tie silk.
Rib: Orange tinsel; substitute fine copper flat.
Thorax: Peacock herl.
Hackle: Well-marked feather from under the woodcock's wing which shows grey and white.

Variant: A body of red-bronze peacock herl ribbed with orange tinsel.

Witches

This group of flies was created by Rolt as a development of the Green Insect. The common factors are a body of green peacock herl, a rib of flat gold or silver and a red tag. As with any successful fly, variations have been made by several people. The main examples are:

The Original Rolt Witch
Hook: Sizes 12–18.
Tie silk: Brown.
Body: Bright green sword peacock herl, two or three strands twisted together.
Rib: Fine flat gold.
Tag: Ibis or scarlet-dyed swan.
Hackle: Light honey dun.

Woolley's Grayling Witch
Body and tag: As above.
Rib: Flat silver.
Hackle: Pale or medium blue dun.

Silver Witch
Tie silk: Black.
Body and tag: As above.
Rib: Silver flat.
Hackle: Badger cock.

RON BROUGHTON

River Derwent above Calver

White Witch
Tie silk: Brown.
Body and tag: As above.
Tip and rib: Silver wire.
Hackle: Palmered white cock.

Norman Roose's Olive Witch Norman Roose knew very well what he was doing when he called this a Witch variant, but it is on the border of being a different fly.
Tie silk: Green.
Body: Green peacock herl.
Rib: Green tying silk.
Hackle: Medium olive cock.

Woodcock and Hare's Lug (*See* col. illus. 1) This is undoubtedly a stone-fly replication, with its two tails, dark body, lack of long hackle and a soft wing which clings to the back of the fly. I have used it as such and found it very effective.
Hook: Sizes 10–14, or even 6 and 8 where the large stone-flies exist.
Tie silk: Yellow.
Tail: Two fibres of brown mallard.
Tag: Two turns of flat gold tinsel.
Body: Dark hare's ear with a small amount of dark green wool; left rough
    and with a thick pad at the shoulder to be pricked out as a hackle.
Wing: Inside of a woodcock's wing feather.

Substitutes

Some mention must be made of substitutes and where to find them. Throughout this list of flies I have tried to indicate reasonable alternatives for now unobtainable materials.

The feather substitutes are easy enough. Woodcock wing, from its lighter and darker sides, the reddish-brown feathers of pheasant and the innumerable red and brown hen wings are all adequate as alternatives to owl and landrail.

Dotterel wing feathers are a little more difficult. They are a fawnish-dun shade with golden tips and are very soft and mobile. Stewart in the 1850s was finding it necessary to use the under-coverts of starling in their stead, and there are the small wing feathers of the golden plover that make good substitutes. Touching up the tips of the feathers from under the wing of a starling with a yellow felt-tip pen, if not overdone, is useful. That lightest of blue feathers from a tern's wing happily can be substituted for, with similar feathers from a herring-gull.

Scandinavia

*Danish and Norwegian Flies
Tied by Hans van Klinken*

Ants

Para-ant A very good pattern for when there is no hatch at all. I have strong belief in the feeding memory of fish, and this is the steak to offer them!
Hook: Partridge 1EA1 #8–18.
Tie silk: Uni 8/0 black.
Body: Black foam and thread.
Hackle: Dark dun, tied as parachute.
Head: Black foam.

Wet Ant A secret weapon for hard conditions.
Hook: Partridge E1A#10–12.
Tie silk: Uni 8/0 orange.
Body: Golden acetate floss.
Legs: Partridge hackle fibres.
Head: Bronze peacock herl.

Caseless Caddis
Hook: Partridge GRS15ST#8–16.
Tie silk: Uni 8/0 black.
Underbody: Fine lead wire.
Ribbing: Clear monofil 0.25 mm.
Body: Furry foam, yellow and greenish colours.
Back: Flexibody, grey transparent.
Thorax: Dark brown mink dubbing.
Head: Tie silk.

Crazy Sedge (Leon Links) An excellent fly for sunny and windy conditions.
Hook: Partridge E1A#8–14.
Tie silk: Uni 8/0 brown.
Body: Tie silk.

Rib: Brown hackle, close-wound.
Wing: Reindeer hair from belly, extra long.

Culard The smallest fly in my collection, and I am sure it is the size that makes this pattern so successful.
Hook: Partridge 1EA1#16–18.
Tie silk: Uni 8/0 black.
Body: Herls from a peacock's wing feather (black).
Rib: Fine gold wire or yellow silk.
Wing: Cul de canard feather cut in the middle.
Hackle: Dark dun.
Head: Tie silk.

Hodal Emerger No. 1
Hook: Partridge GRS15ST#8–16.
Tie silk: Uni 8/0 black.
Body: Green or olive-green furry foam.
Back: Green transparent flexibody.
Rib: Clear monofil 0.25 mm.
Legs: Partridge hackle fibres.
Wings: Natural Swiss straw.
Thorax: Mink dubbing.
Eyes: Monofil, burned at ends.
Antennae: Black bear fibres.

Hodal Emerger No. 2 An excellent fly for lake fishing in the north.
Hook: Partridge GRS15ST#8–16.
Tie silk: Uni 8/0 black.
Body: Gold SLF dubbing.
Wings: Natural Swiss straw.
Thorax: Fiery brown SLF dubbing.
Antennae: A bunch of black bear fibres.

Klinkhammer Special My best fly for broken water.
Hook: Partridge GRS15ST#8–14.
Tie silk: Uni 8/0 tan for body, plus Danville's spiderweb parachute.
Body: Fly-Rite Poly dubbing No. 19.
Wing: One strand white poly yarn.
Thorax: Three strands of bronze peacock herl.
Hackle: Blue dun hackle.

Leadhead
Hook: Partridge H1A#8–12.
Tie silk: Uni 8/0 brown.
Underbody: Tie silk.
Tag: Fluorescent green flexibody.
Tail: Partridge hackle, in the form of a collar around the tag.
Body: Hare, rabbit or squirrel dubbing.
Head: Lead shot.

Once and Away A fly with similar effect to the Klinkhammer Special, but for slow-running and still water.
Hook: Partridge GRS15ST#12–18.
Tie silk: Uni 8/0 grey.
Body: One peccary fibre.
Rib: White tie silk in four open turns along the body.
Thorax: Bronze peacock herl.
Wing and wingcase: Three CDC feathers.

Russian Flies

Pheasant Tail Nymph
Hook: Size 10–12.
Tie silk: Black 8/0.
Tail: Six cock pheasant centre tail fibres.
Body: Cock pheasant, wound flat.
Thorax and cover: As body.
Legs: Ginger cock hackle fibres, beard style.

Klinkhammer Special
Hook: Curved size 10–14.
Tie silk: Tan 8/0.
Body: Tan fly-rite poly dubbing.
Thorax: Two strands of bronze peacock herl.
Wing: White poly-yarn/antron.
Hackle: Ginger or grizzle cock hackle.

Olive Hare's Ear Gold Head
Hook: Sedge size 10–12.
Tie silk: Olive 8/0.
Tail: Dyed olive hare's mask.

Body: Olive hare's fur.
Rib: Fine pearly lurex.
Head: 3 mm gold bead.

Mating Shrimp (Goddards)
Hook: Wide-gape 10–12.
Tie silk: Light olive.
Underbody: Fine lead wire, formed into a hump on hook shank.
Body: Blended seal's fur or substitute: olive, dark brown and pink, ratio 6:3:1.
Rib: Oval silver tinsel.
Back: Clear polythene.

Swedish Flies

Supplied by Lars Olsson

See colour illustration 2.

Black Bibio A representation of small black flies, ants, etc.
Hook: Sizes 14–18.
Tie silk: Black.
Body: Black or dark brown fur formed into two balls on either side of the waist.
Hackle: Black, dark brown or dark blue dun, cut off on top and bottom, tied in the waist.
Wings: Brown or blue dun cock hackle points.

Copper-ribbed Hare's Ear A representation of a sedge larva or a general wet-fly pattern.
Hook: Sizes 10–12.
Tie silk: Brown.
Body: Four layers of copper wire, covered by dark fur from a hare's ear, trapped between two pieces of tying silk and spun on a spinning block to create a fluffy body.
Rib: Copper wire.

Gim River Fly A representation of an egg-laying, fluttering and bouncing female stone-fly, and a good general pattern.
Hook: Sizes 12–16.

Tie silk: Olive.

Body: Olive (dyed) fur, or strands from a wing feather.

Hackle: Palmered with either two long blue dun cock hackles wound together or two grizzle hackles or one blue dun cock hackle and one grizzle similarly palmered together.

Green Caddis Worm A representation of a sedge larva.

Hook: Sizes 10–12, bent with a pair of pliers to form a humped body.

Tie silk: Olive.

Body: Four layers of copper wire, covered by strands of feather or fur, dyed medium olive. A head and neck are formed by a brown mottled feather from a capercaillie.

Grey Mallard Dun

Hook: Sizes 12–16.

Tie silk: Black.

Tail: Two microfibett fibres.

Body: Three to five strands from a grey mallard wing feather.

Hackle: Dark blue dun.

Wings: Dark grey or grey-dyed breast feather from a mallard drake.

Olive Mallard Dun

Hook: Sizes 12–16.

Tie silk: Olive.

Body: Three to five strands from a feather, or else hare or beaver fur, dyed light, medium and dark olive.

Hackle: Dark blue dun.

Tail: Two microfibett fibres.

Wings: Dark grey or grey-dyed breast feather from a mallard drake.

Sedge Pupa

Hook: Sizes 12–16.

Tie silk: Brown.

Body: Fur from a hare's ear.

Legs and antennae: From one of the small, brown-mottled feathers from the outside of a cock capercaillie wing (marginal coverts).

Rib: Copper wire.

Squirrel Sedge

Hook: Sizes 8–14.

Tie silk: Brown.

Body: Red-brown fur from a summer squirrel, trapped between two pieces of tying silk and spun on a spinning block to make a fluffy long-haired body.

Hackle: Brown, palmered and cut off on top to make room for the wing.

Wing: A bunch of hair from the same squirrel's tail, twice the length of the finished wing, tied in the middle just behind the eye of the hook with five turns, the forward-projecting portion is then folded back over the rest and whip-finished behind the small cushion/head. The wing is then cut to the proper length and tear-drop shape with scissors.

Polish Flies

Three woven flies as illustrated.
See colour illustration 4.

Welsh Flies

Tied by Louis Noble

See colour illustration 4.

Droitwich
Hook: Sizes 12–16.
Tag: Orange silk.
Body: Rear half, narrow oval silver tinsel; front half, green peacock herl ribbed with narrow oval silver tinsel.
Hackle: Badger cock.

Y Diawl Bach
Hook: Sizes 14–16.
Body: Green peacock herl.
Tail and hackle: Ginger-brown hen.

Tied by R.B. Broughton

Colonel's Game Pie Nymph Another fly that can be weighted to swim deep. The name comes from Col. George Ellis, who created it from materials whose donors would make a Tudor Game Pie, and I first heard of it through Michael Leighton's book.
Hook: Size 12 Captain Hamilton International.
Tie silk: Brown.

Tail: Brown mallard.
Body: Dark hare's ear.
Rib: Fine gold wire.
Thorax: Underbound with lead or copper wire; rabbit fur, guard and under-fur well mixed.
Wing cases: Cock pheasant tail feather.
Legs: Brown partridge, tied beard fashion.

Grizzly Bourne This was created by Michael Leighton and has been used by him on chalk streams as well as on Welsh Border rivers. The final effect is of a glowing translucent-bodied fly with a sparkling wing.
Hook: Sizes 12–18, Captain Hamilton Featherweight.
Tie silk: Orange.
Whisks: Honey cock.
Body: Rabbit, blue underfur.
Rib: In larger sizes use one strand of Pearsall's golden yellow floss; in the smallest sizes use yellow tie silk. Rib very closely – six turns on a size 12 hook – to create narrow bands of yellow and grey blue.
Hackle: Grizzle cock, (four open turns) and light red cock (on a size 12 hook, two turns behind the grizzle, four through it and two in front).
Variants: Using olive blue dun or white hackles together with the grizzle is highly useful.

William Rufus There was a gentle correction in *Trout & Salmon* of February 1992 to Michael Leighton and myself from the originator of the fly, James Evans of Leominster. The dressing first appeared in his book *Small River Fly Tying for Trout and Grayling*, and is as follows:
Hook: Sizes 14–16 TDE, bound full shank with fine copper wire.
Body: Crow herl, or any well-flued herl from a black corvid.
Rib: Narrow silver lurex.
Hackle: Black hen dressed square, with the concave side facing forward to impart movement.
Tag: Fluorescent red wool or floss.
Fish either upstream or across and down.

Flies for the Ardennes

By Hugo Martel

Universelle
Hook: 10–18.
Tie silk: Brown.

Tail: Two pheasant-tail fibres.
Body: Dubbed hare's ear.
Rib: Yellow floss.
Wings: Two double wings of hen-pheasant feather.
Hackle: Brown-red cock.
Method: Dressed with four wings in two pairs, each pair glued together at the base to aid tying in. The Belgian style is to place them on either side, with the points upwards.

Mohet d'Ambleve (Mohet is dialect for 'sedge').
Body: Green tie silk.
Hackle: Black cock.
Wings: Dark starling.
Method: As with the Universelle.

Austrian Flies

Tied by Walter Bloch

See colour illustration 3.

Buck Caddis
Hook: Sizes 20, 22.
Tie silk: Black.
Body: Grey, brown or olive synthetic material (bodygills).
Hackle: Palmered with a grey or brown cock hackle.
Wings: Grey or brown deer hair.

Diptera
Hook: Sizes 20, 22.
Tie silk: Black.
Body: Black synthetic material (bodygills).
Hackle: Black cock.
Wings: Two white hackle tips.

Dun
Hook: Sizes 20, 22.
Body: Grey, olive or brown tying silk.
Hackle: Grey cock.
Tail: Grey cock fibres.

Wings: Two grey-brown hackle tips.
Variants: Without wings and with white, brown or olive cock hackle.

Humpy
Hook: Sizes 18, 20, 22.
Body: Orange, green, yellow or red tie silk dubbed with a dark elk mane.
Hackle: Brown cock and grizzle cock.
Tail: Dark elk mane.
Wings: White or light brown calf tail.
Variants: Without wings.

Canadian flies

Supplied by Patrick Michiel

See colour illustration 4.

Renegade
Hook: Sizes 16–18.
Tie silk: Black.
Tag: Flat gold.
Body: Bronze peacock herl.
Rib: Fine gold wire.
Hackle: Rear, brown cock; front, white cock.

Tom Thumb A deer-hair fly of great durability and floating power.
Hook: Long size 10.
Tie silk: Grey monocord, thick.
Body: Formed by the thick tie silk showing under the hook as a pale
   abdomen, the bulk supplied by the deer hair, bound down along the top
   of the hook.
Tail: Tip of hair, long.
Hackle and wings: The body hair is lapped forward to make a suitable
   hump and, after tying in at the eye end, left long. Whether it be allowed
   to spread at right angles or lean forward at 60° is to the fly-tyer's taste.

Dutch Flies

Tied by Fer von der Assen

For use in the Eifel region.
'Frutsels' or 'Trashy Baubles'

Hook: Sizes 18–26.

Green Frutsel
Tie silk: Black.
Body: Apple or olive green floss, thin.
Wing: Clear polypropaline floating yarn.

Black Frutsel
Tie silk: Black.
Body: Black floss, thin.
Wing: Grey polypropaline floating yarn.

Iron Blue Frutsel
Tie silk: Claret.
Tag: Four turns of tie silk.
Body: Dubbed dark grey rabbit.
Wing: Grey polypropaline floating yarn.

Coachman Frutsel
Tie silk: Black.
Tag: Narrow, flat gold tinsel, two turns.
Body: Bronze peacock herl, tied thick.
Wing: White polypropaline floating yarn.

French Flies

Supplied by Raymond Rocher

See colour illustration 3.

Some descriptions of dressings of these flies are not included, as French professional fly-dressers, though happy for their creations to be photographed and displayed, do not want the precise dressing made available to all (indeed, many dressings are patented).

By M. Bresson: Culs de Canard de Bresson
                 Tinsel-bodied flies (Tinsel de Bresson)
By M. Devaux: Bécasse de Devaux
                 Jeck Sedge de Devaux (Jeck being the name of M. Devaux's dog), Jean-Marie de Devaux.
By M. Guy Plas: Emergente No. 48, H16

Incomparable No. 39, H16 (This is tied with a beard hackle of a rare cock feather called the Parados. For further information see Dr Pequegnot's *French Fishing Flies*.)

Thyma-Tag No. 109, H18 (These are tied with natural-coloured red cock hackle.)

Caddis Nymph.

Bécasse de Devaux No. 960
Hook: Size 16.
Tie silk: Yellow.
Body: Tie silk.
Hackle: Woodcock.
Tails: Light red cock.

Gloire de Neublans
Hook: Size 16.
Tie silk: Dark Brown.
Body: Tie silk.
Hackle and tail: Grey cock (i.e. light dun).

La Favorite
Hook: Sizes 15–16.
Body: Quill dyed brick-red.
Hackle: Purple cock.
Tail: Cream white cock.

La Loue
Hook: Sizes 14–16.
Body: Quill dyed salmon-pink.
Hackle: Salmon-pink dyed cock.
Tail: White cock.

Peute de Bresson Henri Bresson of Vesoul's fly and a killer either as a dry fly or as an emerger. In eastern French dialect 'peute' means 'the ugly one'.
Hook: Sizes 12–18.
Tie silk: Yellow or red for a body.
Hackle: Mallard breast, with the fibre tied back over the body to look as untidy as possible. Clip the hackle to fit the size of the hook.

Tricolore
Henri Bresson's series. Palmered with three different-coloured good cock hackles placed side by side.
Hook: Sizes 16–22.
This fly is almost a hundred years old, being based on a nineteenth-century fly, the Chenille. Of the three palmered cock feathers, the lightest is often at the bend, and the darkest at the eye of the hook. It appears to be one of the most used flies in France. See Dr Pequenot's *French Fishing Flies*.

Grayling Fishing in Austria

Michael Hofmaier

AUSTRIA HAS ONLY a brief tradition of fly-fishing in the modern sense, although forgotten sources mention it as far back as the Middle Ages. Spinning has predominated in suitable waters ever since the establishment of more advanced angling techniques, and this has meant that most anglers have been unable to catch the grayling consistently.

On the other hand, the book *A Fly Fisher's Life* by Charles Ritz exerted a tremendous influence when it appeared in German in 1956. Ritz regards the grayling as the best of all the salmonids. It was inevitable that his opinion should be widely accepted in the German-speaking countries.

This is one reason why the grayling is a highly rated game fish in Austria. Unfortunately, it led to many anglers attaching prime importance to success when fishing for grayling, caring little for truly sporting methods.

The Grayling Season

The grayling is very common in Austria in both limestone and granite waters. It can be found in lowland rivers and in mountain streams. This variation in habitat is the reason why the best grayling fishing can be had at quite different times of year, depending on the type of water. The main criterion is – and here exceptions prove the rule – clear, not too high water. The fish should be visible.

The grayling recovers quickly after spawning and provides excellent fishing as early as May, when the season opens in most of the Austrian federal provinces. The beginning of the grayling season is the best time in small to medium-sized mountain streams, already clear due to their lower-

MICHAEL HOFMAIER

Dr Hofmaier fishing the River Ybbs

lying catchment areas. The fish are then regularly distributed throughout the stream, whereas in autumn, with falling water levels, they tend to congregate in the deep runs and pools. If there is any possibility of doing so, the grayling moves from big alpine streams, high and discoloured by melting snow, to spawn in clear tributaries, where it may remain. There it offers good sport, while fishing in the main river is not at its best until several months later.

In early summer the grayling competes with the trout, which at this time is in prime condition in low-lying rivers. One should not waste too much time on grayling now, and the wise angler will tend to regard it as a 'chub with an adipose fin' and avoid it. Where big hatches of the Green Drake (*E. danica*) are observed, the activity of the trout is more uniform than that of the grayling. But there are days when every grayling in the water seems to be active, and such a feast should be enjoyed.

In big alpine rivers like the Drau, the Mur, the Enns and the Inn one has to wait for low water after the melted snow has gone to find good angling conditions. Depending on the altitude of the river's catchment area, the season extends from the beginning of August till the end of November.

147

However, the following points should also be considered. The grayling's active periods, which during the summer last until the evening rise, become shorter as the autumn progresses; towards the end of the year they are often limited to only half an hour at around midday. In view of the fact that the rise depends on the presence of insects on the water, the prospects of sport dwindle as the year draws to a close. As a result, in November and December fishing is often worthwhile only for the angler who lives on the river and can reach for his rod when he sees rings on the water. Lucky man!

Tackle and Flies

Size is not the important thing when it comes to grayling fishing. Really big grayling are found in very few rivers, and there only occasionally. In most cases it is virtually impossible to catch them by sight. One has to guess the size of the fish by the rise-form or the shape of the ring. This is why grayling fishing normally involves going for medium-sized, well-spotted fish that are rising, or at least willing to rise. However, as the number of fish caught – and released – in well-populated stretches leaves nothing to be desired, the real attraction of grayling fishing lies in making sport more difficult by deliberately refining one's method.

The tactics of grayling fishing have already been dealt with in detail in the abundant literature on the subject. At this point, therefore, it is sufficient to mention only the following maxim: in its supreme and most satisfying form, grayling fishing involves fishing fine with a dry fly for individual, active fish. Fishing the rise without seeing the fish comes second. Nymph fishing and fishing with emergers upstream or across can be compared with dry-fly fishing if the movements of the fish can be closely observed. On the other hand, there are strong objections to chuck-and-chance fishing with heavy nymphs. The angler who uses such methods misses out on the real pleasure of grayling fishing.

Dry-fly fishing can be very easy under ideal conditions, such as broad, fairly deep, smooth-flowing water over gravel. The grayling is much less shy than the trout, and during its periods of activity it will also rise very close to the angler, making it possible to take it virtually at rod's length. In such a case an angler looking for satisfactory sport should cast for the fish at a distance representing a compromise between easy success close at hand and the frustrating failure of casting further afield: a compromise, in other words, between the angler's skill and his sportsmanship.

Grayling fishing demands a delicate technique, so a short and light six-to seven-foot rod – in the author's opinion a split cane – for a No.4 line will suffice. This is not a handicap in view of the fact that one wades wherever possible. A slow rod is helpful, as it facilitates striking, which can indeed be difficult. Normally such light equipment is not a disadvantage because there is no need for excessive casting speed: the grayling tends to rise badly in windy weather anyway. A heavier rod and a stronger cast are only to be recommended in fast water, where it can be very difficult to land the hooked grayling with light equipment without following the fish as it drifts downstream. However, it is also possible to fish upstream with a short line and try to keep the fish at the surface immediately after striking. The current comes to one's aid with such surprise tactics, as the fish, often motionless for several seconds, drifts towards the angler on the surface, making it possible to land it even with light tackle after playing the fish for an extremely short time. It gives the angler a supreme feeling of satisfaction to be able to release the victim again before it has even realised that it has been taken.

There is a widespread notion that the grayling can be caught only with small flies. This is entirely untrue. When fishing in early summer, the best results are to be obtained by 'exact imitation' of the insects on the water, which often leads to the use of large flies. In autumn, on the other hand, the choice of fly can be made on more practical considerations in view of the relative scarcity of food. In this case, it is most important that the fly should be equally visible to both fish and fisherman. In deep, fast-flowing water this will result in the use of large sedges or attractors to get the fish rising.

Nevertheless, the principle of smaller flies is, of course, not wrong. The number of midges (chironomids) has grown significantly due to the increasing pollution of our rivers, resulting in a trend to smaller flies. In addition, the up-winged flies found in autumn are smaller than their spring counterparts.

Though autumn fishing is often very difficult, the following general recommendations can be made. There is no objection to selecting a fly on the basis of trial and error. This is less problematical with the grayling than with the trout, as the former is seldom put off after rejecting several flies, and continues to rise. However, in more heavily fished rivers an unsuccessful strike may cause the grayling to stop feeding temporarily. In smooth waters, flies with a hook size of 20 or 22 are often an absolute must, making it necessary to use a cast down to 8x.

A further hint: it may sometimes happen that the grayling rises rather frenziedly to take the duns drifting on the surface. This may easily result in a poor strike, or worse still, in a broken cast. In such a case it is advisable to replace the high-riding hackled fly by a no-hackle which sits deeper in the surface film. The fly will then immediately be taken more quietly.

Some flies that have proved successful on Austrian rivers are detailed on page 141. I often use a Buck Caddis, which is very simple to tie, with size 18 to 22 hooks, a pale dubbed body and a deer-hair wing. I leave off the hackle in order to reduce the silhouette; this hardly has any effect on buoyancy, and the weight of the bend of the hook keeps the fly floating on the water properly. The body hair is provided by my yellow Labrador 'Spanker'.

Grayling Rivers in Austria

Austria has many rivers that offer outstanding grayling fishing. However, conditions in some rivers are no longer ideal, due to a number of power-station and regulation projects (many of them of questionable value) and a general deterioration of water quality.

Especially in autumn, the bottoms of the rivers are heavily covered in algae, as a result of which fishing by sight is only possible in particularly good light even in shallow reaches. Rivers flowing through limestone formations once used to be remarkable for their brilliant white beds. Nowadays it is often beneficial if the river has been scoured by spates before the start of the grayling season. This should not, of course, have an effect on the insect life of the river. Too much flooding shortly before or during the grayling season may completely spoil the fishing even if the water flows away quickly and optimal low-water conditions are soon reached.

The following references to grayling rivers have deliberately been kept general and brief. Detailed descriptions of specific beats can be found in the relevant angling guides.

The main grayling rivers are the Traun, the Steyr, the Teichl and the Alm in Upper Austria, the Saalach, the Lammer and the upper reaches of the Mur in Salzburg, the Drau (renowned for its big grayling) and the Gail in Carinthia, and the Mur, the Enns, the Mürz and the Salza in Styria. The Inn in Tyrol (though not really a dry-fly river), and the lower reaches of both the Bregenzer Ache and the Ill in Vorarlberg, should also be considered to a lesser extent.

The foothills of the Alps in Lower Austria – easily reachable from Vienna – contain many good grayling streams: the Pielach, the Traisen, the Erlauf, the Ybbs and the Schwarza.

MICHAEL HOFMAIER

River Enns at Gesäuse

More than thirty years ago my father took me to the Gesäuse to fish for grayling. Our family doctor came with us; his friend, the owner of a hotel with a water on the River Enns, had given us a day's fishing. I had already been fly-fishing for trout, but had never been after grayling, and I was very excited.

The tiny village of Gstatterboden huddles beside the river at the foot of towering cliffs. Looking up at the peaks, you feel giddy. The Enns alternates between wild, rocky falls and quiet, turquoise stretches.

The weather was fine, and the river looked perfect, but when we arrived at one of the broad gravel beds, no fish were rising. Nor did they rise in the hours to follow. Just as my father and the doctor were packing up, depressed by their lack of success, I caught the only fish of the day: a tiny grayling. With a radiant smile, I showed it to the two older men, and put it back into the river.

My father and the doctor spoke little on the way home, though time and again they returned to the subject of our failure. When I reminded them that we had caught a grayling they were silent for a moment, and then continued talking as if I had said nothing.

One October day recently, I came back to the Enns at Gstatterboden. Although I can remember clearly where I caught my first grayling, the river now looks different, and I could not find the exact place. I had a good day and enjoyed my fishing: but what is the satisfaction of a man compared to the delights of a boy?

Translation by Andrew Smith

Grayling in Belgium

Hugo Martel

THERE IS STILL a good stock of grayling in the south of the country, mainly in the Meuse basin (14,630 km²). Most of the rivers of the Ardennes offer good fishing for grayling (and trout) in very attractive surroundings (which one often fails to appreciate). Many stretches – mostly the best ones – are completely private, but it is still possible to fish good public water and private water. For public water you only need a licence from the Région Wallonne, which you can buy in any post office in the south of Belgium (about £25).

There are many, many kilometres of public water, and the fishing can be very prolific if one avoids places that are easy of access. Take a good map, go for a long (and perhaps not very easy) walk, and you will be rewarded. Try the tributaries, too, where it is much quieter but not bad in terms of results; approaching an overgrown river is sometimes rather difficult, but mostly it adds charm and excitement to the fishing. Each spring the magazine *Le Pêcheur Belge* gives a complete survey of fishing available, including practical information and a very fine and detailed map of the rivers.

The Rivers

This is a rough guide; some strictly private waters or small tributaries are not mentioned.

The Ourthe, which is formed by the confluence of the Western and Eastern Ourthe at Engreux (Nisramont dam), is one of the most beautiful rivers of the Ardennes (along with the Semois). It runs for 135 km through unique scenery and attracts a lot of tourists during the summer. Thousands

153

of fishermen are also attracted to the river every year, and many fishermen means shy fish! The Ourthe is sporadically ravaged by sewage, but cleans and regenerates itself naturally.

The Western Ourthe (53 km) and the Eastern Ourthe (38 km) both have grayling from their sources to the junction. Thereafter there is a grayling zone from the junction to Melreux, a barbel zone with a lot of running-water cyprinids, and grayling as far as Esneux. There is 30 km of public water from the bridge at Nisramont to the bridge at Jupille – good fly-fishing water in nice surroundings – and 97 km from the bridge at Jupille to the junction with the Meuse.

Many of the Ourthe's tributaries contain grayling. One of them is the Aisne: 'une merveilleuse petite rivière', 33 km long. Another is the 92-km Amblève, which, in spite of occasional pollution (fortunately it regenerates itself every time, and grayling are back after a short disappearance), is an interesting river to fish and runs through nice country. Some parts, like the Fonds de Quarreux, where the bed is strewn with quartz boulders, can be compared with well-known foreign rivers. There is public water down-stream from the bridge at Remouchamps as far as the junction with the Ourthe (11 km). The Amblève has its own tributaries, the Salm (18 km) and the lovely Lienne (26 km).

River Lienne

OPT/KOUPRIANOFF

The Semois

The SEMOIS (190 km in Belgium) is justly called 'the queen of rivers'. Grayling now prosper in it, though this is only a recent development – the same applies to its tributaries the VIERRE (32 km) and the RULLES (22 km). There is 80 km of public water on the Semois between Herbeumont (Le Moulin Deleau) and the border with France downstream of Bohan.

The LESSE, 99 km long, is the wildest and most unpredictable river in the Ardennes: one day it is quiet and clear, the next wild and dark after heavy rain and bad weather. Its upper reaches are a trout zone for some 15 km. The grayling zone stretches for some 40 km from Transinne to Eprave (the junction with the Lhomme). Downstream of Eprave the barbel zone starts, and grayling become scarcer.

The LHOMME (42 km) is a capricious river, difficult to fish, and its biological balance is sometimes disturbed by human intervention (pollution, works on the banks). Grayling are found from Mirwart downstream, and from Grupont to Jemelle there is a clear grayling zone with very rich fauna, while from Jemelle down to the junction at Eprave there is a fair stock of grayling.

The BOCQ (46 km) is a very beautiful little river that holds a lot of happy memories for me, for I have fished it for more than twenty years with my late father. It is sometimes polluted around the little town of Spontin, but it always recovers very quickly, and the grayling soon return. After the accidental pollution of the Bocq (9 March 1992) and the Sûre (8

April 1990) it was decided that more attention should be paid to the rearing of grayling, and research was carried out in the fish farms of the Fishery Department of the Ministère de la Région Wallonne.

The CHIERS, in the extreme south of Belgium, is formed by the confluence of the TON, the VIRE and the CHAVRATTE. It is 112 km long, but most of its length lies in France, where it joins the Meuse.

The VIROIN, only 17 km long, is formed by the junction at Dourbes of the EAU BLANCHE and the EAU NOIRE and flows across the border into France, where it joins the Meuse. At the moment it is the best grayling river in Belgium, as a result of the strict and grayling-friendly management policies of local fishing clubs.

The OUR and the SÛRE are part of the Rhine basin. The Our, 122 km long, meanders through the south-east of the province of Liège along the German frontier and joins the Sûre in the Grand Duchy of Luxembourg. The upper reaches of the Sûre (German: Sauer) run for a short distance through Belgium, but most of its 165 km lies in Luxembourg, where it eventually joins the Moselle.

The HOEGNE, 33 km long, is a high peat-moor river, and both it and its tributary the WAYAI (20 km) have a grayling stock. Both rivers are now protected by the Government. The Hoegne runs into the VESDER, which also has a small grayling stock in its upper reaches.

The MEHAIGNE, although not a typical salmonid river, is the most northerly grayling river in Belgium. A tributary of the Meuse – which it joins at Huy, after a run of 63 km – it has been badly affected by the regional sugar industry in the past, but it is now recovering.

There are no grayling in the northern part of Belgium. In April 1990, after a successful introduction of brown trout, 1,000 young grayling of about 10 cm were released in the Dommel and the Bolissenbeek (which are lowland brooks). However, all the salmonids died as a result of pollution, and in November 1993 electric fishing found no trout (the grayling had disappeared before that). There are plans to introduce grayling into the Zwalm – a small, idyllic river in south-eastern Flanders – but purification plant needs to be built first.

Books and Guides

There are no recent fishing guides or books about fishing in southern Belgium. One must still refer to the *Guide de la Pêche en Ardenne* by H. Balzat and A. Dussart (1978) and the older (but still interesting) *Guide du*

Pêcheur Belge (*c*. 1949), edited by P.A. Legrand. Ippa's *Ardennengids van Belgie* (Lanno, 1996) devotes a lengthy chapter to the rivers of the Ardennes and is a very good guide to a lovely part of Belgium that is well worth visiting.

Flies

As there are many fishermen on the banks of the rivers, fish are very shy, which means thin leaders, small flies and a stealthy approach. The 'classic' grayling flies are generally used (including the Red Tag, which is very popular and successful) and sparsely dressed imitations of up-wing flies give good results. Cul de canard flies have long been known to Belgian fishermen and are widely used in small sizes.

It is worth drawing attention to a specific and original Belgian fly, the Universelle (or Universal Sedge). This suggests a sedge but is a good general pattern as well, besides being useful as a small mayfly. An excellent grayling fly in the smaller sizes, it is well described in Dr J.P. Pequenot's *French Fishing Flies* (which notes the error, in flies originating during the 1930s, of giving tails to representations of *Trichoptera*). In the same style is the Mohet d'Amblève ('mohet' being dialect for sedge).

River Amblève: Fonds de Quarreux

HUGO MARTEL

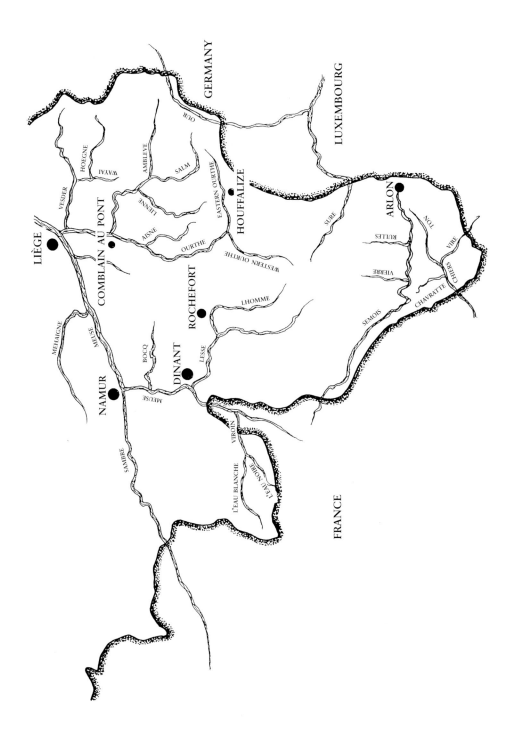

Grayling in Denmark

Hans van Klinken

DENMARK, A PEACEFUL land of farmers and agriculture, is the most southerly of all the Scandinavian countries. It is almost completely surrounded by sea, which makes it very interesting for fishermen (my friend Mogens Espersen tells me that for ages the fishing gods have been very kind to the Danish people, and I believe this is true). In general, fly fishing in Denmark is not easy but the rewards can be enormous. There is excellent salt-water fishing on the eastern coast and around the islands, but it is on the mainland (Jutland) that you will find superb river fishing for grayling: when you hit the right conditions, it really can awaken your heart and soul. More than once I have had some memorable fishing, but there have also been times when the only success went to the fish. Grayling fishing in Denmark is special, different and a real challenge. If all you want is to catch loads of fish, then you never should go there, but if you want to really enjoy your fly-fishing, then I can highly recommend it.

The present

Because of the publicity about salt-water fishing, Denmark's excellent river fishing gets overlooked. The country is a real fishing paradise, especially for the decent fly fisherman, and the prospects are getting better every year. I believe that if people focus only on salt water they overlook a great opportunity. They miss an extra challenge, beautiful wetland scenery and some great fly-fishing. Fly fishing on Danish rivers means peace, quietness and a lot of pleasure – even in high season you always find a wonderful and lonesome spot to wet your flies.

In comparison with England and some other European countries, fly fishing in Denmark is quite young, but the Danes have learned a lot from others' mistakes. Fishing clubs have done a great job in cleaning up their waters, and the Danish Federation of Fly Fishers has made an enormous contribution to popularising our great sport. The reintroduction of salmon and sea trout seems to be meeting with great success; they have returned in many rivers, and the new populations seem to grow every year. Many farmers now take good care to maintain buffer zones close to the rivers and pollution has been severely restricted all over the country. The bad times are really over now, and there are good populations of grayling and trout in the upper courses of many rivers, streams and brooks.

The rivers, streams and tributaries.

I like Denmark because I am always sure of an enjoyable trip, and that's the main reason why I visit it twice a year – normally for four- or five-day trips each spring and autumn. Just to be out for a couple of days, to find some peace, produces such a renewal of inspiration for so many things: it's like recharging your batteries! I also like to fish in small brooks and streams, and Denmark is an excellent place for this. There are dozens of nice streams, most of them still following their natural courses. In spring and autumn many migrating birds break their journeys north or south to take some rest in the fields, bringing extra life to the landscape, and birds of prey are hunting day and night. The rivers, small and very picturesque, beautify the landscape with their meanderings, but those deep, eroded meanders produce perfect lies, shelter and hiding-places. The current runs fast, there are many marvellous feeding seams between the beautiful weedbeds and high, sandy banks, and the conditions are perfect for insects to grow and reproduce. Caddis and mayflies abound, and in several streams large populations of *danica* attract not only fish but also a large group of dry-fly fanatics. Late in the season, when terrestrials fall into the water from the overgrown banks, you sometimes see those pools boiling from activity – I easily can watch this for hours in search of a new trophy fish. When the weather conditions are right, catching up to ten large fish a day is perfectly possible.

There are dozens of excellent grayling waters to fish. You need a state licence (*fisketegn*), which is easy to get at post offices, and for river fishing you have to buy an extra licence for each stream. The prices are very cheap and vary from D Kr 20 a season up to D Kr 100 a day. Hotels (KRO), tourist offices, camping sites, sports shops and local shops are the best places to buy a day ticket. To locate some good river fishing, there are a few place-names you should remember: Ribe, Varde, Skeni, Rolstebro and Skive. These are bigger towns and easy to find on every map. For fishing itself you need a good map – a scale of 1:200,000 or less is highly recommended.

You can get a very good impression of the grayling fishing on Jutland if you work your way up the west coast from south to the north. With a few exceptions, the grayling is native in most of the rivers that flow out into the North Sea – the result of the ice age.

In the south-west the first noteworthy area is around Ribe. Here you cross the Ribe river system, which holds trout, sea trout and a good number of grayling. Take some of the small country roads to follow the river upstream. Driving around in the country, it is easy to get lost, so good map-reading is essential. Search for the wonderful Gels Å tributary (the Danish name for a river or stream is Å), a rather long but narrow stream that offers loads of opportunities and excellent grayling and trout fishing. It is fishable from Immervadbro to Gels Bro. Look for parking areas close to bridges, and don't worry if you don't see any fishermen; just walk up- or downstream and try any good-looking or fishable places. The Gels River has good hatches, and even on rainy days I have seen fish rising. Look for holding pools, and I am sure you will catch some nice fish. Don't be surprised if you hook a large sea trout on a dark day or at sunset!

Gels Å, Ribe river system

161

Hans van Klinken fishing the River Konge

A little further north, between Ribe and Esbjerg, you come to the River Konge (which translates into English as 'the King's River'). Some people consider this the cream of the Danish rivers, and it is definitely one of the best waters for large grayling in the 50-cm range – but often trout will take your fly too. The best stretches are between Gredsted Bro and Foldingbro; this area can be a bit busy at weekends, though, and I personally prefer to fish further upstream. My largest grayling in Denmark to date (59 cm) was hooked and released in a small tributary of the Konge, the Vejen Å.

North of Esbjerg you will come across the Varde river system, which also holds salmon and rainbow. Two of its feeders, the Grindsted Å and Ansager Å, are extremely important for the grayling angler. The Grindsted is one of the best places to go when rain has coloured most of the streams in the area. It is one of the clearest rivers in Denmark and has plenty of attractive weedbeds and hundreds of wonderful holding pools – which can be very deep in places. Besides grayling, the Grindsted also holds large and beautifully marked brown trout which are easy to catch on a dry fly.

You can't miss the Skern river system in the centre of western Jutland.

It is huge and has lots of beautiful tributaries to explore, like the Fjederholt Å and the Vorgod Å. In the main river you will find grayling, trout, sea trout, salmon and coarse fish. The most popular places to fish are from Sønder Felding down to the mouth, but the upper parts are the best for grayling. Many of those who fish the Skern concentrate too much on the main river, however, and in their ignorance avoid its upper reaches and tributaries, so the fishing pressure on most of these stretches is extremely low. A lot of fishermen still believe that the small brooks and

R.V. DUIJNHOVEN

Roger Kenyon fishing the River Guden

163

streams hold few fish or only small ones – this is the biggest mistake a fisherman can make in Denmark. Another reason is that not many people know where to get licences for the tributaries, but that's just a matter of asking. Some farmers offer some excellent private fishing. Be prudent, and always ask first if you are not too sure about the area your licence covers. I have generally got permission quite easily when I have explained that I fish, catch and release only.

The longest river system in Denmark is the Guden Å, which starts not far from Tørring and flows through several lakes before reaching the sea in Randers Fjord on Jutland's east coast. This was one of the best salmon rivers in Denmark, until the spawning grounds were destroyed when a dam was built. Today, however, restocking projects seem to have been unbelievably successful, and a salmon population has returned. The Guden flows eastwards, so the grayling was not originally native here, but fish of up to 50 cm are now common, although not easy to find. For grayling I like to fish from Tørring down to Brædstrup. If you are not familiar with the area have a look at Gudenå Camping at Brædstrup, which is right on the river and has a very nice fly-only stretch to try.

Finally the brooks

To fish the brooks of Denmark successfully you need a lot of patience, good legs and a little skill. The obstructions (high banks, trees, grass, plants) and much clearer water make fly fishing more difficult but also more challenging. In my explorations of the smallest brooks and streams I have found some wonderful waters; the Vorgod Å, Gels Å, Vejen Å, Fjederholt Å and Grindsted Å are among my favourites.

Equipment for river fishing

Rods rated 3–5 of up to 9 ft and a floating line will do the work perfectly. Chest waders are not necessary. Most favoured are weighted nymphs, size 10, like the Leadhead, Peeping Caddis and Caseless Caddis in sandy colours. Shrimps abound in many rivers, and rusty colours provide the best imitations. Dry flies such as the Parachute ant (size 16), *Baetis* imitations (size 14–16) and small parachute flies work well; the Klinkhamer (size 12–14) is highly recommended. During the summer large sedge imitations are excellent. The banks are high and the water can be very deep. Wading leaves traces of mud behind, which can reducing the taking mood of the fish.

R.V. DUIJNHOVEN

A typical Danish stream, the Fjederholt Å

Rules for River Fishing

Size limits: Trout 30 cm; sea trout 40 cm; grayling 33 cm; salmon 60 cm. Most rivers and streams open on 1 March and close at the end of October. The close season for grayling is from 15 March to 15 May. There is no close season for Rainbows.

Notes from a Dutch Grayling Angler – The Eifel Region

Ferdinand von der Assen

THE RATIO OF GRAYLING to grayling anglers in the Netherlands is probably negative. There used to be a natural population of grayling in the Geul, a small river in southern Limburg, but it disappeared due to lead-poisoning in 1885. Nowadays small numbers of grayling occur in some of the brooks and rivulets in the south-eastern part of the country, and these are probably errants from stocking programmes in neighbouring countries.

Despite this dearth of their favourite prey fish, there exists a sizeable band of dedicated grayling anglers in Holland, quite a few of them united in the Dutch branch of the Grayling Society. It is mostly in the grayling rivers of Germany, Belgium and Denmark that you will find them, and some venture farther afield into Scandinavia, Austria or the former Yugoslavia. Many Dutch fly fishers get their first river training on the streams of the Belgian Ardennes, such as the Ourthe, the Lesse and the Amblève, or the rivers of the German Eifel, particularly the Ahr, the Lieser and the Kyll. Hugo Martel writes about the Ardennes elsewhere in this book, and I will limit these notes to the Eifel region, which lies in the triangle between Aachen, Koblenz and Trier, and to the Kyll river in particular.

Like the Ardennes rivers, the Eifel streams have their sources in the Hautes Fagnes (High Moors) of eastern Belgium, but while the Belgian rivers flow into the Meuse, the German streams discharge into the Moselle and eventually into the Rhine. Over bottoms of fine gravel and silt they flow through gently rolling fields and vineyards, and for much of their course the bedrock is carboniferous limestone, which provides good conditions for plant and insect life. Although in places there is some eutrophication due to sewage effluent and nitrate seepage, the water quality is generally quite good, and fly hatches are varied and prolific. All these

JOOP LEIBBRAND

River Kyll

rivers sustain healthy populations of brown trout, grayling, chub and barbel, and in most of them the stocks have been supplemented with rainbow trout. In the Kyll the grayling average about 1 to 1½ lbs (13 to 15 inches), with a sprinkling of larger fish up to 3 lbs.

In the small market town of Kyllburg one can lean over the bridge parapet and watch the big rainbows, up to 7 lbs, weaving in the clear stream below, with the odd dark shape further down indicating a large grayling lying in wait for morsels which the trout may overlook. At Kyllburg the countryside is more spectacular than in the upper reaches, with steep wooded hills and some narrow gorges. The autumn colours and the tranquil atmosphere make this place a favourite haunt for anglers from the cities of western Holland who, like me, often come here for a few days' angling in September or October. The fishing season generally extends from mid-April to mid-October, but on some stretches the local fishermen are permitted to fish for grayling until January or February. Visiting anglers need both a state licence, which costs DM 20 for a year, and a river permit, costing on average DM 20 per day. On some stretches day permits are available only to anglers who spend at least two nights at a local inn. Depending on the river or the area, special fishing restrictions may apply, such as a bag limit or a 'dry-fly-only' rule.

Where it is permitted, nymph fishing can be very good, especially during the early season, and a small olive goldhead (size 14–16) or an upstream emerger is often used. During the summer, depending on the location, there may be large hatches of mayflies, olives, sedges and stone-flies, and most of the fishing is done with dry flies imitating or suggesting these insects, such as Blue Dun, Tup's Indispensable, Little Red Sedge and Yellow Sally. Later in the summer small midges become more prevalent, and falls of ants regularly occur, making the angler reach for such patterns as Black Gnat, Humpy and Red or Black Ant.

In September and October the grayling fishing in these rivers reaches its peak. The fish are in top condition, fishing pressure eases as the holiday season peters out, the weather is often calm and sunny, and fly life, although perhaps not as rich as earlier in the summer, is still abundant enough to bring the grayling to the surface. On a good day it is not uncommon to catch thirty to forty sizeable grayling from only a few pools. Especially when the waters are low and clear it is necessary to go down in fly size. Sometimes sizes 18-20 will do, but more often one has to resort to smaller sizes and leader tippets down to 0.10 mm (8x). Among the local anglers a popular fly at this time of the year is the Graue Hexe (Grey Witch), which is really a Red Tag with a silver ribbing

JOOP LEIBBRAND

An average Kyll grayling

and a grizzly hackle, and in recent times the Klinkhammer fly, an invention of fellow Dutchman Hans van Klinken, has become a favourite with many.

In the mid-1980s a group of flies became very popular among the Dutch grayling anglers with whom I used to fish, though nobody I know claimed to be the inventor. Suddenly they were there, and, although I first saw them used by Dutch anglers on the Kyll, their fame spread quickly and they are now firm favourites with many grayling anglers in Holland and neighbouring countries. It started with a simple fly that consisted of no more than a few turns of green floss for a body and a tuft of clear polypropylene yarn for a wing. Inevitably, we soon began tying variations to cater for different conditions of light and water. Although some of these flies are based on well-known trout patterns, such as Coachman and Iron Blue, they were designed specifically for grayling fishing, and we enjoy great success with them especially in low water conditions. We call them 'Frutsels', which means something like trashy baubles, and we usually tie them on size 18 hooks, although sometimes we go down as far as size 26. These flies are very simple to tie and very cheap: perfect for the average Dutch grayling angler!

The French Grayling and Grayling Fishing in France

Raymond Rocher

Terminology and Distribution

THE GRAYLING IS called *ombre commun* in France because it used to be much more common than it is today. It is sometimes called *ombre de rivière*, so as to avoid the frequent confusion with the *omble chevalier* (*Salvelinus alpinus*), which is a lake salmonid. The fact that it was called *ombre d'Auvergne* at one time shows that it was very common in the Massif Central. It no longer is, and, though our *Thymallus* is still well worth fishing for in a few rivers of central France, the best region for grayling nowadays is the east. The distribution of the grayling has always been limited to the east, the south-east and the Massif Central.

Situation of the French Grayling

Our grayling stocks have generally declined since the early part of this century for various reasons: pollution, the building of many hydro-electric dams which has altered the natural flow of our rivers and interfered with spawning, overfishing with natural larvae and, of course, the immoderate use of the motor car.

Our grayling stocks are very variable, depending on the stream or part of the stream, and on the year. They vary from still very good to poor. But, as the French love grayling, and as there has been a great demand for grayling fishing from the younger generation of fly-fishers, angling federations and associations have made notable efforts in recent years to stop the decline, maintain stocks at an acceptable standard, and even improve them to a certain extent. As far as I know, attempts to re-introduce

171

grayling to trout waters where they had died out for a number of reasons, have generally not been very successful. But results have been very good in two or three rivers where grayling were introduced for the first time and where they have become established and even very prolific.

Great progress has been made in France in the artificial breeding and in the transport of the delicate grayling. Restocking with grayling fry or *ombrets* (three to four inches) from abroad, and now from our own hatcheries, has become quite common. Our most important grayling hatchery, at Augerolles (Puy de Dôme) in the Auvergne, is owned by the Conseil Supérieur de la Pêche, our highest administrative fishing authority, and run by M. Cuinat. A new grayling hatchery is to be built in the lower Ain Valley by Piam, one of our top fly-fishermen.

To give an idea of the work done in France in this respect, I will relate briefly the history of the Seine grayling. The angling federation of the Côte d'Or in Burgundy had tried very hard to establish grayling in the upper Seine system. In 1952, and again in 1954, a number of mature grayling from Ain and Jura were turned into the Seine. This was followed in 1956 by the incubation of 50,000 grayling ova sent from Yugoslavia by Mr Svetina, Head of Slovenian Fisheries; fifty per cent of these were lost, and 22,000 grayling fry introduced. Again in 1958, 50,000 ova were sent from Yugoslavia, with a fifty per cent loss and 21,000 fry introduced. The same operation was repeated in 1959 and again in 1962. These experiments were carried out by the Côte d'Or Federation with the advice of Mr Svetina and under the technical authority of M. Vivier. Now grayling have become fully established in the river Seine, where they find ideal spawning conditions.

List of Grayling Waters and Locations

Grayling now occur in the French streams and rivers named below. The stars that appear against them indicate their quality as far as grayling fishing is concerned. Thus, three stars mean 'good' or 'very good'; two stars mean 'fairly good'; one star means 'moderate to poor' or 'variable'; and no stars at all means either that there are grayling in the lower reaches only, or else that the river has recently deteriorated a great deal.

Eastern France:	Vosges: Moselle* and Moselotte**
	Doubs: Loue***, Lison***, Dessoubre***, Cusançin***, Doubs**
	Jura: Ain**, Saine*, Cuisance*

Ain: Ain**, Bienne**, Oignin, Furan*, Séran, Pollon
Haute-Saône: Ognon**, Lanterne*, Breuchin*, Planey, Semouse, Combeauté, Augrogne
Côte-d'Or: Seine*** and tributaries

South-eastern France: Isère: Bourne*, Guiers*
Savoy: Rhone*, Fier*, Guiers*, Isère
Vaucluse: Sorgues* (our southernmost grayling stream, only thirty miles from the Mediterranean coast and well below the 45th parallel)

Massif Central: Cher: Arnon**
Doubo: Loue**, Lison**
Haute-Loire: Loire, Anc du Nord**, Allagnon**, Allier*
Loire: Anc du Nord*, Lignon de Boën
Allier: Besbre
Puy-de-Dôme: Dore (where grayling may be coming back after a successful struggle against industrial pollution); Sioule
Cantal: Allagnon**
Lozère and Ardèche: Allier**, Espezonnette, Chapeauroux* (our highest grayling stream; grayling occur up to 3,800 feet)
Haute-Vienne: Vienne**
Corrèze: Dordogne*** (where grayling where successfully introduced in 1975). Other Corrèze streams have been stocked with grayling in recent years (Corrèze, Diège, Vézère), but we cannot say yet whether they have become established. Some grayling are also to be found lower down the Dordogne outside the Department of Corrèze.

I may have forgotten one or two, but the best and most famous ones are in the list. A few years ago the Huisne**, which rises in Orne (Lower Normandy) and flows south into the Sarthe through the department of Sarthe, was stocked regularly with 'ombrets', and now grayling breed and have become established in this river – which is first- and second-category. They are also to be found in its tributaries. There are no grayling in Brittany and the south-west, nor in any other Normandy stream.

RAYMOND ROCHER

Good trout and grayling water on the Upper Loue

Back in the 1960s, when I used to fish with Frank Sawyer, André Gagniard, the publisher of our then leading game-fishing magazine, told me to ask Frank to let him have some of his adult grayling to try to introduce grayling into one of our Normandy chalk streams, the Charentonne. Of course, Frank's answer was obstinately and furiously negative, which was quite understandable after his long struggle to keep down the numbers of grayling in his beloved Avon.

Types of Grayling Stream

Apart from a few slow-flowing weedy streams, like the Seine, the Lanterne, the Breuchin and one or two others, our typical grayling streams flow comparatively swiftly over rock, stone and gravel. They usually consist of a regular succession of more or less deep pools or reaches, long gravel shallows called *gravières*, and fast broken water. As in most grayling streams, our fish will lie on the bottom of the pools when they are not rising, and they will move to the tails of the pools or on to the *gravières* when they do rise. They are often caught in broken water or just below the small waterfalls made by the *Nassis* which are natural tufa weirs across some of our eastern limestone streams. Some of these are rivers, not streams, and they require breast-waders to fish effectively.

RAYMOND ROCHER

A 2 lb 4 oz (1 kg) grayling taken on nymph from the Seine

175

In the so-called grayling zone of our salmonid streams, grayling are usually mixed with other species, mostly trout and/or coarse fish. In recent years, they have had a tendency to become established further upstream and invade the trout zone.

Due to the size and variety of our country, there are some differences between the grayling streams and the grayling in them. The Seine, which is a very cold river, much like the Yugoslavian Karst rivers, produces very strong, fat and deep grayling somewhat different from those of the limestone rivers further east, like the Loue, which are also rich waters but have a faster, more irregular and more abundant flow. Most of the Massif Central streams run through peat or poor soil and over a granite bottom, especially those flowing at high altitudes, such as the Chapeauroux, the Ance or parts of the Allier. The food there is not nearly so rich, and, though they can produce large grayling too, much bigger than their trout, their fish are not shaped like the grayling of the Loue, Ain or Seine. They are more streamlined and longer, weight for weight, than the latter. They may taste a lot better too, and their coloration may also differ.

I have never found notable differences of behaviour between our grayling types, nor between our grayling, more generally speaking, and foreign grayling. The most marked difference between French grayling

RAYMOND ROCHER

River Chapeauroux

176

and other Continental or British grayling lies in the fact that ours are probably harder-fished because we have more people fishing, and therefore they are harder to catch.

The Status of the Grayling in France

The status of the grayling in France is very high indeed, so high that in some regions *Thymallus* is treated as an even better fish than the trout. It is much the same in other Continental countries where I have fished, and where it is even more strictly protected than in France. The French have

Y. RAMEAUX

Two famous French grayling anglers. Foreground: Pierre Bourret of Lyon.
Mid distance: Aimé Devaux of Champagnole, celebrated fly tyer

always appreciated grayling as a game fish, and the finesse required in grayling fishing on the fly. They appreciate the fish as a gastronomic delicacy too, and though this quality varies depending on the river, grayling is preferred to trout if it is cooked well and eaten shortly after capture. No grayling man can remain insensitive to the beauty and majesty of such famed grayling rivers as the Loue, the Ain or the Doubs, or even the uncertain upper Rhône, especially at the end of the season.

To sum up how we feel about the grayling, I cannot do better than to quote our late L. de Boisset, probably our greatest French angling writer.

> The grayling is a true game fish. With the trout and the salmon, it is the loveliest inhabitant of our streams. With trout fishing, and well before salmon fishing which is a rough game of chance, grayling fishing is a pastime for the cultured man. It is full of delicacy and nuances.

Seasons, Rules and Fishing Conditions

The grayling season in France does not open until mid-May in most departments, whereas on the same streams, trout fishing starts as early as March. In some regions of the east, Doubs particularly, the rules are stricter than elsewhere: delayed opening, drastic bag limits, prohibition of certain methods, no deep wading or breast waders, no fishing on certain days, etc. There are few fly-only stretches; those at Goumois on the Doubs and at Chenecey on the Loue are the exceptions. We have two categories of streams in France: first-category, where the game fish, trout and/or grayling, are the dominant species; and second-category, where the coarse fish predominate. This is important, because on the former grayling fishing ends at the same time as trout fishing (i.e. it runs from mid-September to early October, depending on the department). On the latter, though you are not allowed to take trout after the first-category closing date, you can continue fishing for grayling until 31 December, and for coarse fish throughout the winter.

Therefore, on our first-category rivers the season is rather short: mid-May to the end of September or early October. Perhaps this is just as well from the point of view of conservation, as most of our waters are harder fished than grayling waters abroad. Our best grayling fishing is on first-category waters. For various reasons – including heavy fishing pressure in the spring and low water levels or even drought, as in Central France – grayling fishing in the summer, especially with fly, is not very good, so that on these first-category rivers the best fishing is in May and June or early July and at the end of the season. In its lower reaches, the River Ain, which is first-category throughout from its source to its confluence with the Rhône, is classified as a grayling river and can be fished until late November, but with the fly only (including wet fly with bubble-float) after the close of the trout season.

Second-category grayling rivers are very few and, with one or two exceptions, not very good for grayling, even in the autumn. The stocks are very variable from one year or one stretch to another, and the sport is often spoilt by seasonal spates or high water from the dams. The fishing on the lower Ain, for example, is often disturbed by high water from the Vouglans dam, except on Sundays or occasional weekdays. The upper Dordogne, which produces some of the biggest French grayling and is second-category, is much the same. Our alpine rivers, which are usually unfishable in July and August due to the thawing of the high snows and glaciers, can be beautifully low and clear in the autumn and winter. The upper Rhône in Savoy is a majestic river and still contains quite a lot of grayling, and large ones too; they do not often rise, but when they do, they sometimes come up like rockets from very deep water and will take large flies. The landscape is of breath-taking beauty.

Apart from the lower Ain, the upper Dordogne or the Rhône, autumn grayling fishing can be had on the Doubs, the Allier, the Vienne, the Allagnon and the Huisne. Quite acceptable hatches of olives, small stone-fly and midges can be expected even in December if conditions are right. The heptagenids, so common on French streams, stop hatching in November.

In most French streams and rivers, grayling spawn in March and April. Though they may migrate for spawning, they never migrate over long distances. Some cock grayling are already mature at the age of two years, but our hen grayling are no good as spawners until their third or fourth year. Hence our size limit: twelve inches, throughout the country, from the tip of the nose to the end of the forked tail. One or two associations have raised the limit to twelve-and-a-half inches. Most of our private water is in the east, where private water and public water are often mixed. But this does not always mean that such unsporting methods as bubble-float fishing for grayling are not practised on some of these private stretches. Generally speaking, the younger generation of fly-fishers are more conscious of ecological and conservation problems, which means that they fish for sport rather than for the pot, and on public water will sometimes be seen to return their sizeable fish to the water, even on very difficult streams.

Y. RAMEAUX

A lower Ain grayling

To finish with rules and fishing conditions, I must add that on our large grayling rivers, canoeists can be a nuisance in spring and summer – especially on the rivers of the east, which are periodically invaded by canoeists from local clubs or from across our borders. On broad waters it is not so bad as on small waters. At times conflicts arise between anglers and canoeists, so that in some places, like the Loue valley, canoeing is forbidden before 10 a.m. and after 4 or 6 p.m. Notices to that effect have been put up. They are generally observed.

Fishing Methods

Maggot fishing is forbidden on all first-category rivers, but fishing with aquatic larvae is still widely practised and takes a heavy toll of our grayling. So does wet-fly fishing with bubble float, which is practised on wide rivers with a spinning outfit, and means several flies can be cast to great distances. It is the easiest, ugliest, most barbaric form of fishing, and it catches grayling of all sizes, including small fish. Fortunately the number of flies that may be used has been reduced to a maximum of two by law. I have seen bubble-float fishing practised, either with a transparent bubble float or with a weighted white cork, in other countries, but in France this most unsporting method has completely superseded the traditional method of wet-fly fishing for grayling. It is a very great pity indeed. The famous *mouchettes de l'Ain* probably still linger in the memories of our fathers and grandfathers. I do miss the country people and local wet-fly men of yore whom one used to see working the river downstream with their team of three wet flies, especially in Central France. Times change.

By far the most popular form of grayling fishing in France now is dry-fly and nymph fishing. Owing to improved information and advertising, casting and fly-dressing courses, fly-fishing clubs and magazines, even (God forbid) fly-fishing competitions, it has become so popular that some of our grayling and trout streams are getting overfished by these methods. This has made our fish very shy and educated, and compelled our anglers to improve their technique, tackle and artificials, and to alter their general approach. After a visit to the east of France, the late Oliver Kite said that he considered the Besançon school of dry-fly fishermen to be the most advanced in Europe. That was years ago; what would he have said if he had lived and fished the Besançon rivers now? Oliver Kite meant not only that the dry-fly men of the east caught difficult fish from hard-fished rivers, but that they had open minds and were always looking for improvements, for something new. In other words, they were not the slaves of tradition. To fly imitation they prefer 'the impressionistic style of fly-dressing with a generally simpler approach'. And one of the reasons why they took to the Sawyer style of nymph fishing just as a duck takes to water is that this style is a simplification and a good example of impressionism.

I do not want to give the impression that our grayling are uncatchable. On many rivers they can be easy or even suicidal at the beginning of the season. In rough or small streams, they are comparatively easy to deceive on large hackle flies, wet or dry. I have caught many a big fellow from some high-plateau streams of Central France while casting for trout or by just fishing the water. Traditional English wet or dry flies for grayling, fancy or imitative, are quite sufficient in some cases, as are traditional tackle and techniques.

Y. RAMEAUX

Grayling from the lower Ain, the most famous grayling river in France

Most of our good streams harbour the same species of flies as British streams, from the tiniest smut, midge or *caenis* to the largest sedge or mayfly. Do not think, as many a chalk-stream man does, that rivers other than chalk streams have little or no fly! The fly life on our limestone waters, even now, is just as rich, and usually a lot more varied. You still get fantastic hatches of small olives even below our dams, when conditions are right. On the whole we have many more heptagenids, large sedges and midges in our grayling rivers. Chironomids (midges, snow-flies) play a more and more important role in fly-fishing here, because they tend to outnumber the traditional small flies below impounded waters or villages or towns where pollution is on the increase.

Although grayling are commonly taken on large flies, including sedge and mayfly, on our large rivers most of our anglers use lightly dressed small or very small flies. The dressings of four of our classical grayling patterns – Gloire de Neublans, La Loue, La Favorite, Bécasse de Devaux and Peute – are detailed on pages 143–5. The Bécasse de Devaux, is a good example of the taste of French grayling fly-fishermen for artificials dressed with soft feathers. In recent years they have adopted the *cul-de-canard* patterns, generally unwinged, and dressed with the soft downy feathers from the rump of a duck, as tied and commercialised by Bresson and Devaux in the east of France.

Another very popular series of dry-fly patterns for grayling is the French Tricolore series, dressed and sold by Bresson. A French Tricolore is simply a palmer fly dressed with three good cock hackles of the same size and of three different colours, wound side by side round the hook shank in any order. When dressed well on first-class small hooks (16-22) it is a very good grayling artificial. It is often taken by choosy grayling rising consistently to spent or duns. As for the Culs-de-Canard, which lend themselves to a great variety of dressings, when lightly dressed they are good imitations of the emerging duns. A tiny Cul-de-Canard is the best possible imitation of a midge.

To fish for grayling our dry-fly men favour a comparatively long, light, supple rod (nine foot, DT4.5), silk lines and very fine long leaders (up to 6 yards ending in 6 to 8x), even where the fish are large. They nearly always cast long lines downstream to a rising fish, so as to present the fly first. Downstream, or across and downstream, this is the way I fish, and I think it makes a great difference. Presentation is all-important. Simple reels, very often of English make, small hand nets, or no nets at all, and, generally speaking, light tackle and equipment are the rule. Graphite is now preferred to cane for rods, for the same reason.

For nymphing we use good Sawyer patterns or variations of these, and the Sawyer style of fishing. Some of our young fishermen have become experts at nymphing. Most grayling caught on nymphs over here are caught on small patterns fished on long lines and very fine leader points, usually cast to visible fish in comparatively shallow water – one to three feet deep – in June or July.

Some of our streams and rivers are excellent for summer nymphing, because their water is very clear and our grayling will move in shoals on to the gravel shallows or wander about in the shallow water near the banks at midday or in the afternoon. It is not nearly as easy as tackling a shoal of chalk-stream grayling in a deep pocket or a pool on a summer afternoon. These grayling of ours are really a challenge.

Deep-nymphing with heavy nymphs in the pools or in deep water is, with a few exceptions, much more difficult, because we have fewer grayling and they are usually scattered over a larger area than in a chalk stream. This sport is practised by only a few experts. It is often the only way to catch big grayling in rivers like the Seine, where the whoppers do not often rise to the surface except on odd days in the early part of the season. One should not forget either that there is no weed-cutting on weedy rivers in France, except in some Normandy chalk streams, so that it is sometimes next to impossible to get your nymph down to the good fish because of the abundance of weed.

I remember two particularly good years for grayling when I fished with both small and deep nymphs on the Seine in late July. These were 1985 and 1986. The water levels were low, the water gin-clear as always, the weed scarce, especially in 1986, and the weather conditions ideal. The grayling I caught ranged from one to over two pounds. They were some of the best grayling I had ever caught in my country; the same sort of grayling that you catch in Yugoslavia: fat, powerful summer fish that will keep you running down the bank or floundering down the river for over a hundred yards before you can net them out. Yes, they were some fish, and in those years, so much better than the trout.

The Seine, the Dordogne and the Loue produce our largest grayling. In the Corrèze Dordogne, between Argentat and Beaulieu, fish of over two pounds are not a rarity, and fish of over three pounds have been caught. The Dordogne grayling are highly selective, and, because of the abundance of bottom food, most grayling over two pounds can be caught only on deep nymphs, which should be imitations of caddis nymphs, so common in this great river. The special patterns dressed and sold by Guy Plas of Marcillac-la-Croisille in Corrèze usually do best.

The Future of the 'Ombre Commun'

Although the management of our game fish waters has improved, it is still far from scientific. In recent years, for example, the season has closed in mid-September instead of December on the lower Ain, a typical *Thymallus* river. In eastern France, on the Loue, artificial nymphing has been banned while bait-fishing is still allowed. Every winter some of our best waters are invaded by cormorants which fly in from northern Europe and wreak havoc on the vulnerable grayling stocks.

To make up for that, some Associations have been trying to introduce grayling, or re-introduce the native breed of grayling – in some rivers with good results, as on the lovely Ain. But the future is still very uncertain, for the grayling are very demanding fish and won't accept *any* water, especially if polluted. And the cormorants are still protected and keep coming in to take a heavy toll of these wonderful fish every year.

Grayling in Germany

Robert Thomas

THE GRAYLING IS found in all the major German river systems: the Rhine, Weser and Elbe systems flowing into the North Sea, and the Danube system flowing south-east into Austria, Hungary and Romania to the Black Sea. The German name for the grayling is Äsche, or *Äschen* in the plural. (Strangely, the mullet is known as *Meeräsche* (sea grayling), so somebody once obviously found a similarity between the two species! Historically it has always been regarded as a fine game fish and on a par with the trout as a table fish, and it has never been regarded with the disdain accorded to its English relations on the chalk streams.

To what extent the grayling has spread in Germany as a result of stocking, it would be impossible to say, but where it is found today it is regarded as a native fish. Although grayling are found in all the major river systems, this obviously does not mean that they are found throughout Germany in great numbers. Generally, the north German flatland, with a few exceptions, is not noted for its grayling fishing. The better grayling fishing is found in the hilly central regions down to the mountainous south of the country, and it is here that we find the better-known grayling rivers which I shall describe later.

As far as fishing methods are concerned, it should be noted that fly fishing is nowhere near as widespread in Germany as it is in the UK, and there are estimated to be only around 30,000 fly fishers in the whole of Germany. One of the reasons for this is that much of the prime salmonid waters has historically been in private hands, so that there were fewer accessible stretches of water than in many other countries. Today access is available through clubs, hotels or towns, which manage their own stretches (mostly in the tourist areas), but probably the majority of grayling water is still private. Fly fishing does however probably account for the majority of grayling caught.

ROB THOMAS

Ahr Valley, Eifel region of Germany. British Embassy fly fishing water
in February

Flies and tackle used for grayling are more or less the same as those
used in other countries or as those used for trout. Standard grayling or
trout dry flies will work fine in most situations when fish are rising.
Standard wet fly fishing is not very widespread and seems to have gone
out of fashion. As far as nymph fishing is concerned, goldheads have
become very popular for both grayling and trout, and are fished upstream
or down. One system of nymph fishing which is not widespread is the
Czech system of a team of three heavy nymphs fished on a long rod and
short line, which has become popular in the UK. Where it has been used
it has accounted for some very large grayling indeed – which had presumably previously been fished over. It should be noted, however, that teams
of flies are often not allowed, and the rules may state that a single fly only
shall be used. This should obviously be clarified before one starts to fish.

Laws, Rules and Regulations, etc.

No chapter on fishing in Germany could be without at least an attempt to
describe and clarify some of the unique, misunderstandable laws pertaining to fishing in this country, which are sometimes illogical, often

contradictory and always complicated. Basically, it should first be understood that Germany is a Federal Republic, and that laws regarding fishing are decided upon by the State and not the Federal government – which means that there are likely to be some differences between individual States on such things as size limits or seasons, although in general they do not vary too much. Bag limits are set by the owner of the fishing rights.

The licensing system is similar to the UK inasmuch as an annual rod licence (*Jahresfischereischen*) is required, which is issued by the State authorities, and additionally permission is required from the actual owner of the fishing rights (e.g. club membership, hotel guest permit, etc.).

Seasons are also similar to those in the UK, and the grayling season is usually from the beginning of May until the end of February, and the trout season from mid-March until mid-October (although clubs can vary the closed seasons within those set by the State). The reality of grayling fishing in waters which are shared with trout, however, is that the season closes with the trout season, and only a few clubs tend to keep the fishing open for the sake of the grayling.

At this point the similarities between German laws and those of most other countries tends to stop. Two further laws are the cause of much confusion and, when explained to other nationalities, account for much head shaking disbelief. These lay down that:

1. That anyone resident in Germany who wishes to obtain a State licence (*Jahresfischereischein*) shall first pass a one-time written and practical test on fishing. These tests can usually be taken in one's town of residence, but usually only on one set date in the year.

This is a State law, and some differences may occur from State to State. This law should not concern the visiting angler too much, however, as guest licences for a limited period are available through the local authority in the town or region where one wants to fish. The office responsible for issuing these licences is the Lower Fishery Authority (*Unterfischereibehöde*), which can usually be found in the local town council offices (*Rathaus*). It will also be useful to contact the local tourist information office (*Fremdenverkhersamt*), especially in the major tourist areas, which will usually be only too willing to point one in the right direction. At the end of this chapter I have listed a few tourist information offices and hotels in areas which cater for anglers, which will help visitors get the appropriate licences and also issue permits themselves for local waters. Remember, however, to take two passport photographs of yourself with you, together with your national rod licence from your country of residence.

An additional tip here: You may, especially in the larger towns and outside the usual tourist areas, come up against civil servants in the Lower

Fishery Authority offices who will not know of the existence of guest licences for foreign visitors, or who may tell you that they cannot issue them. In such a case please remain calm and polite, but tell the person dealing with you that you know that they are available and ask him to find out how to issue one. Do not allow yourself to be put off!

2. That any fish which is caught, which is in season and of takeable size shall be immediately killed and taken (i.e. catch and release is effectively illegal).

This law is actually not a fishing law at all but derives from a Federal law (Federal laws are always above State laws) pertaining to the prevention of cruelty to animals. It effectively states that no person shall inflict pain or harm on an animal without good reason.

In various cases of precedent in the courts, brought on by animal-rights activists, it was considered that fishing for pleasure constituted a breach of this law, but fishing for the bag was legal. Now, although the law in question is a Federal law, the fishery law it was applied to was a State law, so, again, various states have ruled differently on this subject. Be that as it may, very few people actually abide by this law, and most anglers do release those fish that they do not want to keep for the pot – indeed many fishery owners stipulate catch and release, and are thereby themselves effectively breaking the law.

Winter snow, River Ahr

One consequence of this law is that it has tended to take the wind out of the sails of the anti-fishing movement in Germany, where it is today far less widespread than in the UK. It would, however, seem to be a shame that fish cannot give their opinion on the matter; if given the choice of being returned to the water alive to live another day or be killed, I am sure I know which they would choose.

It is, however, important that visiting anglers are aware of the existence of this law and that they act responsibly, especially if people are looking on whilst they are fishing.

Grayling Waters in Germany

Grayling in Germany are found almost exclusively in rivers and streams (I am only aware of one stillwater in which grayling are regularly caught: Obermaubach Reservoir on the River Rur between Cologne and the Belgian border). Between 1900 and the mid-1970s, in an access of well-intentioned tidiness and order, most West German rivers which ran through towns or adjoined farmland were straightened, graded and canalized for land reclamation purposes, to allow quicker drainage and, supposedly, to reduce flooding risks. (The results are often still evident today and are seen every time lower reaches of major rivers flood because of the lack of water meadows in the upper part of the river system.) With many of their natural hiding places taken away from them, many fish, in particular salmonids, were adversely affected.

The pattern of many rivers and streams was therefore often one of long straight stretches with the odd bend, interspersed with weirs to break the speed of the water flow. It was only from the late 1970s on that people and the authorities began to realize the error of their ways and to stop further grading and sometimes try (usually unsuccessfully) to renaturalise rivers. With the passing of time and winter high waters, much of the damage caused has been hidden, banks have grown over, and gradually rivers and streams are returning to their natural state. The longer ago the original grading took place, the more advanced is the return to nature. Since the 1980s this, together with the general decrease in industrial pollution, has even led to the return to the Rhine and its tributaries of the once plentiful salmon and sea trout. For these rivers, then, the future is looking positive. Grayling, however, have been generally declining in numbers for many years now, to the extent that they have even been placed on the red list of endangered species in several areas of Bavaria. The reasons for this decline, when many other fish are making a comeback, are not clear, but would seem to be the results of many factors. Certainly the grading of rivers adversely affected grayling; so has the resultant silting up of spawning beds; and in several successive winters cormorants have also taken their toll. However, this does not entirely explain the decline, since it is also often evident in rivers not greatly affected by any of the above factors – and indeed trout do not seem to have suffered as much as grayling.

In the former East Germany, there was never the same degree of grading as in the West, because of lack of state money, and it is probably in the former East that the biggest improvements to water quality have occurred. After the fall of communism and the unification of East and West Germany at the beginning of the 1990s East German industry almost ceased to exist, and as a result the once-rife pollution which had voided many rivers of fish life, rapidly declined. Now, almost ten years on, those rivers have made an almost complete recovery and are again full of aquatic life.

The following then is a list of some of the rivers in Germany in which the grayling is found today. It would be impossible to list *all* the rivers and streams holding grayling, so I have restricted my choice to those that I can comment on from experience.

Lower Saxony

The northern part of Germany is not renowned for its grayling fishing, but two rivers that lie between Hamburg and Hanover in Lower Saxony are worth mentioning. One is the Örtze, just north of Celle – and in particular in the area round the village of Hermannsberg, where tickets are available. The other is the Ilmenau, which flows north through Lüneburg to join the Elbe. Both are in the Lüneberg Heath region on typically sandy ground. Grading and straightening of these rivers in the past has created problems with grayling spawning beds silting up.

The Eifel

The Eifel region is, broadly speaking, bordered by the Belgian border in the west, the Rhine in the east, the Moselle in the south and a line drawn between Aachen and Cologne in the north. Grayling are found in the Kyll, Ahr, Rur, Our and Prüm rivers, and in the lake at Obermaubach on the Rur.

Of the above, the Kyll probably has the most accessible stretches of guest-ticket water, tickets being available in most villages along the Kyll, (though mostly in conjunction with stays of at least two nights in local guest houses or hotels).

Bergisches Land/Sauerland

The area lies to the east of the Rhine at Cologne. Grayling rivers here are the Dhünn, Agger, Sieg, Lenne, Diemel and Lahn. Guest-ticket water is very limited but may be available through local clubs.

Spessart/Rhön

Roughly in a triangle between Frankfurt, Fulda and Schweinfurt. Rivers are the Sinn, Fränkische, Saale, Jossa, Lüder, Schlitz and Altefeld. Guest tickets are available on several stretches.

Black Forest/Schwäbische Alb

The Black Forest region, in the extreme south-west of Germany, and the Schwäbishe Alb region south of Ulm are two of the most picturesque parts of the country, and it is in the latter that the Danube begins its long journey to the Black Sea.

Rivers where grayling are found are the Nagold, Neckar, the Upper Danube and the Blau. Tickets are available on all rivers.

Fränkische Schweiz/Bayerischen Wald

The Fränkische Schweiz region is north of Nuremburg, and the Bayerische Wald lies between Regensburg and the Czech border.

The Wiesent and Pegnitz rivers in the Fränkische Schweiz have long been known to grayling and trout fishermen and are probably, historically speaking, the centre of German fly fishing. The Wiesent has suffered badly in recent winters from cormorant predation. Tickets are available at several points along the river, in particular in Waischenfeld and Streitberg. On the Pegnitz tickets are available in Velden.

Southern Bavaria

The main rivers in southern Bavaria where grayling are found are the Iller, Lech, Ammer, Loisach, Isar and Inn. Since the mid 1980s the grayling population throughout these rivers has been declining at an alarming rate. The exact reasons for this are not evident, although, (as we have said) many factors seem to have played a role, and to what degree natural causes may be to blame has not been fully researched. The fact is, however, that the water quality is excellent in most cases. Natural predation by birds has not helped but cannot be the sole cause, and the presence of rainbow trout has

River Ahr, lower limit of British Embassy water at Ahrdorf bridge

been mentioned, but they were also present during periods of excellent grayling stocks. Fishing pressure by anglers has been reduced, even to the extent of a complete ban on taking grayling in some areas – and still the situation is one of grave concern. It does seem that complete generations of grayling are missing for some reason; large grayling may be caught as well as small grayling, but everything in between seems to either have never been present or to have disappeared.

The extent of the decline can be seen from the following examples.* On a 44-km stretch of the River Inn an average of 4,633 grayling per year was caught from 1973 to 1978 inclusive. A peak was reached in 1979, with almost 14,000 grayling caught, and in 1980 a total of almost 8,000 grayling were accounted for. But in 1981 there was a dramatic downturn, with fewer than 2,000 fish caught. The decline has continued steadily, and catches in the years 1993 to 1996 inclusive have been below 200 fish per year.

On a 45-km stretch of the River Isar catches averaged 2,433 grayling per year from 1968 to 1970 inclusive, 666 grayling per year from 1971 to 1973 inclusive, and 1,233 grayling per year from 1974 to 1976 inclusive.

* Data taken from Dr Elisabeth Mathus and Dr Oliver Born, *Bestandsituation der Äsche in Bayern* (1997).

From 1977 to 1987 inclusive the number of grayling caught remained relatively steady, at an average of 2,954 per year, with a peak in 1981 of just over 4,000 fish caught. From 1988 to 1991 inclusive, the catch averaged 1,186 fish per year, but from 1992 to 1996 inclusive, it fell to 236 fish per year.

Former East Germany

The best-known grayling rivers in the former East Germany are the Stepenitz, Nebel, Werra, Felda and Sächsische Saale. Owing to a duplication of names, the Stepenitz is the river which ends in the river Elbe with the town nearest the fishing being Pützlitz. The Nebel flows into the Baltic with the town nearest the best fishing at Hoppenrade being Güstrow. In contrast to the southern Bavarian rivers, these eastern rivers have improved greatly within the last ten years due to the rapid fall in industrial pollution after the collapse of communism, and today the grayling is found in good numbers in all of them. This would seem to contradict the theory of grayling stocks dwindling due to unknown natural causes, as seems to be the case in Bavaria – if some unknown factor were causing the decline elsewhere, this should also affect the eastern German rivers, but this does not seem to be the case.

Tickets are available on the Felda in the village of Stadtlengsfeld and on the Sächsische Saale below the Hohenwarte Stausee (Reservoir) down to Saalfeld. Both these waters offer excellent grayling fishing – the result of a lot of hard work put in by local clubs to improve stocks and water quality.

On Italian and Balkan Grayling

Antonio Sabbadini

ITALY AND THE Balkans are on the south edge of grayling distribution in Europe, the southernmost population being found in the River Luča and Lake Plavsko – in Montenegro, close to the Albanian border.

Grayling Distribution in Italy

Thymallus thymallus, (*temolo* in Italian) is restricted to the country's northern regions: Valle d'Aosta, Piedmont, Liguria, Lombardy, the Veneto, Trentino-Alto Adige and Friuli-Venezia Giulia. At the start of the twenty-first century, the situation of the Italian grayling seems to be improving, at least where its environment is improving, and above all where fishing rules are conducive to its defence rather than its destruction. There are signs that in many quarters increasing attention is being paid to this peerless, irreplaceable fish (one of them being the foundation of 'Thymallus', an Italian society promoting awareness and conservation of grayling). If its future looks better, this is reassuring and promising, but the fishing effort is increasing, and many knotty problems remain to be worked out. The battle against grayling's enemies must go on!

Valle d'Aosta Region

Dora Bàltea Grayling are found only in this river, especially from Nus, below Aosta (the regional capital), down to the village of Pont-St-Martin on the borders of the Piedmont region. The best stretches, in descending order of merit, are at Hône, Arnad, Issogne, Verrès, Champdepraz, Montjovet, Pontej, Chambave, the junction with the Clavalité, Fénis and Aymavilles. Specimens over 50 cm are not rare, and the fly fishing is very pleasant, but the flow is frequently broken up by weirs, and the river is afflicted by periodic water abstractions.

Piedmont Region

Verbano-Cusio-Ossola Province

Toce This freestone river in the Ossola valley (home of the nymph-like artificial flies known as *camole*) is well endowed with grayling, from its outlet into Lake Maggiore almost up to Crevola d'Ossola. It has a good flow and offers fine fishing, in spite of some water abstraction.

Province of Verbania

Melezzo This river flows into Lake Maggiore. Grayling were introduced downstream of the village of Re some years ago and now appear established.

Province of Vercelli

Sesia The Sesia valley is the home of the Italian rod and line combination called *frusta valsesiana* and of the little flies known as *moschette valsesiane*. The river harbours grayling over nearly the whole of its course (grayling zone), but the best reach runs from Piode down to Quarona. Until the 1970s its grayling population was numerous and included fine specimens. Then a decline began, principally owing to disastrous spates and overfishing, though this has now been reversed, thanks to strict fishing rules. The Sesia's very beautiful surroundings make autumn fishing for grayling much sought after.

Province of Turin

Dora Bàltea Following on from the stretch described under the Valle d'Aosta region, this section, from Carema to the river's confluence with the Po, has numerous grayling of good size. Here, too, weirs and water abstraction may cause considerable change in water levels. Downstream to Ivrea, from Crotte to Vische, the river flows through particularly wild surroundings that are very attractive, although difficult of access.

Chiusella A tributary of the Dora Bàltea, this beautiful torrent harbours many wonderful grayling, especially upstream of the Strambinello dam.

Orco Again, overfishing, too many weirs and resulting water abstraction somewhat spoil this otherwise first-rate grayling river that until a few years ago was much renowned. Even so, it is well worthy of a visit – especially the stretch from Cuorgnè to Locana.

Stura di Lanzo and *Stura di Viù* These rivers have grayling in abundance – respectively, from the village of Pessinetto down to Villanova Canavese, and from the little town of Viù to their junction.

The Po and its tributary the *Péllice* Grayling can be found in the Po from Cantogno to Casalgrasso, and in the Péllice for many kilometres upstream from the confluence.

Province of Cuneo

Stura di Demonte This wonderful river contains grayling, albeit localised, from Demonte for several kilometres downstream to Cuneo, the provincial capital.

The Po There are grayling from the bridge at Staffarda to the border with Turin province.

Liguria Region

Province of Genoa

Aveto Plenty of grayling, although they are very small, from Rezzoaglio to the Boschi dam; overfishing and too low a size limit are mainly responsible.

Lombardy Region

Province of Sondrio

Adda (Valtellina) This long water course – which flows into the north end of Lake Como and then out of the southern end and on to join the Po – is a real refuge for Lombard grayling. In about 50 km of the upper section, from above the village of Chiuro to Delebio (near the lake) grayling are everywhere. Fly fishing only and catch-and-release are increasingly stipulated in many places.

Mera In this river, which flows firstly into Lake Mezzola and then into Lake Como, grayling are well spread downstream from Chiavenna.

Province of Bergamo

Brembo A small population of indigenous grayling still exists in the short reach between the villages of Zogno and Stabello; downstream a few catches are reported now and then.

Serio This beautiful river once had plenty of grayling, but the population was wiped out by water abstraction and the building of several dams and weirs. The upper reaches have been successfully restocked with Slovenian grayling.

Provinces of Milan, Bergamo and Cremona
Adda (downstream of Lake Como) Long ago this was a grayling-fishing Eldorado, but, owing to pollution, water abstraction and overfishing, now only a few disparate stocks remain in some sections, such as Cassano d'Adda, Rivolta d'Adda and Spino d'Adda, and more particularly around Cavenago d'Adda and Bertonico.

Provinces of Varese, Milan and Pavia
Ticino This river, too, was once a grayling-fishing Eldorado, but today its stocks are sadly reduced for the same reasons as those on the Adda. However, water abstraction and pollution have been reduced, and some restocking is being done with apparent success.

Province of Brescia
Chiese Upstream and downstream of Lake Idro there are some grayling, from Ca' Rossato to about Carpenedolo.

Trentino-Alto Adige Region

Province of Bolzano
Aurino There are grayling from the village of Campo Tures down to the confluence with the Rienza below Brunico.
Rienza Grayling from Brunico to confluence with the Isarco.
Passirio Grayling from St Martino in Passiria to Merano.
Isarco Grayling from Fortezza to the junction with the Adige.

Provinces of Bolzano and Trento
Adige Grayling can be found from Glorenza to Lasa, from Merano as far as Salorno on the border with Trento province, and from there as far as Borghetto.

Veneto Region

Province of Verona
Adige From Borghetto, on the border with Trento, to Verona the number of grayling has improved as a result of stricter fishing rules.

Province of Vicenza

Brenta There are grayling from Martincelli down to Bassano del Grappa, especially around Primolano, St Marino, Valstagna, Pove and Bassano.

Provinces of Belluno and Treviso

Piave There are grayling in the stretches from the village of Ponte nelle Alpi down to Pasa, from Segusino down to Vidòr and from Falze di Piave to Nervesa della Battaglia.

Province of Treviso

Livenza Along the border of Pordenone province, downstream from Cavolano to Brugnera.

Friuli-Venezia Giulia Region

Province of Udine

Tagliamento There are a few, scattered grayling between the confluence with the Fella (at Stazione per la Carnia) and the bridge at Pinzano, and in the lower reaches of some minor tributaries, such as the Leale, Melò, Arzino and Cimano. This river is subject to severe water abstraction, drought, spates and some pollution.

Fella This river, the largest tributary of the Tagliamento, harbours grayling in reasonable quantity from Chiusaforte to the confluence. Subject to spates and drought.

Resia After repeated introductions of fish, this tributary of the Fella holds a successfully breeding grayling population of good consistency, distributed from Stolvizza to Peeves.

Ledra This is a splendid short river, like a chalk stream. However, owing to overfishing and diversion of water from the Tagliamento, it has suffered an appreciable and progressive decline in grayling numbers. What a shame!

Natisone Past introductions and translocations have produced a self-perpetuating grayling population of good consistency and fine specimens from Stops down to about Cividale del Friuli. Subject to spates and drought.

Stella (river system) The river Stella, along with the Stalla, Varmo, Corno, Ghebo, Torsa and other streams of minor importance, makes up a system of spring-fed water-courses, like chalk-streams, that meander across the lowlands before reaching the sea. (Ernest Hemingway loved fly fishing on these streams on his trips to Italy). Grayling (and trout) used to be found almost everywhere, but today they are scarce and in continuing decline. The causes are water abstraction, canalisation and diversion of water, and also growing pollution from the fish-farms concentrated here and from intensive agricultural practices, which have created severe eutrophication.

Province of Gorizia

Isonzo (called *Soča* in Slovenia) This river is renowned for its grayling population and its marbled trout (*Salmo trutta marmoratus*). The Italian section supports grayling in fair quantity and quality, especially from Gorizia to Gradisca d'Isonzo.

Province of Pordenone

Livenza and *Meduna* In spite of excessive fishing and some pollution, there are still grayling in the reaches of these rivers that flow across this province.

Characteristics of Italian and Balkan Grayling

Grayling occupy the so-called 'grayling zone' or 'grayling region' of the above rivers where their physical, chemical and biological qualities, and with favourable climatic conditions, provide them with a fit habitat. Unfortunately, parts of the rivers are, for technical reasons, suitable for hydroelectric development schemes and for diversion of water to uses such as irrigation, drinking-water, and fish-farming. This and the building of weirs for lamination purposes often results in the complete destruction of the habitat and of the grayling population. In Italy, a thickly peopled country and heavily industrialised, such events are very frequent and widespread.

It is well known too that grayling are sensitive to pollution, so common today; nevertheless, in various places they are showing clear signs of recovery after extended agony. So they occupy again parts of Italian rivers, even rivers still severely polluted where they had disappeared or had been seriously affected, showing that they are getting used to chronic pollution. Such happenings are evident in other European countries, too.

Even if esteemed long go – Izaak Walton says, 'and in Italy, he is, in the month of May, so highly valued, that he is sold there at a much higher rate than any other fish'; and adds, 'St Ambrose, the glorious bishop of Milan, who lived when the Church kept fasting-days, calls him the flower-fish, flower of fishes ...' – in Italy the attitude toward grayling has provided feeble protection: an inadequate close season that starts too soon (from 1 or 15 October) and ends too soon (1 April, when grayling are still spawning or are highly vulnerable post-spawning), a legal size of only seven inches, no bag limits, and all baits and lures allowed.

In the last few years, however, an increased interest in grayling in some regions has resulted in the introduction of a legal size of eleven to twelve inches, a close season extended to 1 or 15 May, bag limits and often a fly-only rule. But the persistent, indeed increasing fishing pressure, is excessive beyond measure and, combined with quite inadequate keeping, makes the aforesaid restrictive rules useless. All things considered, the Italian waters are little sought-after, although some retain their beauty, attraction and interest, together with grayling populations of value.

The present Italian grayling distribution very likely matches the natural ancestral distribution, connected with the basin of the River Po and the Adriatic Sea. This lack of certainty is due to the matching lack of particular historical research and study, and to small-scale stocking or restocking of grayling in the areas already mentioned and elsewhere. For example, their introduction into some watercourses in the Appennines in Central Italy has recently been promoted.

These introductions or reintroductions were and are carried out usually with yearlings from heterogeneous sources, very seldom Italian, but rather Swiss, Bavarian, Austrian and Slovenian – that is to say, coming from transalpine countries.

Apart from the complicated question of sub-species it is worth mentioning the morphological differences between Italian grayling from the Adriatic river system and those from the Danube Basin and Black Sea river system. There has been no complete and methodical study; nevertheless, the available partial results show that there are real racial differences expressed in characteristics, such as the number of radii in the pectoral fins, the number of pyloric caeca, and so on, in populations from different river systems, such as the Black Sea and from the Adriatic. These findings support a presumption of the complete ecological isolation of the Italian grayling population from other European populations in general.

It is a complex question, however, because European grayling in general, and Middle European grayling in particular, have not been racially studied – as indeed the Italian ones have not. Thus it is not possible to draw a definite conclusion.

Apart from the significant differences in many morphometric characteristics, the 'presumed' Italian or Adriatic grayling has the following peculiar external features, obvious to the ordinary fisherman. The basic general coloration, within limits of well-known variability, is grey, shading into dark blue tinged with dark olive on the back; the sides, scattered with blackish spots, are silvery grey with a light golden hue; the ventral part is white, sometimes with a fringe of gold; the pectoral and ventral fins are grey or yellowish grey; the anal fin is dark grey, with a hue of pink or gold; the large tail is a dark transparent blue-grey; the adipose is dark grey or olive-grey, often fringed with pink. Most importantly, two of the peculiar features of the transalpine grayling are absent; first, a black spot in a brilliantly white field on each side of the throat, in the under-part of the mouth, and second, a large spot (or rather stain) of irregular shape above and behind the ventral fin on both sides, suffused and sprinkled with deep magenta or claret.

Transalpine grayling, at least those of the Danube Basin, are characterised by a greenish-yellow grey body and a dark olive-brown back; the ventral part is pale grey with a striking yellow-gold shade from pectoral to anal fins; pectoral, ventral and anal fins are greyish yellow, shaded with pale orange or a pale reddish colour; the tail, a very distinctive feature, is at least reddish yellow, if not hot orange or red. Of course, there are the black spots on each side of the throat and the claret stain above the ventral fins. Other characteristics, such as the dorsal fin or punctuation on the sides, are similar to the Italian ones and not worthy of note.

Incidentally, Danubian grayling, unlike their Adriatic brethren, are very prone to leap whilst being played, and to leap repeatedly, especially in colder months or in colder waters, adding much to the pleasure of the pursuit.

The males of both Black Sea and Adriatic grayling are darker, and their colours are very pronounced during spawning.

Outward appearance is certainly not an absolute indicator. Its interpretation is subjective and may sometimes even be unreliable, for it is well known that the features already mentioned may change with environment, season, sex, age, etc., and may also over weaken or conceal some of the distinctive pattern coloration. However, the identification of grayling based on the disposition and number of black spots on the sides is certain.

As mentioned above, the flanks of grayling are generally studded with little spots which vary in number and position. Thanks to Dr H. Persat (1982) of the Département de Biologie Animale et Ecologie, Université de Lyon, we have an ingenious and interesting way to identify grayling individually and also to recognise grayling strains. Dr Persat became interested in these spots, and distinguished juvenile spots, variable in the distribution patterns and number, from those of adult fish, which are stable and for life. The latter characteristic was confirmed by capture/recapture method and by recording the side-punctuation system for each fish marked by adipose fin clipping.

The quickest, most accurate and most practical way to do this was to take a photograph of each specimen from one side, usually the left. The photographs were stored as black and white negatives mounted in slides. Only specimens longer than seven inches were considered, because the spots of the smaller ones are not always clear enough to be accurately located on the photographs and may also be confused with juvenile spots in the dorsal area. The number and disposition of the spots are not symmetrical between the two sides, and some cases of specimens without spots on one side were photographed on the other side.

After the recapture, the simple comparison of photographs gave easy identification of each specimen, since the disposition of the spots did not change. Some problems arose with spot numbers, but they resulted either from the bad definition of some spots (due to the bad quality of the photograph – these were always visible subsequently) or from masking of spots by the pectoral fin, and are hence technically soluble. Some odd instances of fish without spots, or with only one spot (which is usually near the head and the lateral line) are solved by examining the disposition of the scales along the flanks and their irregularities, or other morphological aspects.

Obviously, sorting and comparing photographs becomes a long and tedious business, but today the matter is an easy task for the computer! What is more, Dr Persat spotted another use for the computer: identification of grayling strains by differences in the frequency distribution of the mode, mean and variance of spot numbers between different populations.

As an example of some practical use and preliminary results, it appears that grayling of the River Ain in France are characterised by few spots, usually between five and twenty, scattered with relative evenness both above and below the lateral line on the anterior area of the body. Those of the River Soča/Isonzo of Slovenia and Italy have a greater number of spots – between thirty and sixty – gathered below the lateral line and on the anterior third of the body; those of the River Ance in France have yet more spots – between sixty and one hundred and fifty – scattered both above and below the lateral line almost as far back as the tail.

To sum up, we have a new way, worthy of wider application and investigation, to recognise grayling strains and racial or sub-species differences.

Finally, the last word in research appears to involve the use of genetic variations detected by electrophoresis – using isozymic gene frequency data to understand the genetic structure of fish populations – or DNA (mtDNA or nuclear) analysis. This recent, efficient approach (which, more generally, will make use of population genetics in the conservation of fish populations and in fishery management) seems to be the path to follow for the future.

Grayling Distribution in the Balkan Peninsular

Balkan *Thymallus thymallus* (called *liplien* in Serbo-Croat and *lipan* in Slovenian) is found from Slovenia and Croatia to Bosnia-Herzegovina, Serbia and Montenegro in rivers of the Danube Basin-Black Sea river system, and in some of the lakes and reservoirs too. It is found in only one watercourse of the Adriatic river system. Before World War II this stream flowed entirely in Italian territory and was called the Isonzo; after the war the new international boundary divided it into two sections, with the source, the upper and middle course in Slovenia, where it is called the Soča, and the lower reaches in Italy, known as the Isonzo.

The most important Balkan rivers that harbour grayling are the following.

Slovenia

Soča Grayling are found in particular from the junction with the Lepena to the boundary with Italy, near the town of Nova Gorica/Gorizia, a reach of about forty-five miles that includes three reservoirs, notably that of Most na Soči. Grayling are also present in the terminal reaches of some minor tributaries – the Lepena, Koritnica and Tolminka – and in the major tributaries – the Idrijca, with brooks Bača and Trebuša, and Vipava.

Unec Here grayling were introduced with great success after World War II. This watercourse has a unique karst feature: starting as the Pivka, it flows in the open air for about seven miles, then sinks underground and runs through the well-known Postojna Caves, from which it flows out as the Unec and meanders through a plain before disappearing again; it finally reappears near Ljubljana, the Federal capital, as the Ljubljanica, before flowing into the Sava. The Unec, formerly renowned for its brown trout, is now celebrated for its grayling too; its abundance of water-insect life is prodigious. The hatches of mayfly are impressive, as is the quality and quantity of sedges, so that the growth of the fish is very quick and the size they attain considerable.

Sava This is formed by the joining of the Sava Dolinka and the Sava Bohinjska. It harbours good grayling in both its upper branches, and in the principal course down to the town of Kranj.

Savinja It harbours grayling from Letuš to the town of Celje.

Croatia

Kupa From Brod na Kupi to the town of Karlovac.
Dobra From Toplice Lešce to the junction with the River Kupa.

Bosnia-Herzegovina

Una From Donji Srb to Otoka.
Sana Vrblja to the confluence with the Una.
Vrbanja From Siprage to the town of Banja Luka.
Ugar Grayling are found in the reaches above the junction with Vrbas.
Pliva From above Šipovo to the Vrbas, near the junction with the town of Jajce.
Vrbas From above Gornji Vakuf to the town of Banja Luka.
Usora From about Blatanica to the junction with the Bosna, near the town of Doboj.
Lašva From Vitez to the junction with the Bosna.
Bosna From about Ilidža, near the town of Sarajevo, to the confluence with the Lašva.
Drinjača From Kladani to the junction with the Drina.

July wet fly fishing on the River Sava, Slovenia

Cehotina From Pljevlja to the junction with the Drina, near Foča.
Sutjeska From Tjentište to the confluence with the Drina.
Tara From Mataševo to the junction with the Drina.
Piva From Boan to Šavnik to Pivsko lake, to the flowing into River Drina.
Drina From Foča to the junction with the Lim

Serbia

Jadar From about Osečina to the confluence with the Drina.
Uvac From Lake Zlatarsko to the junction with the Lim.
Studenica From Brezova to the junction with the Ibar, near Ušće.
Ibar From Rožaj to the confluence with the Stitnica, near Titova Mitrovica.

Montenegro

Luča From Gusinje and Lake Plavsko to the junction with the Lim.
Lim From the junction with the Luča to the confluence with the Drina.

The major part of waters holding grayling are thus in Bosnia-Herzegovina. The Drina river basin is the most remarkable, but many others are very

A. SABBADINI

The Mill of Slap, River Idrijca, Slovenia, with the pool where the grayling feed on wheat grain

interesting, although some are difficult of access or do not always offer very comfortable accommodation. (Bosnia was one of the places selected by G.E.M. Skues to spend his holidays.) Other interesting waters are, for instance, the River Kupa in Croatia, and Lake Plavsko and the rivers Luča and Lim in Montenegro. There are yet others, fairly recently stocked with grayling, but with mixed success.

The best-known rivers are those of Slovenia, such as the Soča (together with its tributaries Lepena, Koritnica, Tolminka, Bača, Idrijca, Trebuša and Vipava), the Unec and the Sava. Factors that help to make Slovenian waters very interesting include fewer problems of pollution and water diversion, lower human presence, picturesque surroundings, good accessibility, comfortable hotel accommodation and conservative fishing rules (grayling up to sixteen inches and over and a frequently selective, fly-only rule). These qualities justify their renown, even if today they are a bit overcrowded and over-exploited.

Incidentally, Slovenia produces for propagation purposes about half a million grayling fingerlings every year. These are obtained from pairs of mature specimens netted or electro-fished in spawning grounds or whirlpools at spawning time, reared to the age of about four months before being used to stock rivers in Slovenia itself or in other countries.

Habitats and Feeding Habits

Apart from lakes or spring-fed waters that meander in a plain as chalk streams do – usually rich in weeds, and with a relatively moderate current – Balkan and Italian grayling occupy mainly the typical zones of rivers or river-lake systems. As described by Huet in 1954, the grayling zone is characteristic of rivers and larger rapidly flowing streams. The gradient is usually less than in trout waters, and the riffles and rapids are generally separated by pools. The more rapid stretches are inhabited by both trout and grayling, and the calmer waters in between by the running-water cyprinids, such as barbel and chub. In summer, the waters of the grayling zone are relatively less oxygenated than those of the trout zone, and the temperature is higher. The stream bed is usually of finer material than is common in the trout zone, often consisting largely of gravel, spread out and washed clean by the current.

As Sir H. Davey wrote over 150 years ago, grayling require a combination of stream and pool; they like a deep pool for rest, and for some bottom feeding, a rapid stream above and a gradually declining shallow below. The temperature of the water and its character, whether still or moving, seem more important than its clearness.

Leaving the deep pools, sub-adults and adults move downstream to the shallows, where they occupy the best places and continue and intensify bottom feeding, but principally they rise to mid-water or up to the surface, intercepting drift-food at various levels.

As is well known, the interception is accomplished by rising almost vertically from the bottom to seize sub-surface or surface food, and then returning as steeply to the depths in an elliptical movement. This procedure provides feeding fish with the advantage of being able to command a particularly wide view of the surface and to choose at will between floating fly, insect in mid-water, or nymph on the river bed.

The intimate affection for the bottom lie can be neglected in still water, such as lakes and reservoirs, and in large and deep pools of running water, where the surface 'food lane' becomes important as an alimentary source. Here grayling position themselves in mid-water, sometimes a few inches sub-surface, like trout or more often at a depth of two feet or more, and from this position they rise and come down again, intercepting food in their individual fashion.

Italian and Balkan grayling also feed all the year round mainly on bottom fauna organisms. In spring, summer and early autumn they rise to collect sub-surface or surface organisms, exploiting the abundance of exogenous creatures which fly over the water, swim on the surface or are carried by wind or water from the land. At this time, according to Müller in 1961, the weight of stomach contents shifts from about half of each kind, to about fifteen per cent of bottom fauna organisms and eighty-five per cent of surface organisms.

Since the grayling have such a wide geographical distribution, it is understandable that their feeding differs in particular rivers, lakes or regions. Nevertheless, the common main food items during all seasons are: *ephemeroptera* (mayflies), *trichoptera* (sedge or caddis-flies), *plecoptera* (stone-flies) and *diptera* (midges, crane-flies, gnats, etc.), both in larval, nymphal or adult stage. *Orthoptera* (grasshoppers), *odonata* (dragon-flies, damsel-flies), *hemiptera* (bugs), *Neuroptera* (lacewings), *lepidoptera* (moths and butterflies), *megaloptera* (alder flies), *coleoptera* (beetles), *hymenoptera* (wasps, ants, bees, etc.), *arachnida* (spiders), *mollusca* (water snails), and *crustacea* (freshwater shrimp, etc.), are generally representative of seasonal feeding, or are found only in small numbers in the course of the entire year, but on several waters some of these form a substantial source of food.

Of course, the diet of grayling may include other organisms locally available, such as shrews in the Pechora river, or more rarely, aphids – a proof of their extremely keen eyesight. Like other fish, grayling can easily develop a peculiar taste for unusual dishes! I do not refer to temporary, induced habits created by fishermen through repeated groundbaiting, but to an almost natural learning connected with local availability of a particular edible matter.

Years ago, I came across two noteworthy cases. In the first instance, a deep and whirling pool below a partly natural mill-dam on the River Idrijca in Slovenia harboured some brown trout, an occasional rainbow, and grayling. Many autopsies in successive seasons frequently revealed the presence of wheat grains in the stomach contents of grayling. This rather old mill, the only one within a radius of several miles, worked hard – so that wheat grains were frequently spilled and fell in the water – and the grayling had gradually learned that the particles passing by were something pleasant and nourishing. (But is this vegetable matter sufficiently digestible for grayling?)

In the second instance, the freestone River Soča in Slovenia, near the village of Kobarid, had formed a subsidiary channel along the right bank, where there was a dairy farm not far off, on the adjacent land. The results of washing and cleaning the dairy machinery were daily discharged at close intervals late in the morning into this minor watercourse, inhabited and frequented by grayling. The milky effluent impressed the fish which were already feeding there, and attracted further good specimens, most of whom were soon engaged in actively feeding there on something.

They were feeding near the surface film, two or three inches under the water and also well below, but assorted wet artificials and nymphs proved useless. The depth of the principal watercourse made an approach from the left bank impossible, the right bank was almost vertical and encumbered with boulders and bushes right up to the water's edge, so close-range inspection of what the fish were feeding on was out of the question. But, after the discharge from the dairy farm ceased and the water had cleared up, an odd specimen, at last deceived by an occasional wet fly or nymph of some kind, disclosed through post-mortem examination that the fish was feeding greedily on scrapings from the cauldrons used in cheese making! A strange and perhaps insoluble problem for the ingenious fly-tyer!

In the summer months, and into early autumn, you sometimes catch grayling that reveal, through examination of the gastric content, the presence of strange creatures, with an unusual life history. Together with insects and other more or less usual invertebrates one can find very long, slim, thread-like beings which are opaque, greyish or coffee-and-milk coloured, often only one or two in number, but sometimes so numerous to nearly fill the cavity of the stomach, curled up or entwined round each other, mostly still moving and living. From a technical point of view they are worms: members of the class *Gordiaceae* or

Nematomorpha (from the Greek, thread-like), order *Gordioidea*, families *gordiidae* and *chordodiae*.

Leaving aside the matter of sub-families, genus and species, a matter for the specialist, they are commonly called 'hairworms'. Owing to their close resemblance to thick hairs, and their habit of appearing quite suddenly in small bodies of water such as drinking troughs, and even in domestic water-supplies, the superstition arose that they were horsehairs that had fallen into the water and come to life! Their other name, Gordian worms, refers to their occurrence in masses so tangled as to suggest a Gordian knot, the intricate knot fastening the yoke and pole of a waggon, dedicated in Greek mythology to Zeus by Gordius, father of Midas. (It was said that whoever could manage to untie the knot would inherit Asia. Alexander the Great severed it with his sword, giving rise to the expression 'to cut the Gordian knot': to take drastic or unorthodox action to resolve a problem or impasse.)

These worms are also found in freshwater habitats, springs, brooks, torrents or spate rivers and streams, and even in damp soil. They represent the adult form of the creature and are of separate sexes, with the males usually identified by a forked rear end. The adults, from four to over twelve inches in length and from one-fifth to two-fifths of an inch in thickness, do not feed and are merely the reproductive stage in the worms' development.

After mating and fertilisation, the eggs are laid in long whitish, gelatinous strings attached to water plants or stones. The next stage in their life history is somewhat quaint. After a brief free-swimming stage, the larvae – about seven-thousandths of an inch long and very unlike adults, encyst on vegetation or some other support at the water's edge. These cysts remain for several months, and when the cysts or the vegetation bearing them are eaten by a variety of insects, the larvae are released, and they bore through the gut wall of their hosts into the body cavity, where they lead a parasitic life growing into long thread-like creatures. Hosts include the larvae or adults of *coleoptera* (aquatic or terrestrial beetles), *trichoptera* (caddis-flies), *Odonata* (dragonflies), *orthoptera* (grasshoppers, cockroaches and crickets), *myriapoda* (scolopenders, millipedes), *neuroptera* (alder flies), and *arachnida* (spiders).

Cysts may of course be eaten accidentally by other creatures, such as nymphs of *ephemeroptera* (mayflies), *plecoptera* (stone-flies), and the larvae of chironomids, snails, tadpoles and fish – in which case they do not develop by re-encysting. They either die or continue their development when the abnormal host is itself eaten by a normal one, for example, water-beetles *dytiscus* can become infested through tadpoles of the common frog *Rana temporaria*, or *carabus*, through chirinomids.

Growing into the adult hairworm within the host takes several months, presumably being dependent on favourable conditions for development. There is some evidence that terrestrial hosts tend to seek water when their parasites are about to emerge, and any newly emerged worms soon die if they have not access to water. If the worms emerge from their hosts in spring or summer, reproduction takes place soon after, but when emergence takes place in autumn they hibernate in damp surroundings until the following spring.

The presence in the grayling's menu of one or two hairworms together with other invertebrates might be due to worms parasitising one or two of the hosts eaten by the fish. But to gorge with them is a different thing; it is during the free existence devoted to reproduction that the filiform adult hairworm, in search of the other sex, comes across grayling, who evidently do not waste the opportunity of a tasty (though thin and difficult-to-swallow) morsel, creating another intriguing problem for the 'matching the hatch' fisher and ingenious fly-tyer!

But turning back to 'normal', how can the fisher, and particularly the fly-fisher, take advantage of the above-mentioned grayling's feeding-habits?

A. SABBADINI

Contents of a grayling stomach, including several Gordius

Bait fishing is a first answer, as this makes it possible to use different naturals and to test the skill in various conditions. Earthworms, gentles, brandlings, red marshworms, caddis, wasp grubs, small caterpillars, stone-fly nymphs, maggots and so on are all effective; usually worms and maggots are used, but Austrian fishers employ tiny bits of white bacon fat – like maggots – in November and December, and H.G.C. Claypoole, in 1957, tells of grayling even taking hempseed, probably under the impression that they are water snails. Neither Italian nor Balkan fishermen have developed particular or specific methods of bait fishing for grayling. Usually they employ the outfit they use for cyprinids, and often catch grayling when fishing for cyprinids.

But the fly-only rule, already operative in many Slovenian and Croatian grayling waters since World War II, at last is spreading to Italian waters too. Of course fishermen passionately fond of fly-fishing, and dedicated to it, existed before there were such rules, and their ranks are constantly increasing. Among them, in Italy as well as in Slovenia and Croatia,there are a few noteworthy experts in casting, fly-dressing, rod making and so on – some of international renown, others of more restricted celebrity. They have achieved remarkable results, such as new or improved fly-tying tools, materials and fly-patterns, improved fly-casting techniques, new rods and reels, books, etc.

Italy, Slovenia, Croatia and Bosnia do not have a fly-fishing heritage, an old tradition with a corresponding fly-fishing literature; fly-fishing, namely wet-fly fishing, was merely a way of angling, followed by a minority; dry-fly fishing in particular was followed by very few. However, there are two noteworthy exceptions: the traditions of Val Sesia and Val Ossola. In the former valley there evolved a tapered fly-line of horsehair, *frusta valsesiana*, attached to a long rod and furnished with several little flies, *moschette valsesiane*, – spider pattern, like those of W.C. Stewart, or the French *mouchettes de l'Ain* – fished wet-fly style. In the latter, there developed nymph-like or grub imitations, *camole della Val Ossola*, together with little flies like the *moschette valsesiane*. Both were tied on eyeless and barbless hooks of peculiar shape: in practice fine needles, strongly bent and offset, the bend and point first set to the right and then to the left, to give quick penetration and good hold.

Both Valsesian flies and the *camole* and flies of the Val Ossola have known a wide reputation. They were and are used, in particular the *camole*, especially for grayling fishing, in up to a dozen different dressings or colours, as droppers on a cast called *moschera* or *camolera*. The cast does not end with a tail fly or tail *camola*, but with a weight, such as a piece of lead wire, a plastic-coated lead rod or a leaded wood stick. Today these are industrial products and come in a range of weights to suit different depths and different current velocities. They are called *temolino*, and the cast plus load *temolera*. This outfit is used with a long spinning-rod and a fixed-spool reel. It allows fishing with all the usual wet flies, nymphs, etc and on all occasions – even in seasonal and environmental water conditions that do not allow the usual wet-fly or nymph fishing, even with a fast-sinking line and leaded nymph. In particular, it allows the fisherman to cast anywhere with ease, and to present several patterns of artificials at various depths down to the river bed (on which the load swims and hops along, keeping in constant touch with the artificials, the hook setting being almost automatic). This method of fishing, although highly successful for a beginner, is indiscriminate, and indeed often devastating, in its efficiency. Although it is a method of employing artificial bait, it is banned or severely restricted in all the waters where grayling are esteemed, and the rule is 'fly-only' on these waters.

This rule involves, it goes without saying, the entire world of fly-fishing, from rods, lines and leaders, to entomology and fly-dressing, from dry and wet flies to nymphs, from 'parachute' and 'paradun' to 'stillborn' and 'emerger', from fishery management to fishing tactics.

The choice of artificials to employ is dictated by the circumstances, of course, but sometimes personal fancy can bring success, thanks to the well-known catholic taste of grayling. This obviously does not deter the determined purist from 'matching the hatch', even if the capriciousness of their feeding habits may lead grayling to ignore the best imitations offered in a perfect manner.

In Italy and the Balkans the fishing season begins after spawning, when the fish are exhausted and hungry. The time for the best fishing is shortly towards the end of summer, but improves and lasts longer in the autumn, when the water temperatures are more favourable and the fish are in prime condition. This is largely caused by active preparation for spawning, so that the metabolism increases as the need for storing reserves becomes more urgent. In winter, where grayling fishing is allowed, the catch is reduced to its lowest, owing to very low water temperatures and lack of insects, forcing fish to feed on bottom fauna.

Thus, all through the season, one can use the tribe of olive imitations, as well as those of other *ephemeridae* and of midges, *chironomidae* and other *Diptera*, from the classic Blue Dun and Olive Dun to the Iron Blue Dun and Tup's Indispensable, from the wet March Brown female to the Greenwell's Glory, etc., as well as the corresponding nymphs – classic or leaded – and midges and chironomid pupae imitations.

In this section the dressings of the patterns cited refer strictly to the

Dictionary, by A. Courtney Williams, except where stated; the hook size is the standard one, although sometimes it is necessary to go down to diminutive sizes, matching the leader accordingly. On other occasions, a big mouthful attracts grayling more than a small one. Some excellent patterns – with their correct dressing – are impossible or difficult to find on the market. (Here is a task for the amateur fly-tyer!) The patterns of Devaux, the well-known French fly-tyer, have wide use and success.

On occasion, mayfly imitations are required, as well as those of fresh-water shrimp, classic or modern. During the first days of July, the winged ants, male and female, red, brown or black, small or large, begin to swarm and to fall on the water surface. When the river or lake is bordered by woodland in mountainous country, the presence of the conspicuous ant, *Formica rufa*, is very important. Grayling are particularly keen on these *Hymenoptera* and can gorge themselves on the ants, even on those of diminutive size, to the exclusion of anything else. A good imitation, or a modern version, is therefore imperative.

Then the imitations of the sedge tribe must enter the lists, to be used from sunset until dark during the summer. They are: Silver Sedge, Grannom, Little Red Sedge and Little Brown Sedge. Very effective results can be obtained until November, and in colder months during the daylight hours, from a dry pattern of Slovenian origin, tied on hook size 18, dressed as follows:

Body: hazel-brown wool.
Wings: brown hen, bunched and rolled, sloping back over the body and parallel to it.
Hackle: red cock (Rhode Island Red), small.
Tie silk: brown.

The needle flies come next, fellow members of the *Plecoptera* (*Perlidae*) or stone-flies, very important towards the end of the summer and all through the autumn. Willow fly, for example, occur on most of the waters in question, and good imitations are a must. Split Willow and Willow Fly as dry flies, Light Spanish Needle as wet, but fished on the surface, are very effective, as well as the Mistigri by Pequenot (1975), a sensible French pattern.

This review, obviously partial and incomplete, concludes with some general classic patterns that are very useful, if not indispensable, such as Coch-y-bondhu, West's Coch-y-bondhu, Partridge and Orange, Snipe and Purple, (Snipe and Yellow, Snipe and Orange), Dotterel Dun (Dotterel and Orange, Dotterel and Yellow), Gold-ribbed Hare's Ear, Cul de Canard,

Grey Duster, Jassid, hook size up to 24! Standard patterns must be mentioned too, of course: Red Tag, the capital Rolt's Witch and Woolley's Witch. Another capital fly, perhaps my favourite, in October and November, is ...

There, that's done! I have emptied my grayling fly box on the table, and listed those I cannot do without when pursuing Italian or Balkan *Thymallus thymallus*. Tight lines!

Mongolia: First Impressions

Naïl Jones

I AM FORTUNATE IN having a job which takes me to most parts of the world, not least so that I can indulge in my favourite pastime – fishing, and fly-fishing at that. It was with some misgivings therefore that I heard that we were to spend the next two years in the Mongolian People's Republic or, as it is more popularly known at home, Outer Mongolia. With the Gobi Desert in mind, I thought the chances of any fishing, let alone fly, would be pretty slim indeed.

In fact I was quite wrong. The northern part of Mongolia in which the capital Ulan Bator is located, is reasonably fertile, and apart from the extreme winter climate where temperatures can drop to as low as -49°F (-45°C) the late spring and summer are not unlike those in south-east England. The River Tuul near the capital is where six months ago I cast my first fly in Mongolian waters, much to the amazement of my local colleagues, who had never seen anything like it before! Despite being warned off because of over-fishing, pollution and other horrors too ghastly to mention, I tackled up and selected a small Gold-ribbed Hare's Ear, size 14, just as I would do at home. The sport was truly excellent. Within a couple of hours, I had around a dozen good-sized fish, mostly grayling, but some of them Arctic char.

The grayling were practically identical to those I have taken in Europe, with the males' purplish dorsal fin bright and shiny in the evening sun. Although I was fishing fairly late in the season, the grayling proved to be very active on an eight-foot Hardy's carbon-fibre rod and a 5/6 floating line. The char, which look like trout except for the mouth, which is more round, also fought well and were perfectly delicious. I did not use specifically grayling patterns, nor for that mater trout patterns, since the water I was on was completely unknown to me, and at that stage one fly in my view was as good as another. Several trips later, it seems to me that any of

215

JOHN BAILEY

A fine Mongolian grayling

the classical dry-fly patterns work perfectly well here. Since I am not very good with the wet fly, I have not as yet tried it. No doubt this will change later in the year. Currently the ice on my river is several feet thick, and apart from the foolhardy who ice fish with the same avid enthusiasm as I fly fish, the rest of us must wait until late May at least, before the river has properly thawed out. As for the locals, they too seem to be enthusiastic anglers, although it is true to say that if they were to apply their usual techniques for catching fish on one of our better-known chalk streams, many a Club Secretary would need resuscitating.

Fishing the artificial fly is of course unknown, but the Mongolians do fish with lures, they spin and they 'live bait'. Grasshoppers are perhaps the most popular bait, being impaled on a small hook and tossed into the fast-flowing water. Wobblers are made from small blocks of wood shaped to resemble field mice over which a piece of fur is stretched and a treble attached to the end. Since one cannot buy anything of this nature in Mongolia, the Mongolians are left to their own ingenuity to come up with the right tackle. They also trot with worms and use deadbait, but the grasshopper technique is by far the most popular. Given the sparse population of this vast country – around two million, which works out at

JOHN BAILEY

Fishing the River Tengis, Mongolia

roughly two people per square mile – there is little danger of all Mongolia's rivers and lakes being overwhelmed by pollution or misuse. But there is already a sense of conservation in the country, and the authorities are taking steps to ensure that their natural resources are not abused.

Despite the growing influx of Western tourists, including a number from the UK, it will be some time yet before we experience organised fly-fishing holidays in Mongolia.

Naïl Jones

The above was originally an article appearing in the spring issue of the *Journal of the Grayling Society* in 1986. In a book attempting to be international in its scope, and intending to show the wide distribution of grayling throughout the Northern Hemisphere, this was too good a piece to miss. Naïl Jones gave his permission for its inclusion, and, though pressure of work did not permit him to enlarge or supplement it in any way, he allowed that the editor might add to it in any way that he considered useful.

As I knew next to nothing about Mongolia, nor could I find anyone who did, I had recourse in the first instance to the Embassy of the Mongolian People's Republic and then to the John Rylands Library in Manchester. Even then, there is not a great deal to find written about this magical land and its people: a travelogue, one or two books on sociological-political history, a few recorded lantern lectures by intrepid explorers of the nineteenth century, and a great deal about Genghis Khan.

If I were a young man again and wanted to travel to the most mysterious land on this earth, I would remove all obstacles to go in search of Mongolia. In days gone by it was a land of nomadic peoples, through which ran the Great Silk Road from China to Bokhara and Samarkand. Though now it is most easily approached from the West by train or air, it was once quicker to go by sea to Peking and thence by camel or horse to the old capital of Urga, where now stands Ulan Bator, the 'Red Hero'.

It is a land and a people with a long history, going back in civilisation to at least 1500 BC, and it has archaeological remains from the Old Stone Age. It contained the great trade route between China and Europe, whose beginnings are lost in the mists of time, and developed into the great Empire which, under the rule of Genghis Khan, became the scourge of medieval Europe. For a long time it was under the influence of the Chinese, but the Russians became paramount about the turn of this

JOHN BAILEY

The River Tengis, Mongolia

century. Two revolutions occurred, and by 1921 the new independent state of the People's Republic was created.

Mongolia's territory is vast, its population small, and the continental climate is severe. Spring comes in May and the first snows in September. Surrounded by ramparts of mountains, the Mongolian plateau is higher than the surrounding regions of China, Siberia and Turkestan. But beyond the 15,000-feet high mountains to the west, with their eternal snows, there is a rich country of pasture, forests, rivers and lakes. At the eastern end of the Tula-Orkhon Basin lies the capital, Ulan Bator. A great, modern industrial city, it lies in the wide valley of the River Tula. Beyond to the south is the Great Gobi Desert, and eastwards the Great Wall of China winds its way over high mountains.

Mongolia was opened to a few Western travellers in 1954, and within ten years small parties of tourists were admitted in order to travel the country around Ulan Bator. Though the countryside around the capital is being urbanised and industrialised, there still appears to be a very considerable interest in horses and hunting, both to produce extra food and also for sport.

But of fishing there is nothing. I think Naïl Jones has created a 'first'.

Certainly nobody before, that I can find, has written about angling in the Mongolian People's Republic.

Ronald Broughton

North America's Arctic Grayling

Patrick Michiel

WHERE PEOPLE ARE found in North America, Arctic grayling are not. As with all generalisations, there are exceptions to this rule, but not many, and they usually don't last long.

The Peace River in northern British Columbia is one of the lasting exceptions. Although it is a typical Canadian Arctic grayling water in the physical sense, a number of factors have saved its grayling population from encroaching civilisation.

Within British Columbia, the Peace River flows eastward, out of the Rocky Mountains, in a large river valley. The north valley slope is mainly open and grass covered, with a sprinkling of aspen forest, juniper and even prickly pear cactus. The south shore must look much as it did in the late eighteenth century when explorer Alexander Mackenzie travelled through the area searching for a route to the Pacific. It is forested, mainly with spruce, but also with pine, aspen and birch. The wood buffalo that Mackenzie observed along the river are now gone but the Arctic grayling survive.

At one time the Peace River extended westward into the Rocky Mountain trench, where it began at the junction of the Finlay and Parsnip Rivers. Now a 600-square-mile reservoir covers the upper Peace behind the W.A.C. Bennett Dam. The Peace Canyon Dam was subsequently constructed twelve miles downstream. Prior to the hydroelectric projects, which were built in the late 1960s and 1970s, the river used to freeze over in winter; but now, because of the fluctuating water levels caused by the variable demand for electricity, the river remains open all year round, even when the winter temperatures hit 40°F (-40°C) and colder.

In Alberta, the Peace turns north and flows into the Slave and Mackenzie River system, through the heart of Arctic grayling range, northward to the Arctic Ocean.

221

PATRICK MICHIEL

Fishing the Muskwa River, Northern British Columbia

The principal element in the survival of the Peace River's grayling populations is that the Peace is a very difficult river to fish. It's a large, swift river, and the standards of Canada, where the vast majority of the land belongs to the Crown rather than being privately held, access is fairly difficult, even in the settled areas. Further discouraging anglers, the major hydroelectric projects west of the village of Hudson's Hope, cause water-level fluctuations as great as thirteen feet on an irregular basis. Not only does this represent a degree of danger to anglers, it also means that fish-holding areas fluctuate constantly. Without using the shore background above the high water mark for reference, simply recognising a specific stretch of water, from one day to the next, can be difficult.

A Day Afield on the Peace River

One windy day in late August we crossed the Peace River west of Fort St John, in a square-stern canoe equipped with a four-horsepower outboard motor. The river is over 270 yards wide at that point. As we moved downstream along the south shore, at several places I caught glimpses of fish rising, but was unsure whether they were grayling or Rocky Mountain whitefish.

Approximately half a mile downstream from the launch point, we landed in a back eddy and tied up the canoe. After assembling our fly-rods, we sat on the rocky river bank eating lunch and watching the river for signs of fish. From our vantage point on the shore, we could see many fish rising along the intersection of water flow in the eddy fence. Even in the swift pocket water above the eddy, fish were rising. A small rise of dark mayflies (*Rithrogena virilis*) appeared to be under way. As they accumulated in the eddy fence, fish were picking them off.

While my companions watched, I tied on a size 10 Red Quill dry fly (Mustad 94840) and from below the start of the first eddy, quartering upstream, I false cast to get some line out, then dropped the fly just above the eddy line. I began stripping and mending line furiously to keep pace with the fly in the current. As the fly passed the current line, I saw a splash and tightened up on the line. I was rewarded with the solid feel of a good fish. It fled upstream taking back most of the stripped line. I recovered the balance on to the reel, and soon the weight of the fly-line in the current and my continued pressure pulled it back into the eddy. It stayed deep. When it tired, I waded into the edge of the eddy, in my hip waders, and netted the fish. It was a lovely male Arctic grayling, sixteen inches long and weighing about one pound ten ounces. That's large for a river this close to civilisation.

I washed the fly off and checked the knot; then I tried to dry it with a few false casts. It wouldn't float, and the remaining grayling wouldn't touch it below the surface. I changed to a Black Gnat dry fly of the same size. Arctic grayling are not selective in the sense of 'matching the hatch'; however, they are selective in terms of whether they are taking wet or dry flies. The reasons I had initially chosen the Red Quill, were to match the obvious rise of dark mayflies and because of the additional presence of more selective rainbow trout. By matching the mayfly, I could increase my odds of catching the rainbow, while maintaining the prospect of catching the grayling. Once I knew grayling were present, and knowing they usually travel in herds (they are not true 'schoolers'), 'matching the hatch' was no longer important. The main point was to pick a fly that would remain afloat in the swift water, and one I could see without difficulty. The Black Gnat would float well, and the slate-grey mallard wing quill would show up on the smooth swift surface water. With the Black Gnat dry fly tied on, after three or four casts, I soon caught a fourteen-inch mate to the first fish. I released it carefully.

PATRICK MICHIEL

Patrick Michiel with an Arctic grayling

On another day, with the same equipment set-up – a dry line with a long leader (or sinking-tip line) – a Black Gnat wet fly will take grayling from just below the surface film. But dry flies will not work. On one occasion I fished for more than half an hour over a grayling hole where others had been catching grayling for several hours. With a wide assortment of dry flies, I didn't elicit a movement from a fish. Then, after switching to a barbless wet fly, I caught and released over thirty Arctic grayling in less than two hours.

The Peace is so swift at that point that the outboard was not powerful enough to ferry all three of us back upstream to our car. I volunteered to work my way along the shore to a section of slacker water. My companions would ride the boat up and collect me in a few hours. I began working my way upstream, while they walked downstream to fish holes they knew from previous visits. In the fast water, I had numerous rises, but managed to catch only two rainbow in the sixteen-inch range. I gently released both of them.

About 500 yards upstream, a break caused by a small intermittent stream enters the Peace Valley. Gravel, flushed from this smaller valley by the spring run-off, has built a gravel bar out into the river. Mindful of the power dam sixty miles upstream and the fluctuating water levels, I took note of the water level at the base of a large boulder on the shore, and cautiously waded out on to the bar. (The water levels do not change too suddenly; they are somewhat like tides in the ocean, just less predictable.) I had observed fish rising along the upstream edge of the bar when we had passed by on our way downstream in the canoe.

The water was only slightly over my knees, but, because of the swiftness of the river, I was only just able to keep my balance. I could feel the water pressure bouncing stones by my feet. About ten yards from shore, I began casting upstream into the wind. The wind was gusting to 25 mph, and I was able to cast only a short distance, but it didn't seem to matter. My presence was not deterring the fish, which were rising all around me. I had to move occasionally to improve my deteriorating footholds in the gravel. (A person in chest waders can end up in trouble very quickly, if he succumbs to the temptation to take that extra step into deeper water.)

Most of the grayling were rising along the upstream side of the bar and further upstream. I laboured to cast against the wind and had many hits just as the fly touched down. By this time I was using a hairwing Royal Coachman on a No. 8 hook – it seemed to be the only thing I could keep afloat.

During a lull in the wind I was able to put one cast out farther than most of my casts from the bar. Stripping madly, I followed the fly in the

PATRICK MICHIEL

The modern headwaters of the Peace River below Peace Canyon
hydroelectric dam

fast water. When the grayling struck, I tightened up at the correct time, and the fish fled into the fast water and headed downstream with my fly. I moved it into the eddy on the downside of the bar and eased myself ashore, keeping the line firm, then netted the fish in the back eddy. My third grayling of the afternoon was in the fifteen-inch range. I had just taken it ashore when my companions came to collect me for the trip home.

It was very tough fishing – not the fishing part, just the place: wind gusting downstream from the west; swift, clear water; cold and dangerous. But, Arctic grayling were there. It was wonderful!

Morphology

Arctic grayling are one of the most beautiful freshwater fish on the North American continent.

At first glance, one immediately notices the large, sail-like dorsal fin. In the female the dorsal fin is substantially smaller than the male's, which extends back as far as the adipose fin. In some populations there seems to

226

be a tendency for the male to have a slight indentation in the dorsal fin, between the main portion and the final three or four rays (it is not known whether this is a genuine genetic characteristic or simply a common injury). The male pelvic fins are also substantially larger than those of the female.

The fish are vividly coloured. The back is dark blue or purple, and there are scattered black spots along the sides. A distinct stripe is visible from the pelvic fins forward to below the pectoral fins. The dark dorsal fins are fringed with orange and have orange and turquoise spots. The male's oversize pelvic fins have orange stripes on a dark background. The male colours are even more vivid during spawning.

Arctic grayling are not large fish. The current world record is a thirty-inch grayling, weighing five pounds fifteen ounces, caught in the Katseyedie River in Canada's Northwest Territories in 1967. The previous record was a fish of five pounds eight ounces (twenty-one-inches) from Great Bear Lake. Average angling catches would range between twelve and fifteen inches. They are also slow growing, and do not live particularly long, with eleven or twelve years being the maximum.

Distribution

In North America, Arctic grayling are found throughout the US state of Alaska, throughout the Canadian northern territories of the Yukon and the Northwest Territories, but not in the Canadian Arctic Islands (except for Vansittart Island off the southern tip of the Melville Peninsula). Unlike many North American trout and char species (rainbow, cutthroat, Dolly Varden, Arctic char and brook trout), which have sea-run (anadromous) populations in their midst, Arctic grayling are not found in salt water nor in sea-run situations.

The grayling's range extends southward into the northern portions of the Canadian provinces of British Columbia, Alberta, Saskatchewan and Manitoba. Small populations are also present in remote areas of Montana, Wyoming and Utah. At one time, grayling were found in Northern Michigan rivers flowing into the Great Lakes, but they disappeared in the 1930s.

Massive attempts to reintroduce Arctic grayling into their former ranges and apparently similar habitats, have been generally unproductive, although the Province of Alberta occasionally does some grayling stocking. Attempts are also under way on a few Michigan Rivers, and some work is being done in Montana.

Biology

Grayling are often found at the junctions of small streams and larger rivers. They are visual hunters; consequently – unlike many fish species, which have activity thresholds in the early morning and again at dusk – grayling are most active during the middle of the day. They often swim in the stream, just below the surface, rising to take food in the surface film.

Arctic grayling are spring spawners, spawning just after winter ice leaves the lakes. Where their range overlaps with northern pike, the spawning takes place at the same time as, or just after, the pike's. The fish seek out gravel areas in the streams, and the eggs are shed over the bottom, with no redd being prepared. The males are territorial and use their dorsal fin in a threat display to chase off other males. In observing spawning in the Peace River, I have noticed the fin is also used during mating, where it is curled over the female in an undulating manner. Grayling spawn more than once, but may not spawn annually.

As a demonstration of their adaptability, Arctic grayling are found across several aquatic communities. In the western portion of their range they are found with the *Salmonidae* (the Pacific salmons, rainbow and cutthroat trouts, Dolly Varden and lake char) while in the northern and eastern portion of their range, one finds them living in the same habitat as Dolly Varden and lake char, inconnu, rainbow trout, walleye, northern pike, whitefish and goldeye.

The decline in their range gives observers an impression of delicacy. Many reference texts point to the grayling's sensitivity to pollution and logging practices, and these factors have been blamed for the extirpation of the species in northern Michigan, for example. In reality, an examination of the North American Arctic grayling's distribution reveals that the species inhabits a wide range of freshwater habitats – small creeks, big rivers, large and small lakes. A wide range of water quality also characterises its habitat, from tea-coloured bog water to mountain streams with glacial flour. A species thriving in such challenging environments cannot possibly be described as 'delicate'.

If one must generalise about the Arctic grayling's habitat, several factors appear consistent. North American grayling water is generally clear and cold; therefore, low in productivity.

An important factor in grayling behaviour relates to its small mouth size. A single glance at an Arctic grayling demonstrates that grayling have a very small mouth; a twelve-inch grayling has a mouth one quarter the size of a similar-sized eastern brook trout. Work by biologist C.S. Holling, with other phyla, has demonstrated that predator species have been programmed by natural selection to prey on optimal-sized food items. The Arctic grayling's diet reflects the relative small size of its mouth. Young grayling eat zooplankton, then switch to immature insects, caddis, mayflies and midges, as they increase in size. Adult grayling continue with this diet and add a broad assortment of invertebrates – wasps, bees, ants, dragonflies, grasshoppers and beetles, as well as fish eggs. Other items recorded in the largest grayling include lemmings, a few other grayling and cisco fishes.

The low productivity of the habitat of Arctic grayling, combined with its small mouth size and a history of low fishing pressure, combine to make it a fish 'ripe for the catching'. Grayling are not selective because they cannot afford to pass up any potential food item. They have to feed at every opportunity.

As a result of the need to find suitable food in a barren environment, Arctic grayling easily fall victim to the most unaccomplished angler. Unfortunately, many unaccomplished anglers are also unaccomplished in terms of conservationist ideals.

I believe this gullibility is responsible for the grayling's decline in populated areas. Numerous Arctic grayling streams and rivers were crossed when the Alaska Highway was built, bridging the 1,500-mile gap of wilderness between Dawson Creek, British Columbia, and Fairbanks, Alaska, in 1942. Tourist travel began slowly after the war, and within 20 years concerns

PATRICK MICHIEL

Murray River grayling

229

were voiced about grayling conservation. Currently there is virtually no good grayling fishing alongside the Alaska Highway. To find grayling in that relatively wild country, one must hike several miles away from the highway.

When feeding, grayling will not be 'put down'. It is not unusual for an angler in good grayling waters to catch dozens of fish from a single location. On one occasion I was fishing at a point where a clear stream enters the more turbid Muskwa River. With the sun behind me, and with the aid of polarising glasses to cut the glare, I was able to catch (and subsequently release) about a dozen fish from that single location. As the herd diminished, I could count the fish in the clear water, still keen for the fly, oblivious to the fate of their fellows. Incredibly, I caught them all – the entire pack. As a consequence of the grayling's gullibility, anglers must fish with barbless flies and the concept of 'catch and release' firmly in mind.

Fishing Tactics

When I first began fishing for grayling about fifteen years ago, I thought my success was due to my prowess as a wily fly-fisherman. Naturally, I should have known better. There had been clues that I was dealing with a gullible fish. For example, local jet boaters didn't beach their craft fifty yards away from the grayling 'hot spot' and creep down the shore to cast their lures, as one would with wily eastern brook trout or chalk-stream browns. The jet boaters would roar into the middle of the grayling hot spot – all 300 horsepower and 23 feet of aluminium jet boat – and beach the craft with enough fanfare to put any self-respecting trout down for a week. Then they would assemble their gear and fish off the stern, and catch respectable-sized Arctic grayling. When I suggested more fish might be caught by parking the craft further down shore and walking to the hot spot, they looked at me with the curiosity rural folk world-wide reserve for 'city slickers'.

European grayling have been subjected to centuries of fishing pressure, and this may account for the difference in gullibility. Gullible European grayling were eaten by Isaac Walton and his contemporaries; only the crafty survived.

In northern Canada the bigger rivers are usually turbid after spring run-off or rains, while the smaller streams seem to clear earlier. At these times, grayling anglers can usually find success by fishing at the intersections of small clear streams and the larger turbid rivers. Indeed, throughout the summer season along the Mackenzie, Liard, Peace, Parsnip, Muskwa, Yukon and Prophet Rivers, grayling congregate at the points where the clear water meets the turbid.

PATRICK MICHIEL

Jet boat travelling

August and September usually provide the best river fishing for grayling. By late summer, the spring freshet is well over, the water-borne silt has settled out, and the water is at its clearest. As grayling are visual hunters, this may account for their voracity in the late summer.

Fishing in the lakes is generally good throughout the summer, as their turbidity does not vary as greatly as that of most of the rivers. In lakes, as with many other species, the prime fishing location for fishing grayling is at the mouths of streams and rivers flowing into the lakes.

Gear

The grayling is a fine sport fish, especially on light fly-fishing or spinning gear. Record-size fish, in excess of four-and-a-quarter pounds, are rare, with fish in the one-pound ten-ounce range being better than average. As a consequence, fly-fishermen normally use five- or six-weight rods, between eight and ten feet long. The longer rods, in six weight, would be for use on some of the big rivers in the north-west, like the Peace, the Yukon, or the Liard. The smaller rods would be suitable in the smaller rivers (ten to thirty yards across).

A factor to consider is the host of other species present along with grayling, in the various parts of their range. One never knows when one is going to elicit a response from something a little bigger than the average grayling, which is another factor pointing to the six-weight rod.

231

Good quality, compact travel rods are useful if one is travelling by float plane, jet boat or horseback, to the fishing area. The country where the

Fishing the Murray River in Northern British Columbia

232

best Arctic grayling fishing is found is virtually always rough; therefore, a good sturdy rod case is a must.

While dry-fly fishing, a weight-forward line or a double taper will work equally well. For wet-fly fishing, a sinking-tip line or floating line with long leader will be suitable. Netting experiments have demonstrated that grayling rarely go below ten feet in lakes. A nine-foot tapered braid leader with a 4x tippet is just right for grayling fishing. A 3x might be appropriate if there is a chance of running into a larger species in the same water.

Arctic grayling fly-fishermen don't have to go afield with 165 different fly patterns. In remote areas, two would probably do, a wet fly for below surface feeding and a dry for surface feeding. Of course, only the most parsimonious angler would only have two flies (and parsimony and fly-fishing tend not to go together). A range of flies covering a variety of sizes and styles would not be unreasonable. 'Dark flies on sunny days, lighter flies when overcast' is a good maxim to follow.

In western Canada, the most popular fly pattern for Arctic grayling is the Black Gnat, followed closely by the Royal Coachman (in both their wet and dry configurations). Size 10 hooks would easily be the most common size used. The Renegade is also a popular western North American fly, as is the Tom Thumb, which can be tied in a variety of configurations (*see* page 142 for these two fly patterns). Most of the standard patterns will work. Barbs should be squeezed flat, or barbless hooks used for 'catch and release' fishing, especially when one gets into a real herd of grayling. If one catches two or three right off, there are probably another thirty in the same hole. That's when I switch to barbless hooks.

When travelling in remote Canadian areas, whether alone or with a guide, one should always be prepared to be self-sufficient. Aeroplanes and boats break down; darkness comes, and the boats can't navigate the big rivers at night; weather changes suddenly, and landing sites become 'socked in'. When travelling with a river-boat outfitter, guide or float-plane pilot, never go anywhere in a remote location without a warm coat – and be sure there's a compass, matches and a little food in the pockets.

When I am dropped off at some remote location to fish for grayling, while the guide does something else 'for just a minute', I always bring a compact emergency kit along, with rain gear, a sleeping bag, a Swiss Army knife, fire-making materials and a little food. On one occasion, a river-boat outfitter left me ashore, happily fishing grayling, while he went downstream to deliver some wapiti hunters to a nearby location. The boat broke down, and what was supposed to be a two-hour afternoon idyll turned into a cold night under the stars in grizzly bear habitat. Fortunately I had taken my pack, with a down sleeping-bag and a little food, out of the boat before he left, so I feasted that evening on fresh sautéd grayling and bannock cooked over a hot alder fire, and slept very well in the down sleeping bag, with my .444 cal. Marlin rifle by my side. Indeed, it was quite pleasant – but, had I not kept my pack, it would have been a miserable night. The nearest village was ninety miles away, the nearest road sixty miles. About twenty-four hours after dropping me off, the outfitter showed up, suitably apologetic and embarrassed. Having made certain others know the trip details, one waits, in plain view, at the agreed spot.

Spin fishing is probably the most common form of fishing for Arctic grayling in Canada. Fishermen use small spoons, or spinners, for casting and trolling, mepps in Size 0 and $\frac{1}{8}$-ounce Panther Marten are both popular grayling lures. When fishing swift rivers, many grayling spin anglers put a three-way swivel on the end of the line, then add a short length of light test monofilament with a bell sinker. On the end of a short piece of monofilament attached to the third swivel eye they affix a wet fly with a maggot on the hook point. Using this gear, they ensure the fly is placed below the surface of the water, and if the sinker hangs up, it can be easily broken off and another attached.

PATRICK MICHIEL

Canvas cover-up for the night

Most anglers use boats when fishing grayling. Expensive aluminium jet boats are often used to travel the swift rivers of the northern Rockies in Alberta and British Columbia, and jet boats are also used for river travel in the Yukon and Alaska. Canadian-style canoes are used for short trips on the rivers. Aluminium car-top boats are used on lakes with road access, and float planes are often used throughout the northern areas to reach otherwise inaccessible waters.

Ice Fishing

In Canada and Alaska, Arctic grayling are also sought during the winter through the ice, usually from late February on throughout March, when daylight hours begin increasing.

Anglers bore holes through the three-feet-thick ice and drop down bait or lures. A host of different fishing rigs are used, from simple hand-held lines, to specially made ice-fishing 'pop up' rods. Some people use regular spinning rods propped up to allow the line a straight drop into the hole. Because of the low water temperatures beneath the ice, the fish are not particularly active. A large fish may produce only the subtlest of movement in the rod tip.

Another method of detecting these subtle takes is to use an ice fishing hut of some sort. In the darkness of the ice hut, looking down through the bore hole, one can sometimes see fish moving towards the bait, especially in shallow water. Often one can see a large Arctic grayling holding the lure in its mouth; just tasting it, without the slightest trace of movement in the rod. Huts also take anglers out of the cold. Many people use old tents with the floors removed.

Most ice fishermen use bait. Maggots are available in local sporting goods stores, and seem to work well with Arctic grayling both in winter and summer.

The challenge of ice fishing, aside from surviving the bitter cold, is in detecting the subtle takes in the rod tip, then reaching down and grasping the rod without disturbing the fish, and setting the hook. By then the contest is over.

The Future

In North America, Arctic grayling are not fished with the same fervour as the trouts, chars, walleye and northern pike. They are spoken of in reverent tones because they are such good sport when an angler runs into them, but the major challenge is in the finding, rather than in the artful deception with a fly.

Arctic grayling are found in the northern wilderness roughly above the 55th Parallel of Latitude. The vast majority of Canadians live within ninety miles of the 49th Parallel, so they have little opportunity even to visit Arctic grayling habitat.

In British Columbia, a province where a wide range of angling opportunities is available, fishing statistics are kept. In 1985, on the basis of creel surveys, provincial biologists estimate 87,000 Arctic grayling were caught with 54,000 being kept. This is a very small harvest considering the 5.4 million rainbow trout caught (3.3 million kept) during the same year in British Columbia.

When grayling are caught, it is usually by sportsmen involved in other activities. A wapiti, caribou, or mountain sheep hunter might break out a travel fly rod for an afternoon of fly-fishing after a successful hunt. On the west coast, a steelhead or salmon angler might pick one up with an egg-pattern fly, near a group of spawning pink salmon.

PATRICK MICHIEL

Arctic grayling, Canada

It's no sin to catch and eat a few Arctic grayling as part of a wilderness shore lunch or a nice meal at home, but it is a privilege, and one with no future guarantees. In most areas the daily legal catch is five Arctic grayling per person, with no size limit. I never keep more than two, and I make sure 'catch and release' fish are handled gently and expeditiously.

Arctic grayling in North America are an enigma. Where people are; they aren't. They are wonderful sport for fly-fishermen and good table fare; yet few anglers seek them out. They survive in a tough habitat, but are easily overfished and wiped out.

And yet, the Arctic grayling mystique is there. Tomorrow, I'll be drawn to the Peace River again, in admiration, respect and reverence.

Under the Spell of Norwegian Grayling

Hans van Klinken

WHEN I RECALL my Norwegian fishing trips my heart immediately starts to beat faster. The moment I arrive in Norway I feel as if I am coming home, and it really hurts when I have to leave again. I think those feelings sum up how much I like this wonderful fishing paradise – over the years I have been visiting Scandinavia, Norway has become a second home. When I think of Norway I see the fjords, mountains and mighty rivers as clearly as if I were really standing there. The midsummer nights and the midnight sun have always fascinated me, and they also provide a welcome bonus of many extra fishing hours. When I think of the fishing, it's the 'Lady of the Stream' that impresses me the most; the Norwegian grayling is my favourite fish by far, and I have a strong personal tie with her.

Of course there are hundreds of rivers in Scandinavia that produce excellent grayling fishing, so let me tell you why it was the Norwegian grayling that drove me crazy. It happened in 1981, when I was fishing the River Sömåa in eastern Norway and caught my biggest-ever grayling on a pattern called Rackelhanen. It was a beautiful fish. I have never broken my record again, and – although I have matched that fish's unbelievable size of 61 cm twice more, in 1984 and 1989 – it is the memory of my first 'black grayling' that is the strongest. I never had seen such a large and dark-coloured grayling before. She was well hooked and started to bleed when I took out the hook. When I released her, she turned her head as if to look at me before she slowly disappeared into the depths again. If she really watched me I still don't know, but that look made such an impression that it triggered my passion for grayling. I knew I must have hurt her, and from that moment I learned another lesson; I never used a barbed hook again.

238

R.V. DUIJNHOVEN

Hans van Klinken with his record fish of 2 ft (61 cm) from the
River Sömåa

239

Where to fish for Norwegian grayling

This is a very difficult question, because there are so many good places to fish. The best suggestion I can give you is to buy a good map of Norway and Sweden. Then draw a huge circle taking in Rena, Folldal, Nybergsund, Idre (Sweden), Funäsdalen (Sweden), Brekken and Röros. This is the area in which you will find some of the best wild grayling fishing in Europe; the two most important river systems are the Glåma (Glomma) and Trysilelva (Klara in Sweden). To get the best impression about Norwegian grayling fishing, I only can advise you to follow both rivers upstream to the north as far as you can. Try all tributaries you meet, and don't forget the dozens of smaller rivers in the upper parts; this is exactly what I did, and it is how I have found my favourite spots over the last twenty years. For the Glomma, start your research in Rena, and follow the Klara up stream from Edeback. As you make your journey your experience and catches will improve, slowly but surely, day by day!

How it all started

In 1980 I discovered a few important 'rules' that became the key for my Scandinavian grayling fishing. One of them was to cover long distances along riverbanks and through the forest: do the mileage, and you are sure to hit many hot spots! I walked many miles when I followed the Klarälven (Sweden), camping out beside the river, working my way slowly north and exploring the river with the little knowledge I had built up above the Arctic Circle. Some days I walked more than 10 kilometres, and while I was fishing the silence and peace of the riverside brought me very close to nature and wildlife. In those days I used only dry flies, and my catches were not plentiful, but I enjoyed every single minute of it.

Of course we all like to catch fish, and it gives enormous satisfaction when you see a fish come up and take your fly on the surface, but for me fly-fishing has become a little more than just catching fish. We also like a good and strong fight, with many jumps, and I am happy that more and more people are starting to enjoy releasing the fish afterwards too. I discovered that hooking and playing are very important to build up your skill, but I also noticed that they are not the most important thing about being a good fly fisherman. Maybe that's why I am not competitive at all. Some simple observation of animal behaviour at the waterside can make my day, too. I still remember the time I saw a beaver playing with its cubs, and I simply forgot the evening rise. I learned quickly, and the longer the distances I covered the more I felt in tune with the river, nature and wildlife.

R.V. DUIJNHOVEN

A 1 ft 10 in (56 cm) grayling from the Glomma

Each day brought me closer to Norway, and time and distance taught me how to improve my catches of the larger grayling. Sometimes I couldn't handle the river, especially when fish refused to take, or when I couldn't reach the feeding fish. Instead of getting frustrated I just took a longer break, sitting down to eat my lunch while I scanned the river. I watched rising fish for hours and it gave me many ideas and new inspiration. I started to recognise holding places, food seams, feeding lies, and learned how to read the river. My casting was not very spectacular, so I tried to avoid the busy fishing places; most people fished the quiet water, but my poor distance casting made the broken water and rapids my favourite.

The big change in my fly fishing and fly tying started during the same trip, when I met a solitary old angler who caught a few really big grayling in heavily broken water. Interested in his skills and achievement, I struck up a conversation at the riverbank, and we proved to have a lot in common (maybe that's why he was so generous and willing to help me with good advice and tips). After a long pleasant talk about flies and techniques we exchanged some flies, and before he left he gave me a very strange yellow fly named 'The Rackelhanen'. It was one of his unsinkable and favourite traditional Swedish sedge patterns, which he emphatically recommended me to try. This size 10 Rackelhanen was a huge fly (which was what had attracted my attention to it), but when I used it I had almost as much success as my Swedish friend had enjoyed. It was the perfect fly for broken water and strong rapids, and in no time the Rackelhanen was put with my other favourites. Full of confidence I travelled on upstream, staying at several locations but now catching bigger fish. Then the worst happened: I lost my new 'favourite' and had to revert to my old English shoulder-hackled dry flies again. They were still effective, especially the Red Tag and Greenwell's Glory, but the Rackelhanen had achieved so much that there was nothing for it but to make a copy. After trying several designs I arrived at my 'own' version of the Rackelhanen which seems almost as successful as the original.

I have no idea how my fly-fishing life would look today if I had not come across the Rackelhanen. The success of this creation gave me enormous self-confidence in making my own patterns and stimulated me to start a complete new way of fly tying. Big flies seemed to be the secret of catching the bigger fish, and that's why my Scandinavian patterns increased in size. It was with my own variations of the Rackelhanen that my fly-fishing obsession began and my fly-tying development started. For me, the Rackelhanen is much more than just an ordinary fly – not because it brought me my personal grayling record, but because it led me ultimately to develop patterns like the Poly Sedge and Klinkhammer Special.

R.V. DUIJNHOVEN

Lake fishing for grayling

For me, the 1980 fishing season was one of the most educational. After four weeks of intensive fishing as far upstream as the famous Isterfossen rapids near Lake Femund in Norway, it culminated in a wonderful 51-cm grayling – up to then, my biggest grayling ever. From that moment I knew my destiny for the succeeding years.

The feeders of the Trysilelva

When I next returned to the Femund area I changed my fishing strategy. This time I chose one location for my base, camping out at Johnsgård, a nice camping place right on Lake Langsjöen from which I could cover many new fishing areas. Over years of staying there I began to recognise some of the best grayling waters in central Scandinavia (the four months of wilderness experience I gained in northern Finland were a great help in my research and exploration). Rivers like the Sölna, Sömåa, Hola, Röa, Mugga, Femunsdelva and Glöta must be the Garden of Eden for every grayling angler, and lakes like Femund, Sölensjöen, Aresjöen, Isteren and Feragen were just a few more of my newly discovered paradises.

Most of these waters are between 600 and 1,000 metres above sea level, the weather conditions are tough, and the fishing season is short, although very productive. There is also an enormous population of wild and hungry mosquitoes, and you just have to learn to deal with these (though I guess some people never will or can). This area offers the grayling what I believe it likes most. The lakes provide very good conditions for survival during the severe winters, and they have an excellent food supply: insect life is abundant, with superb caddis hatches and many species of up-wing flies. Most of the streams in the area are very similar, though they vary greatly in width and depth. Sometimes you can walk across easily, but at other places you only can swim to get to the other side; to reach the best places needs a long walk or a canoe.

The Sömåa is relatively short compared to the others, but it is a wonderful stream with loads of deep holding pools. Most of the pools are well fed by nice rapids and have beautiful outflows – perfect conditions for dry-fly fishing. The Sömåa flows between Lakes Langsjöen and Isteren, and access to the river is easy, because it runs parallel with road no. 26 (which makes its grayling population very vulnerable to fishing pressure).

The Hola connects Lakes Langsjöen and Storsjöen. The latter is the largest of several lakes that are better known as the Hodalen Lakes. Over the years the Hodalen Lakes have become one of my favourite areas in Europe for grayling lake fishing. It is a very tough and rough area with strong windy conditions, but take my advice and fish it on sunny and windless days, because only then you are able to locate the fish. The biggest perch I have taken on a fly I caught here while grayling fishing.

The lower part of the Sölna took me a long time to explore, but the reward was unbelievable when I finally found five extremely good hot spots. I still vividly remember how much effort it took me before I could wet my flies – I had to swim across the Femundselva. It would be stupid for me to repeat a trip like that these days, but it was one of my most wonderful experiences from the past. The best way is to fish from the lake downstream by canoe. Unfortunately there is now a road going to Gakseter to the east side of the Sölna and Lake Sölesjöen, which must surely have increased the fishing pressure.

The Rivers Mugga and Röa are located in Femundsmarka National Park north-east of Lake Femund. During my first visits to the Röa I was dropped off at the mouth by boat from Sorvika and rented a canoe. The Mugga I explored on foot, starting from Langen, and I found some excellent fishing on the way up at the crossing places on the outlet from Lake Langtjönn. Both these rivers are exclusively wilderness fishing, and the only way to be successful is to camp out and work your way upstream. I always met one or two 'crazy' fishermen in this unique and quiet place, and a good chat on the way is essential to improve your successes.

When you follow all lakes and rivers you will notice that most of them belong to the same catchment area as the mighty Trysilelva. Even lakes Femund and Isteren are connected by the Glöta. It is a huge river system, still following its natural course, and most of it is totally unaffected by humans. With all the space and perfect living conditions, this system produces grayling that grow quickly and fight very well – that's another reason I return year after year.

Unfortunately, the excellent fishing in the Sömåa has declined enormously during the 1980s, due to too many visitors failing to return their large catches. Today, though, there is new hope again, and catches of larger fish are improving. A few fish of 50 cm or more were caught in 1998 and released, so hopefully they will again reach the magic size in the year 2000!

The Shining River and its Tributaries (The Glomma)

On the Glomma my exploration is not much different, although I make my way upstream more quickly because of greater fishing pressure and man-made regulations. I just bypass all the areas where embankments have changed the natural course and depth of the river. In the early 1980s the

River Rena produced an excellent fishing, but it then declined (I don't know the reason), although it has got better again in the 1990s (today it is one of the tributaries most favoured by the Danes). I stay quite a long time in the Koppang area, to explore and discover superb fishing in the many channels the river has cut for itself (sometimes it is a real challenge to find or even reach the main river). I often catch huge pike that take my hooked fish.

Further upstream you will meet the River Atna. This is a wonderful river, but it has been always a great mystery to me. Some years I have had unbelievable catches, while in others I have hardly been able to find any fish at all. It was in this river that trout fishing became very popular with me! Between the Atna and Alvdal you will never see many fishermen, though I can assure you that there are a good number of hot spots. Perhaps the reason is that the river here runs a bit further away from road no. 3; not many people seem to like to walk any distance these days.

I have had great times in Alvdal, especially when I was learning how to fish the awesome Folla River. If you ever fish the Glomma you surely should explore this river and follow it upstream as far as Sletten. My best fishing pal had his finest-ever grayling fishing in this river; unfortunately he died too soon, and we never could fish his favourite place together.

Between Alvdal and Tynset the fishing is less interesting because of huge regulations. The best fishing is probably on the lower part of the Tuna, especially just above the junction with the Glomma; sometimes this stretch holds a nice population of big fish, but it is extremely vulnerable to fishing pressure. About ten kilometres upstream from Tynset, though, you will hit the area of the shining river. From here all the way up to the outflow from Lake Rien the Glomma can be considered the *crème de la crème* for the grayling angler (this is not just my own experience; many books tell you exactly the same – and they are all right). The only way to be successful is to become at one with the river; look for the shining effect produced by the broken surface water. The area is not only beautiful but also very quiet. There are just a few peaceful towns, which you can easily fall in love with, and the people are extremely nice and friendly and always willing to help you. It is in this area that I spend most of my time, and I am sure I could live here forever.

I can't tell you exactly where to go, because there are too many places. Some people say you should fish only between Tolga and Oss, but I would suggest you stay at least two weeks in the area and explore it for yourself. Concentrate at the Glomma first, and when that seems difficult, just travel to one of the many tributaries. Talk to other fishermen, have chats at camping places, and try to put all the information you can get to use.

R.V. DUIJNHOVEN

Hans van Klinken with a River Glomma grayling

Where and How to Start Fishing the Tributaries

For newcomers to this Norwegian grayling paradise the fishing will be extremely difficult, but, once you have found the knack, it seems very easy. Most rivers have grayling, trout, whitefish, and even perch and pike. The distances will be the greatest problem, for today most fishermen don't like to walk with a backpack any more. Most tributaries flow through large lakes, or just have many little ponds or deep-holding pools along their course, but that can make the fishing much easier – at least if you are not afraid to walk. I usually start at an easy access point where I can park my car and prepare myself well. I never travel without a backpack filled with extra fishing equipment, clothing, food and even some emergency stuff (drinks are not necessary; the crystal-clear water will take care of that). I just start walking, sometimes as much as two or three kilometres, before I start fishing. I watch out for human tracks, for I know most people don't walk very far, and as soon as there are no tracks I start fishing. These are the areas where you have the best chance to catch the bigger fish, because many people still fish for the freezer and where people have been, a lot of fish will have been taken out. I often pass a few fishermen and ask how they are doing. They usually are enthusiastic about their catches so I just leave them to fill their creels – they don't know what other pools can bring!

I have learned that when a river runs into a small pond or a big pool you hit a hot spot. I have also learned that you generally only have one or two chances to get a really good-sized grayling. Never walk into the water before you have scouted it well and know what you are doing. Look at the feeding line first. If there are no rises don't worry; try to analyse the best place for your cast and where exactly you want to land your fly.

Be sure the fly drifts without any drag. Always start with a huge dry fly and let it float with the edge of the current into the pool. Make just a few casts, and if there is big grayling in a feeding mood he or she will surely take it. If this fails, try doing the same with a weighted nymph. In this case cast upstream and use a bite indicator to present the nymph at the right depth and without drag. It must drift into the pool with the bottom current, and not with the surface current. Save a cast with a smaller fly for the way back. Depending on the size of the pool, I never made more than about ten unsuccessful casts. Then I walk further and try the tail of the pool, or else I just walk to the next pool.

If I am successful I only take two or three fish out of a pool, release them and try again on the way back or on another day. This way of fishing leads me to some really nice fish, and every year I get several grayling of 50 cm plus. This is the technique I use to catch the big ones – and it

247

works, as I prove to many of my friends who join me in Scandinavia. Most of them have got their biggest-ever grayling.

Sometimes when you walk from pool to pool the fish start to rise all over the place. You can start fishing, or just try to recognise the feeding lies. I prefer to do both, marking the lies for those times when the weather changes and I have to go back to nymph fishing only. Make notes and write down as much information as you can find: times of feeding, weather conditions and insect life – it will all be useful data for the next time.

Places where rivers run out of lakes are other hot spots. Sometimes the current is very smooth, and even if you try hard it seems impossible to catch anything. At such times try small emergers or midge imitations.

Equipment

My favourite rod for the Glomma is a rate 4 up to 9 ft long. For the smaller tributaries I use an 8½-ft, 4-piece travel rod, weight 4 or 5. It is handy when you have to walk and can leave it in your backpack until you reach the place you want to fish. I still use the small System Two reel with an olive-coloured Cortland Clear Creek floating line. This line is my favourite by far: it has a nice fine taper and is excellent for windy conditions. Because of my preference for huge parachute flies I use a tapered, braided leader from about 9 ft connected with tying thread and waterproof superglue; this prevents wind knots during casting very well. For the tippet I mostly use 0.12-mm or 0.14-mm Stroft monofilament with lengths up to 2 metres.

I have a good selection of dry flies and nymphs. The dressings of the most popular ones are given on p. 134–6.

Grayling in Poland

Stanislaw Cios

SINCE 1985, WHEN the World Fly Fishing Championship was won by the Poles, Polish fly fishing has attracted a lot of attention. It is an increasingly popular hobby in Poland, and the main fish to interest fly fishermen nowadays is grayling.

Distribution

Essentially there are two areas of Poland with native grayling populations: one is the north (mainly in Pomerania) and one in the south (in the mountain region). In Pomerania, grayling thrive in almost all larger rivers, the best known of which are the Drawa, Głda (and all its major tributaries), Brda, Wda, Wieprz, Łupawa and Łeba. All these rivers are typical highland waters, with a relatively gentle gradient. Most are narrow and deep, with many trees (mainly alder) on the banks, a sandy or muddy bottom and, at times, swampy banks. In summer the blackflies often render the angler's life difficult, though not nearly so miserable as in, say, Lapland.

In the southern area almost all the major rivers have grayling. The best known are (from west to east), the Bóbr, Kwisa, Nysa, Soła, Skawa, Dunajec and Poprad. They are submontane waters, usually wide and with a stony bottom. The fishing here is very enjoyable, since there are very few blood-sucking insects.

The very strong interest in grayling has given rise to many attempts to introduce it to waters where it was not native. The first attempts were as long ago as the 1880s, although the first successful ones started in the 1950s. As a result of these activities there are now self-sustaining populations of grayling in some rivers in the Mazury lake district of north-eastern Poland (e.g. the Pasłeka, Wel, Rospuda and Supraśl), in central-eastern

Poland (the Bystrzyca near Lublin) and in the river San (Bieszczady mountains).

The greatest success was achieved on the San. In 1967–8 the river was dammed at Solina, in a stretch of non-salmonid water. The reservoir was very deep (65 m) and, due to draw off from the deepest and coldest layer of water, the temperature of the outflow was low (about 10°C all the year round), which created very good conditions for salmonids. Since 1971 the river has regularly been stocked with grayling, and the fish have acclimatised very well, so that a self-reproducing population has become established. Since the late 1970s the river has been full of grayling, and its excellent fishing and the beauty of the river and its surroundings contributed to the decision to organise the World Fly Fishing Championship there in 1985.

The San (near Lesko) is certainly the most interesting grayling river for a foreigner; it is excellent for dry-fly fishing. Another river in southern Poland that is worthy of interest is the Dunajec, especially the long stretch from the dam in Czorsztyn down to Stary Sącz; nymph experts may test their skill here. Northern Poland should appeal to anglers not bothered by wilderness, swamps, lack of luxurious hotels, difficult access to rivers and abundant blackflies (though only during certain periods). I usually fish on the Drawa (in the Drawa National Park), the Wda (from Czarna Woda to Tleń) and the Brda (from Rytel to Woziwoda); I am sure any foreigner would find a fishing trip there very memorable.

Nowadays, Poland is no longer a grayling angler's paradise. The situation was very good until about 1986–7. Since then the widespread use of the leaded-nymph technique, deterioration of water quality and spawning success, and the recent domestic economic crisis (food shortages, plus unemployment allowing more time for angling) have all contributed to grayling's decline. There are, however, signs of improvement in many rivers.

Ecological and angling notes

My research on the biology of grayling in Polish waters, and especially on feeding patterns, shows that the feeding behaviour differs between the two main grayling areas.

Northern area

In most rivers there is a clear feeding pattern. The main prey in clean (oligotrophic) rivers are:

- the caddis (*Brachycentrus subnubilus*). The larvae are eaten in very large numbers from late June until November. At times as many as over 400 larvae may be found in the stomach of one fish, with very few other prey present. The adults are of no importance to fish or anglers, since the emergence period is usually early May (even trout rarely rise to the adults).
- the shrimp (*Gammarus* mainly *G. pulex*). It occurs in fish stomachs mainly in the cold part of the year. It seems that summer vegetation provides a refuge for the shrimps, and as it dies in autumn the shrimps' propensity to drift greatly increases, enhancing its availability to fish.
- the water bug (*Aphelocheirus aestivalis*). This never occurs in very large numbers (I have never found more than 44 in one stomach) but is a constant and very characteristic component of the diet

In many clean rivers the diet is enriched by the larvae of the caddis *Oligoplectrum maculatum*, Hydropsyche, Limnephilidae, *Lasiocephala basalis* and *Ceraclea fulva*; the Calopteryx damselflies; and the Baetis mayfly (mainly in September and October). In the Wda and Drawa crayfish (*Orconectes limosus*) are also eaten (especially in autumn during high water, when they are more easily washed down with the current). For example on 29 October 1994, in a sample of 35 fish from the Wda, I found 16 crayfish (in other autumns the number has been much smaller). The largest one I have found in a stomach was 5 cm long.

In rivers which receive some pollution the diet is dominated by the shrimp, the water louse (*Asellus aquaticus*), Hydropsyche, blackfly (Simuliidae) and midge (Chironomidae) larvae, leeches (*Erpobdella* – mainly in autumn) and the mayfly *Ephemerella ignita* (mainly July–August).

From the angler's point of view it is very important to note the dominance of food taken in the water column in these rivers. Usually over ninety per cent of the food consists of aquatic organisms (or their aquatic stages, in the case of insects). Hence the weight of the creel is in direct proportion to the weight of the flies and depth of the water in which they are presented. The fish are often catholic in their choice; on most occasions any artificial fly that looks edible may do the job. Some instances of strong selection (and refusal of many artificial flies) occur when the fish are feeding selectively (and very heavily) on *B. subnubilus* and the blackflies.

Surface feeding is not a very regular phenomenon. The best dry-fly feeding occurs in the first half of June (when the fish are still concentrating on the Baetis mayflies) and from late August until October. Late summer and autumn surface-feeding grayling concentrate on duns of *E. ignita* (initially) and Baetis (mainly *B. rhodani*), and on certain terrestrials. The role of terrestrials on some rivers and some days may be exceptionally important. In particular in October, when leaves are falling on the water after the first frosts, the Pentatomidae bugs, and some beetles, become very easy and attractive prey (the characteristic odour of Pentatomidae, difficult to compare with Christian Dior perfumes, in no way offends the fish). Spiders are also a regular component in autumn, though usually in small numbers.

In some rivers some fish show an inclination for taking prey from the bottom. I have seen grayling rooting out such food. This is also confirmed by the presence of large numbers of cased caddis of the Goeridae family (*Silo pallipes* and *Goera pilosa*) in their stomachs. In the river Brda – which has deep but very clean water in which it is possible to observe the fish (at times huge trout, or even pike over 10 kg, may be seen) – I have noted interesting feeding behaviour. Bottom-feeding fish take food in three ways:

- from the bottom, as the prey moves on it. Once, for several hours, I and my friends observed a 36-cm fish in shallow water feeding heavily on a sandy bottom just some 4–5 m from us. None of our flies aroused any interest until, finally, after heavy brainstorming, I tried a tiny nymph that rolled on the bottom. With the first cast I got the fish. The stomach contents proved that my assumption was correct – the fish had been eating mainly tiny gammarids.
- just above the bottom (about 10–20 cm). These fish are interested only in prey passing near their mouths; only occasionally do they make a dart to intercept more distant prey. This happens when the fish are not in a very good mood. In general they are difficult to catch with a fly, but in clean waters, once a fish is sighted, after many attempts it may be induced to take the fly.
- taking food which flows up to one metre from the fish. This occurs during heavy feeding, especially in turbulent water (when the prey is flowing throughout the water column), in water with abundant vegetation, or in slower water during emergence of mayflies. These fish are quite easy to catch, but difficult to find. The weighted-nymph technique, in which the angler seeks the fish 'blindly', to a large extent relies on these fish. One of my friends has told me of seeing grayling pluck food from aquatic plants. This seems highly probable, in view of the large amount of aquatic plants in some stomachs.

Southern area

In the case of the southern grayling populations it is more difficult to present a clear feeding pattern, since the situation differs in each river. However, I would like to draw attention to the following features:

- The major role of the mayfly *Oligoneuriella rhenana* in the Dunajec and Poprad. These large mayflies are eaten in July and August. The main prey are the larvae, but on occasion the adults may be eaten. Emergence en masse occurs at sunset, when at times billions of insects hover over the water, perform the nuptial dance and die off. Fish quite often become interested in bands of males trying to grasp a female; the whole company falls onto the water, which excites some fish. Artificials often imitate these clusters, so the flies are quite big and very 'bushy'. Nymphs, which are usually a very deadly weapon, should be dark brown or black.
- The role of the caddis *Oligoplectrum maculatum*. In autumn, fish in the Dunajec at times have well over 1,000 cased larvae in their stomachs (their length is about 5–10 mm); they probably scrape them from the

River Dunajec

253

stones. Early in June some fish may feed very heavily on the spent adults (in some places near the banks the water may be literally covered with the spent insects).

- The importance of the tiny caddis *Psychomyia pusilla*. In some rivers (Dunajec, Poprad, Soła) very large numbers of larvae and emergers may be eaten. I have found relative adults in the stomachs, but – interestingly – they were all females (the caddis is known to deposit its eggs under the water).

- The feeding pattern of grayling in the San. The temperature of the water released from the dam at Myczkowce is about 10°C. In this very cold temperature the insects behave in a strange way. For example, in summer (when it is very hot) in the stretch just below the dam the insects usually emerge at noon or early afternoon, and not in the evening. The fish rise to them correspondingly. Further downstream, as the temperature of the water rises, the emergence gradually shifts to the evening hours. So do some anglers, who know about this phenomenon.

Angling laws

Grayling (like all other salmonids) may be caught only with artificial bait. In practice this means only flies, since very few fish are caught with lures – mainly spinning ones, though I have caught a 25-cm fish on a plug. Poachers, however, have no esteem for this law (it is no great secret that their very effective baits are maggots and sea trout eggs). Some years ago during an angling competition (natural bait only) on the river Gwda, some anglers caught grayling. The fish were thrown on the scale together with roach, perch and similar species. The judges were completely ignorant of the law, and some weeks passed before the mistake was realised. An earthquake followed, but the pillars of bait fishing have remained unshaken.

The size limit for grayling is 30 cm (in force since 1947), though on a few rivers it is higher: i.e. the Drawa (32 cm) and the Pasłeka (35 cm). In the future there will probably be more rivers with a higher size limit. In some productive rivers the fish grow so fast that they have reached the legal size by the age of 1+, so that they are cropped before their first spawning. Some ichthyologists are therefore advocating higher size limits for these populations.

The official bag limit is a total of 5 fish (trout and grayling together) per day. Since the mid-1990s, though, the limit on some rivers has been reduced to 3 fish.

The close season is from 1 March to 30 May. Since the early 1990s there has been a growing awareness of the need to protect the grayling – especially in winter, when the water level is very low, and the fish are easy to catch. Thus, for example, since 1991 fishing on some sections of the Dunajec has closed from 1 December, and since 1997 from as early as 1 November. On some other rivers (e.g. the Brda and Wda in 1994–6) the fish have been protected by a banning on all angling from 1 December.

In all salmonid waters angling is allowed only during the daytime (from one hour before sunrise until one hour after sunset). On the river Radunia (near Gdańsk) fishing with the leaded nymph has recently been banned.

It is worth noting that, though fly-fishing tournaments have contributed their nail to the grayling's coffin in Poland, they have also been instrumental in the introduction of new laws and in sowing the seeds of conservation-consciousness. Reduced bags and increased size limits were first introduced during such tournaments, and the success of these measures served as a stimulus to the application of similar laws in open waters.

Polish angling laws tend to become more restrictive in response to the decline of the grayling populations in all the country's rivers. However, this often seems to me to be treating the symptoms rather than the disease. The truth is that, apart from the very strong angling pressure (and at times also poaching), the decline is also due to a deterioration in spawning conditions (caused by pollution, regulation, the destruction of spawning grounds, dams preventing migration, etc.).

Historical notes and hypothesis on the origin of fly fishing

The first mention of grayling in Polish literature dates back to 1394: an account-book of Queen Jadwiga, which has miraculously survived the country's tempestuous history, contains a reference to the purchase in Kraków of some grayling for Her Majesty. And in 1412 her successor King Władisław II Jagiello had some grayling from the river Dunajec bought for him. These accounts indicate that as early as mediaeval times the grayling was a very highly prized fish, worthy even to set before monarchs.

The first mention of angling for grayling dates from 1721. Rzączński, in a book on the natural history of Poland (written in Latin, widely known in the West), says of lampreys: 'they are used by fishermen as bait for grayling, eel and pike, and other fish'. In general Rzączyński's information is reliable, and, if he is not mistaken (or didn't copy it from some other source), this information is of great interest. I have found a similar reference in Colero (1645: 857), who described fishing in Germany.

The next item, from 1847, is a brief note by Petruski on fishing in the River Stryj (today in western Ukraine). It reads: 'Angling, which is well known, is also very common here, and doesn't need a broader description. However, it is worthy of interest because, to facilitate angling for trout and grayling, instead of a natural bait (i.e. a fish or a worm) they place on the hook an imitation of an insect, made of the hair of a bear. With this bait they catch the tasty, but indeed unintelligent, fish.' This brief note is interesting because it indicates that fly fishing was already quite common in the eastern Carpathians, and its roots reach deep into the past. However, its importance is greatly enhanced by the following passage, of 1875, by Dziędzielewicz, a well known Polish entomologist who published a description of the habits of the mayfly *Oligoneuriella rhenana* in the same river. At the end of it he wrote: 'The fishermen take advantage of the emergence of the insects, for they need not seek the fish in deep runs; lured by the abundant prey, the fish keep near the water surface.' I interpret this passage as referring to fishing with an artificial fly; fishing with a natural, especially the adult mayfly, should be rejected, since emergence takes place at and after sunset, and it would have been virtually impossible to place the fragile insect on the hook in the darkness – not to mention the difficulty of dapping under such conditions.

If this interpretation is correct, then fishing with flies of bear hair would have been a very reasonable method during the emergence of this mayfly. Today it is a common practice among grayling anglers on the Dunajec to make artificial flies that imitate the copulating pairs as they drop on the water surface (which they do often). The artificial is very big and 'hairy'. Perhaps our ancestors were as smart as we are and, observing the same phenomenon, found the same solution, using bear hair.

If this interpretation is correct, then we may take a further big step. One of the greatest angling puzzles left by the ancient Greeks is Aelian's (170–230 AD) passage on fly fishing in Macedonia. Quite a few authorities quote him, but very few bother to interpret his writings. In my opinion the key to understanding the fly-fishing technique he mentions lies in recognizing the insect 'hippurus', that was imitated. In the literature the following interpretations are known to me:

- Rozwadowski (1900) states that the flies were the adults of the common blood-sucking *Tabanidae*. He probably drew his conclusion from the similarity of the name to 'hippos' (horse), since horses are often attacked by these insects.
- Magee (1995) assumes that the insect was a mayfly, but doesn't give any explanation.

• Scholfield, in his translation of Aelian, states that the insects are the two-winged flies *Stratiomys*, which are very distinctive and similar to wasps. Many species of Stratiomyidae thrive in water (mainly in still water) during their larval stage. However, mountain trout streams are not their typical habitat, and the information available to me indicates that the adults behave like terrestrials. Moreover, nowhere in the European literature have I yet found the role of Stratiomyidae reported as other than a negligible component of salmonids' diet (sometimes single insects, usually larvae, have been found in fish stomachs).

There are four elements in Aelian's writings which indicate that 'hippu-rus' must be a different insect: it flies over the water, it sits on the water, fish often eat it, and it is very fragile. In principle very few non-aquatic insects regularly fly over the water, and none of them sit on it of their own will. This implies that 'hippurus' must be the adult of an aquatic insect. Aelian's description seems to indicate a mayfly (or even a stone-fly); it could be a member of the Heptageniidae (some species of *Ecdyonurus*, for example, have bands on their body).

In 1997, through the assistance given to me by Evangelos Kaplanis, living in France, I had the privilege of studying the stomach contents of five trout from the River Aoos, which flows from northern Greece into Albania (the results were published in the French magazine *Truites, Ombres et Saumons*; see Cios, 1997). To my surprise, one of the most important prey items was the mayfly *Oligoneuriella*, as many as 40 adults of which were found in one fish.

It therefore seems highly probable that the Macedonians imitated this mayfly. It is big, so imitation would have been relatively easy to construct (much easier than, say, an imitation of a blackfly or a midge, as implied by the word 'konops' in Aelian's fragment on grayling); the anglers probably fished with dry flies, because they could see the rising fish. It is likely that they fished at sunset, because in Greece this is the feeding time of the fish in summer (I am sure the ancient anglers were as reluctant as we are to get up early in the morning) and it is also the time of emergence and nuptial activity of *Oligoneuriella*. It must also have been much easier to delude the wary fish at sunset (when the visibility is poor) than in daylight, especially when dapping.

Of course, there are some element's in Aelian's writings which do not fit well into my hypothesis (e.g. red wool, bands on the insect's body, etc.), but how many times have we needed to stretch our mind to understand some of the intricate puzzles of the past? Polish angling has already contributed a lot in the discussion of fishing in antiquity. It was

Rozwadowski (in 1900, well before Radcliffe in 1921) who first drew attention to the reference (however dubious) to fly fishing in Martial's epigram, and the greatest enigma – Homer's famous 'horn of the field ox' – found its explanation in the Polish method of catching catfish, still used in the second half of the nineteenth century on the River Neman near Grodno. Of course, my studies of old Polish literature and the feeding habits of trout and grayling in various European waters, need to be complemented by data from some other countries. Of particular relevance might be old literature from the south-east Carpathians (especially Romania) or the Balkans; maybe some bookworm like myself will be able to come up with new information.

Gesner's (1558) account of fly fishing in Germany – the second oldest reference to fly fishing on the continent – doesn't provide any direct support for my hypothesis. However, from his description of the flies I deduce that at that time fly fishing was already a highly developed art, so we must go back further to seek the roots.

Nymph *a la polonaise*

One of the most important contributions of Polish anglers to fly fishing has been the perfecting of the nymph technique. First, a few words about the roots of this technique in Poland.

Until the mid-1970s fly fishing was practised by a relatively small group of enthusiasts (mainly in the Kraków region) probably numbering no more than 3,000. It started to receive considerable attention when tournaments began to be held in the late 1970s, including the Polish championship (initiated in 1977). These acted like a catalyst, providing a strong incentive to improve technique (due to competition) as well as a means of exchanging information very rapidly.

From the early 1980s grayling gradually became the fish of interest to fly anglers. There were three principal reasons for this:

- the abundance of grayling in many rivers (in 1982 I remember counting ten grayling in one square metre in the River Czemica, a tributary of the Głda);
- the increase in the size limit for trout (from 25 to 30 cm) in 1984. Anglers switched to grayling, since it became more difficult to catch trout of legal size;
- the widespread introduction of the leaded-nymph technique, extremely deadly in the case of this fish. This technique was especially important

in tournaments, where, once a competitor had caught the quota, he was awarded bonus points for each minute until the end of the round – which made it more profitable to catch five (later three) fish very quickly than to waste time on some big fish.

The leaded-nymph technique had been known in Poland since the early 1970s, but was practised by only a small group of anglers, mainly on the Dunajec. However, the Poles were the first to make the best use of leaded nymphs to fish for grayling, mastering the techniques of tying and fishing with leaded flies. (In Poland, in contrast to many other countries, one cannot put lead on the line or tippet when fly fishing; this law was an additional stimulus to the development of some flies.)

The fishing technique is very simple – so much so that, like many other simple things, it took a very long time to invent it. The rod needs to be relatively long: usually about 10 feet, though an expert will manage very well with an 8-foot rod. For nymphing in deep runs and larger rivers I use a 12-foot single-handed rod made of a Fibetube blank bought in 1983 (I believe these blanks were produced for only a short time).

The line is not important, though a floating one is preferred (its light colour enhances the visibility of the take). Some anglers even go as far as to say that their wives' clothes-lines will do the job (there is some truth in this, since casting distances are very short, and the line isn't really needed). In the 1980s, when it was rather difficult to buy good fly fishing tackle in Poland, some anglers used normal nylon line and traditional reels.

The flies need to be heavy, so as to reach the bottom very fast. Quite often the tail fly is a heavy one, while the dropper is unleaded. Some anglers even break off the point of the hook of the heavy nymph, to avoid snags on the bottom – a technique that, although legal in Poland, is deplored by skilled and ethical anglers.

There is no rule about fly patterns. Each angler will use a different one, and will catch fish, as long as he knows his art. In general, however, most anglers prefer to make imitations of the larvae of *Hydropsyche* and *Oligoneuriella* (where it exists), and of the *Gammarus* shrimp. Quite often big flies are used, even Size 1, especially in some deep rivers in northern Poland. Many flies are tied with the weaving technique (for which you need a few dozen fingers in each hand, unless you are an expert), and I believe that the perfecting of this technique (though not its invention) is another Polish contribution to fly fishing. Woven flies are really beautiful and sell well; their fishing efficacy is high (comparable to other good nymphs), but everything depends on the skill of the angler (i.e., if you know how to fish, you will get them with any fly).

The length of the tippet depends on the depth of the water. When fishing in deep runs (*c* 2 m) I use a tippet of about 2.5 m, or even longer. The idea is that the line should be held clear of the water while the flies are running near the bottom. Quite often in very fast stretches of water the whole tippet is composed of thin line (0.20 mm, with the last section of 0.15–0.18 mm). The object is for the flies to sink as fast as possible. In deep runs a fine tippet allows better control of the flies and faster recognition of a bite.

More important than the tackle is the method of fishing. (Anybody can make beautiful leaded nymphs, but not everybody will catch fish with them. Skill makes the difference between an empty and a full creel.) The efficiency of the leaded-nymph technique rests on the following assumptions:

- the angler is very often close to the fish (this is why the method is more effective for grayling than for trout);
- he fishes mainly with the tippet, with just 1–3 m of line swinging in the air (the length depends on the conditions);
- the fish feed mainly near the bottom (generally true; trying to catch surface-feeding fish with a nymph can sometimes be a very disappointing occupation).

The basic idea is to make a short cast upstream and let the nymphs sink to the bottom. Then, keeping the rod more or less parallel to the water, move the tip downstream slightly faster than the speed of the current. The idea is to 'feel' the nymphs, and not to allow them to fall onto the bottom and snag. The nymphs pass over just 1–3 m of the bottom before a new cast is made. And that's it! Very simple to write, but harder to learn, and much much harder to catch fish.

The technique is especially effective in very fast, even 'boiling' water. Very few anglers realise that there are fish in such places; still fewer consider such places fishable.

Fishing with a leaded nymph requires considerable stamina and concentration. Making very fast casts, keeping the arm outstretched and wading in deep, fast, stony places is no easy job. The technique may be especially difficult to learn for anglers used to traditional dry- and wet-fly fishing and to casting over distances of 20 m or more. Fishing with heavy nymphs demands completely different casting skills (to some it might appear to have very little in common with the traditional concept of fly fishing). It also requires three other skills. The angler must be able to locate the fish in the river (he isn't fishing the rise, and not every place that holds fish is equally convenient for the technique); he must know where his nymphs are in the water; and he must know when to strike – usually the signal is the end of the line coming to an abrupt stop (although very few such stops signify a fish) – and in the case of a bite must react very fast, otherwise the fish will spit out the fly.

The Poles did not invent the technique. Hooks with lead attached to them were known 2,000 years ago in Herculaneum (see Waldstein and Shoobridge, 1908:122), Aelian 1.15 and Oppian (*Cynegetica* 1.155; *Halieutica* 111.781) mention lead being attached to hooks for sea fishing. Even in Alaska the 'primitive' ('smart' would be more appropriate) Indians attached small stones to their wooden hooks to make them sink better (see Collins, 1937, tab. 56). And in the first half of the twentieth century lead was being used by anglers to get their flies to the bottom. In 1946 Buxton (p. 18) wrote: 'It has been suggested to me that the general objection to nymph fishing is due to the fact that many people always allow their nymph to sink, and artificial nymphs are, I understand, weighted. This has perhaps given the impression that it is blind fishing and therefore less sporting than dry fly fishing proper.' Later (p. 35) he added: 'Since at least 95 per cent of hatching mayfly are eaten by trout in the nymph stage, it is strange that no one has invented a really good artificial mayfly nymph.' It took some forty years more to develop really effective flies and, more important, the way of presenting them.

How much our views have changed over recent years may be judged from the statement by Frost and Brown (1967: 223): 'In nymph fishing the imitation of a larval aquatic insect is fished only slightly submerged and cast to a rising trout'. Today this is a very long way from the generally held view, at least in Poland!

Experiences of Grayling in Russia

Rod Calbrade

D URING THE LAST ten years, with the improvement in East–West relations, many angling opportunities have opened up in the former Soviet Union. Tour operators have been quick to set up either solo or joint operations with Russian partners, allowing anglers to fish (often in waters unfished before) for a wide range of species, principally members of the salmon family.

The Kola Peninsula, on the north Russian coastline, has become the most productive and famous angling destination, due to the massive runs of Atlantic salmon in its rivers. Its close proximity to both Moscow and neighbouring Scandinavian countries, has brought anglers easily and speedily to the area and therefore helped the growth of angling. The Kola, 250 miles long by 150 miles wide, lies mostly within the Arctic Circle and is completely snowbound from November to mid-April. There are few towns, Murmansk being the principal one, and roads into the surrounding tundra are scarce, so the helicopter is king; to reach any of the outlying areas it is vital. The tundra and peat bogs take up in excess of 60 per cent of the land, with birch forests covering other large areas of ground. The Kola is home to many migratory birds, as well as bear, elk and reindeer, and there is a profusion of wild flowers, arctic plants and lichens. The bog acts as a large sponge, releasing snow melt water steadily during the summer months and providing the life blood for the salmon run.

The vast majority of anglers who visit the Kola to fish, do so for the salmon. Grayling mostly, are caught by accident. Because of this, there is little knowledge of what the grayling eat, or even what food types are present. There are strict controls on the number of salmon taken and the methods used, but the local Russian population, like its counterparts in other areas, see the grayling as a very important food source, and it is not uncommon to see them taken, killed and dumped unceremoniously in buckets with other food fish, such as pike.

This area is ideal for grayling fishing, with perfect rivers, free-taking fish and the opportunity to take fish on traditional patterns. My trip, which was exploratory, was undertaken in mid-July 1993. The rivers had not been fished during the particular week before, and the operators wished to see if salmon runs continued or decreased, or indeed, if there was a midsummer grilse run. Flying into a camp by the lower River Kitza, we initially fished areas close to the camp. Immediately we began to pick up grayling on General Practitioners, Ally's Shrimps and other salmon patterns; even though the air temperature was in excess of 80°F and water temperature at 64°F, the grayling did not seem to be fussy. The river here was quite wide but shallow, and it was not until we went up to the previously unfished region of the river that we could identify specific grayling swims. Here the river was narrower, a little deeper and had more noticeable pools and glides. Lined with pine forest, it was an absolutely glorious picture. But Ally's Shrimps still seemed to be the standard diet! Specific areas with a streamy run at the head proved successful, the faster-flowing water maybe being attractive in the heat. Our other river, the Varzuga, failed to live up to its reputation for both salmon and grayling. This was due, no doubt, to the timing of our trip and the lack of running salmon.

ROD CALBRADE

River Varzuga, the Kola Peninsula

Coupled with my experiences, are the observations of other anglers who have fished on the Kola during recent seasons. Hopefully, with all these observations, a picture of grayling habits and successful techniques may emerge.

Rory Pilkington, Roxton Bailey Robinson's camp manager on the Kola for many years, has noticed that grayling are by no means as common during September as during June/July, maybe because they go to deeper water before the cold winter ahead.

John Wilshaw of *Trout and Salmon* magazine is a confirmed grayling fan. He went to the Kola in 1997 to fish mainly for salmon. However, unlike most anglers, John also took a trout rod and spent a couple of afternoons forsaking the salmon and fishing for grayling. Using a size 10 Klinkhamer, he found shoals of fit and fat grayling, mostly good sized fish up to a maximum of 1¾ lbs. But it was whilst fishing on Ally's Shrimp for salmon that he took probably one of the smallest grayling – 3 inches, the fly virtually dwarfing the fish. He also encountered the local Russians' love of grayling as a food source. John's fish were hung in trees and collected later by his guide, when they were gutted and descaled by the river. They were then taken home and salted to re-emerge at Christmas, when they would be fried and eaten, with glasses of beer, as a local delicacy.

Michael Evans runs trips on the northern rivers where the salmon tend to be larger. He has encountered a small number of grayling there and has taken them on skated Muddlers. On his rivers he has noticed 'colossal' stone-flies; presumably these are a useful food source.

Tarquin Millington-Drake of 'Frontiers' states that over on the Ponoi River they have found the grayling to be very free-taking, particularly near stream mouths. Whilst no anglers fish for them specifically, they have noticed good hatches of up-winged and caddis flies – a possible source of inspiration for patterns to try.

My other trips have included two to the Soviet Far East. It is only when you make this journey that you realise how large Russia is; the region lies ten time zones to the East of Moscow! To get there you fly over vast tracts of rivers and lakes, most of which have never seen anglers.

Firstly, we visited the River Khuchtui, which runs down to the town of Okhotsk in the north-west corner of the Sea of Okhotsk. It is a large river with pine forests along its length. The main species of fish here are the five species of Pacific salmon, with Siberian and Arctic char, grayling and, in rivers not too far away, Taimen.

Although a party of anglers fishing the same stretch two weeks earlier told us of good salmon fishing, my party of six failed totally to catch salmon on a fly. We therefore reverted to spinning Tobies, Mepps and other spinners, which some of us had taken just in case! Grayling were caught in the fast runs and necks of pools, taking the spinners, large and small, solidly and aggressively.

Having heard how sporting the char would be, I included in my tackle a Hardy 'Smuggler' trout rod, with a selection of flies of all types. Shoals of char would come up the river, at times quite slowly, but always with a number of grayling intermingled with them. As the char were virtually straight from the sea, it seemed logical to use patterns such as Medicines, which resembled small sea fish. The grayling took them just as eagerly.

The Kamchatka Peninsula, jutting out into the Pacific, consists of 120 or so volcanoes, 30 of which are still active; part of the Pacific 'rim of fire', it continually gets shakes and quakes. Its population of 500,000 is centred mainly on the capital, Petropavlosk Kamchatsky on the south-east of the peninsula. We flew 700 miles north-west, to the town of Palana, to fish the Palana River – the first Westerners to do so, we believed. This river flows into the north-east corner of the Sea of Okhotsk, receiving the massive Pacific salmon runs of its neighbouring area.

ROD CALBRADE

The Upper River Kitza, Kola

This, too, was an exploratory trip. The other anglers included Clive Gammon, plus a party of six French anglers. It was felt likely that we would take grayling by design or accident. We arrived in mid-September, towards the end of the salmon runs, and caught Coho (Silver) and Chum salmon, Siberian and Arctic Char, plus Rainbows (which were quite spectacular) – but no grayling. In fact we were led to believe that grayling did not exist in the river, although our verbal description may have left a little to be desired.

Since 1993 trips to the Soviet Far East seem to have been curtailed by the major UK operators, although there may still be small individual parties going out there.

My final trip was to an area to the east of the Kola, but still close to the northern coastline. We flew to Archangel, and from there further east, to a small town called Nary'an Mar, which is the major settlement in this desolate area that is home to the Nenetsky reindeer people as well as the local Russian population. The helicopter took us to the junction of the Indiga and Belaya rivers to fish for a shoal of Atlantic salmon which it was thought would move upstream before the onset of winter, rather than spend the winter in the estuarial water downstream. What I and my fellow anglers did not know beforehand was that we were to spend the week right next to the river in a *chum*, or what we would otherwise know as a tepee or wigwam.

As well as salmon tackle, I also took a trout rod, specifically to fish for grayling while we were there. The salmon run did not materialise – only a couple of fresh salmon were taken, along with a good number of large kelts – and so our attentions turned to grayling as well. One afternoon, after earlier taking a number of grayling on salmon flies as well as gold-heads, P.T.N.s and other traditional patterns, I spent three hours fishing a small pool close to an inflowing creek, where I had been successful before. I was amazed by the variety of patterns which the grayling took: two-inch Waddington, Medicine, Mickey Finn, size 16 Shrimp, Dunkeld, Muddler, Stoat's Tail, sedges, plus others. These fish were not in the least bit choosy; all sizes of many different patterns of fly were taken eagerly.

During the course of the week, it rained hard, and the river rose continually until it began to threaten the camp site. We had no boats and no real radio contact with the outside world, so we just prayed that the helicopter would come back at the end of the week as promised. It was impossible to move the tent, because of its size and weight – anyhow there was nowhere to move to, as the edge of the forest was only yards away from the camp. The helicopter flew in on a bright Saturday morning after a night when the region got its first dusting of the winter's snow, and the river, by now

River Indiga grayling

running hard, was only four feet away from the tent. To call the trip a failure would be a major understatement, but we did have some excellent grayling fishing.

Overall, anglers going to Russia are going there to fish for salmon. However, during times of hard fishing or when a respite is needed, a change to grayling fishing could be a welcome relief. The grayling are not hard to catch. Maybe because of the short summer when foodstuffs abound, they gorge themselves for six months or so to make up for the preceding six months of frozen rivers and scarce food. With a little more experimentation with tactics and research into food types, grayling could make a valuable addition to the trips there, offering a challenging alternative to salmon. Russia is a grayling-fishers' paradise and hopefully more anglers will see it as such in future. For the dedicated grayling enthusiast it is a perfect place to go to.

Grayling in Northern Sweden:
The Story of the Idsjöströmmen

Lars Olsson

THE GRAYLING COME down from the lake to spawn during the first week of May. I can see them from the bridge, dark shadows moving nervously around in knee-deep, ice-cold water. Males are chasing off males, and pursuing females, ready to fold their big, long dorsal fins over their slender bodies when the time comes.

Except for the firs and pines, the landscape is grey and brown. There are patches of snow in the forest, and the six-mile-long lake Idsjön, upstream of the Idsjöströmmen, is still covered by three feet of ice. It seems as if the fishing season is far away.

However, nature is moving fast in this part of northern Sweden, supported not only by the sun that rises at 3.30 in the morning and sets at 10 o'clock at night, but also by 24 hours of daylight. So, one day, the spawning grayling are gone, and the 'mouse ears', the first small green buds of birches, aspens and willows, can be seen draping the landscape in promising and inspiring soft green veils. The first Large Dark Olive of spring lands on the bridge at noon, and the elegant swifts traverse the glen faster than anything else.

The upper section of the Idjöströmmen, from the bridge down to the 'little lake' – Lillselet – is still too fast and strong at this time of the year for a rising grayling, but the lower section, which is wider, slower and shallower, can be fished with the dry fly from the first day of the fishing season. In the big pool between the second windbreak, and Jönsholmen Island, a few Large Dark Olives ride the surface. Their big grey wings look like two hands pointing towards the sky, as if thanking the Great Spirit, the Master of Life, for being brought into this new, wonderful world of bright blue and lush green.

LARS OLLSON

River Idsjöströmmen, Sweden

It is 2 o'clock in the afternoon, and the day is warm and windless. Four or five grayling have noticed the hatching olives, and take them with typical splashy rises. More olives show up, confirming that the fishing season has started.

I am watching the lovely picture from the windbreak by the fire with the black coffee pot. Sipping my coffee, I am excited but not in a hurry. Eventually I put my mug aside, take my rod down from the roof, and check the dry fly: a Green Gim River dun, a faithful companion for twenty-five years. It has a wide split tail of microfibbets, a dark olive green body of musk-rat fur, a wing made of the speckled breast feather from a male mallard, and two turns of a dark blue dun hackle which, together with the wing, are placed close to the middle of the hook shank.

The grayling are now rising, splashing and rolling on the surface, feeding on the duns. The first feast of the year is on – big enough to bring the grayling up to the surface, and big enough to feed the soul of the dry-fly fisherman. The first cast goes across and down; a parachute cast makes the line and leader land with a lot of slack on the water. The dry fly with its conspicuous wing comes first. The sparsely tied hackle shows the slender, olive body to one of the grayling – there is a splash, and the fly disappears. When I strike I feel the weight of a big fish. The rod bends heavily, and the fish, supported by the fast current, takes four, five yards of line off my

A 20-inch (50.8 cm) grayling takes the dry fly, River Idsjöströmmen

reel, runs downstream for help, finds nothing there, turns around, and rushes upstream. The rod, and the current work together, and eventually a 20-inch grayling slips into the net.

A 20-inch grayling is a big grayling anywhere, but not too rare on the Idsjöströmmen. During the 1998 season 34 grayling of between 20 and 23 inches (50–57 cm) were caught and released, a huge difference compared to the early 1970s.

The history of the Gim River 1842–1998

In 1972 I came to the village of Gimdalen and the Idjöströmmen, which is a part of the Gim river. The logging that had been going on on the river for 130 years, had just ended, and trucks and vans and roads had started a new era in Sweden's biggest industry. The artificial logging structure was still evident, but had to be removed, and the 55-mile-long Gim river restored.

The logging company started its restoration work by removing the old stone and wood structure, the retaining walls and the floating logs that had been anchored in the river in order to guide the timber down to the sawmills by the coast. But after cleaning up the river, the company 'forgot' to take care of the second, and most important part – the restoration. Nothing came back to the river to make it look, and act, natural again. The old 'logging canal' in the middle of the river had the same smooth surface as before, and its bed lacked the necessary variety for fish and insects; there were no lies, no cover from predators and no protection from the current. The 250 dams in the main river and its tributaries were removed, which caused the spring run off to flush through quickly, and powerfully, and after a couple of weeks the water was down almost to its late autumn level. The fishing was bad; sometimes no fish could be seen for several days, and nothing – not even a small one – rose to your fly. The river could not have been in worse shape!

1976 – A Seed is Planted

In 1976 a group of dedicated fly fishermen formed The Gim River Environment Group. Our logo was a dipper, a bird that cannot live without clean, healthy streams and rivers. At weekends we and the local landowners started to move rocks by hand and put them into the river, hoping to create the variety of contour that the riverbed needed. It was heavy and tiring work which had very little effect on the river, but a seed was planted. The many hours we spent working with the river surprised not only the Gimdalen Fishing Board but, more importantly, the Jämtland County Administration Board. They had never heard of fishermen working with the environment, instead of fishing; at that time the policy for improving the fishing in a stream or river was to stock it with hatchery fish. The County granted the Gimdalen Fishing Board money for hiring an excavator to speed up the work and move bigger stones, rocks and boulders into the river. The restoration created a 'new' river, with the variety that was needed, raised the water level, and, not least, made it very appealing to the eye.

However the next five years saw no improvement in the fishing. The size limit was still 10 inches, and there was no bag limit. It wasn't difficult to understand why the fishing didn't improve: too many fish were caught by too many fishermen using worms, lures and flies.

1988–1998

In 1988 the last section of the Idjöströmmen, as well as the rest of the streams in the 55-mile (80-km) length of the Gim River, were restored after the logging, and before Christmas 1988, the Gimdalen Fishing Board made me a surprising offer – to lease the Idsjöströmmen for five years. A fishing dream had come true!

LEIF MILLING

Lars Olsson with a leaping grayling

I knew what I wanted to do with the Idsjöströmmen: to create a river that would become as good as the best rivers in England and USA. I started by turning it into a fly-only river and limiting the number of rods to eight per day. I doubled the price of a day ticket, increased the size limit from 10 inches to 14 inches, and introduced a bag limit of three fish per day. After five years the number and size of grayling and trout had increased, so I doubled the price again, increased the size limit to 16 inches and lowered the bag limit to one fish per person per day. Most fishermen learning about my philosophy for the river released all the fish they caught, even if they were above the size limit – in practice the Idsjöströmmen became almost a No-Kill river. As a result the number and size of fish increased, and each year turned out better than the last.

In 1995 I worked in the river for 10 hours with an excavator. There were still 'non-productive' areas from the logging days that could be improved. The size limit was now 18 inches, and the bag limit was one fish per person for each visit to the area to fish – virtually a catch-and-release situation. An 11-lb, 31-inch brown trout was caught one year, another year a 6-lb brown trout, and an impressive number of big grayling.

In May 1998 I worked with an excavator for nine hours, bringing more rocks into the river, and removing some of the obstacles left over from the logging years. During this season, which was another record, 34 grayling between 20 and 23 inches (50–57 cm) were caught and released. One of the 23-inch grayling was caught by a fly fisherman with a 'catch-and-release net' that had a weighing balance in the handle: it weighed 4 lbs (1.8 kg). No fish were killed during the season.

The Season on the Idsjöströmmen

The Gim river flows through land that is very rich in chalk, and the pH value is 8.1. The Idsjöströmmen section of the river is one mile long and a fairly shallow stream, which makes it particularly good for fishing the dry fly, the north-country wet fly and the nymph. During the season, there are large hatches of up-winged flies, sedges and stone-flies. The fishing season on the Idsjöströmmen lasts from 1 June to 30 September.

June – the month of the upwinged fly

June on the Idsjöströmmen can be described as the month of the upwinged fly. The first to appear is the Large Dark Olive of spring, a promising sight, and a confirmation that the fishing season has started. Then comes the Iron Blue dun, and a little later the Pale Watery and the Small Spurwing. The English classic the Blue Winged Olive (BWO) is not alone on the Idsjöströmmen; she has her cousins with her, *Ephemerella aurivilli*, which is bigger than BWO and *Ephemerella mucronata*, which is very small. The Large Summer Dun, *Siphlonurus astivalis* and *Siphlonurus aestivalis*, are somewhat mysterious to me, because I have never seen one of their nymphs or duns during my 25 years on the Idsjöströmmen. However, the number of spinners in the air above the bridge on warm summer evenings, can be absolutely astonishing. The conspicuous *Heptagenia sulphurea*, the Yellow May Dun, hatches in small numbers, and one never sees swarms of spinners. Other Heptagenia members are *H. darlecarlica*, and *H. fuscogrisea*. The biggest of all the upwinged flies, the Mayfly, *Ephemera danica*, hatches during the last week of June and the first week of July.

Throughout the month the ever-present stone-flies, the prime proof of a healthy river, are hatching. They are the Medium Stone-Fly, Yellow Sally, the Small Yellow Sally and the Small Brown. The nymphs should be tied heavily weighted, and fished deep. The most fruitful, and also the most enjoyable, thing to do is to fish a dry fly during those beautiful, sunny and windless afternoons when thousands of females fly out over the water to lay their eggs while bouncing and fluttering on the surface.

An excellent, but simple, dry fly that I tie and fish on those occasions has an olive green body of musk-rat fur, one long blue dun cock hackle and one long grizzle cock hackle, palmered together. My idea when I fist tied this fly was

Lars Olsson, the river keeper of the Idsjöströmmen River

LEIF MILLING

274

that, from the grayling's point of view, the two blended hackles would look like the four long wings of the stone-fly as it jumps and flutters on the surface during egg-laying.

On gloomy, overcast, rainy and cold days, the hatches of Baetis can be huge and last from 11 o'clock in the morning until late afternoon. On such days, the Large Dark Olives, the Iron Blues, the BWOs and the Yellow May Duns hatch at the same time, and the grayling will rise and feed on them the whole day long. It is a fly-fisherman's dream come true.

A good representation of the hatching duns will be necessary, because the more duns there are on the water, the more selective the grayling are. Nymphs representing the olives will be needed, too, and north-country wet flies in grey and olive colours, like the Waterhen Bloa.

The controversial Yellow May Dun is actually taken, but the nymphs seldom are, since the dun hatches under the surface. The legs are ready, as well as the tails and the body, but the wings look like two thin, grey, wet dishrags. The hatches are never big; one dun appears here, another there, and very often the grayling feed on the emergers. A Frenchman fishing on the Idsjöströmmen one wet June day caught and killed a nice, steely grey 17-inch grayling, and when we opened the stomach and poured the contents into a bowl of water I understood why my dry-fly fishing that morning had failed. We could see 40 emergers, but not one dun! The grayling had been taking the emergers just under the surface, sometimes showing part of their bodies during the rise, making me believe that they were rising to flies on the surface.

LARS OLSSON

River Dauvaeatnu, Lapland

July – The Month of the Sedge

July is the month of the sedge, and Hydropsyche and Rhyacophilia dominate the scene. Even if the first ones show up at the end of June, the peak of the hatch will occur during the first half of July. Everything else that hatches during this period will be rendered invisible by the incredible number of sedges with egglaying females active in the afternoon and pupae at night between 10 p.m. and 3 a.m. If it is warm enough and there is no wind the females behave exactly like their colleagues, the stone flies. They come back to the river, and, jumping up and down on the surface, release their eggs.

During July very few fish will rise during the day (unless egg-laying takes place). Some fishermen ask why there are no rising fish. A little basic knowledge of entomology would tell them that, since it is July, most of the up-winged flies are gone, and even if a few are still hatching, during this warm period, it takes no more than the blink of an eye for the nymph to split its shuck, transform into a dun and lift from the surface.

August – The Month of Red Tag

August is the month of the Red Tag, a favourite dry or wet fly from the days of Mr Walbran, and Mr Flynn. The insect life is now like the Swedish 'smörgåsbord' – it seems as if everything or nothing hatches; no insect dominates, and the grayling feed on up-winged flies, sedges, stone-flies and all kinds of terrestrials. The river is low and warm, but the fishing is challenging and interesting. The lonely Red Tag with its 'red' palmer hackle and scarlet tag is a very visible bright spot on the surface under the clear blue August sky.

The north-country wet fly, which could not compete during the massive hatches of sedges in July is now back again. The grey- or olive-bodied grey-hackled spider, fished two or three on a long 14-foot leader with a 9-foot rod and a double-tapered No. 4 line, is a perfect weapon for August's low, clear water.

September – The Month of the Small Up-winged Fly

September, the last month of the fishing year on the Idsjöströmmen, is again a month of the up-winged flies. They are small now (sized 18–20), the autumn generation of the Large Dark Olive, the Iron Blue Dun and the little BWO species (*Ephemerella mucronata*). As in June, the best weather for hatches is when the days are grey and rather cold, although the hatches are unpredictable. Some days look perfect, but they are not. Other days look similar, and suddenly after midday the hatch starts. Other September days have no hatches at all but a very rare fall of spinners in sizes 20–22.

LEIF MILLING

A leash of grayling for the River Riman

The stoneflies, those proofs of a healthy river, are abundant throughout the fishing year. From the early days of April, with the *Taeniopteryx*, to the last days of October and the *Leuctra*, the Idsjöströmmen has a long and interesting relationship with stoneflies. Most of them are big, slow, clumsy in flight and easy to distinguish from up-winged flies and sedges. Grayling and trout take them as nymphs and fluttering surface flies.

After the fishing season the grayling move up into the Idsjön lake to winter, and the stream rests for eight months – until one day in May, I can again see them from the bridge. Dark shadows on the spawning grounds, males chasing off males, pursuing the females ready to fold their long dorsal fins over their slender bodies when the time comes ...

Grayling and the Gourmet

E.M. Broughton

WHILE PREJUDICE IN this country against grayling as worthy prey has largely been overcome, doubts still seem to remain in many minds as to their culinary worth. Carter Platts in his *Grayling Fishing* quotes several authoritative fishermen, of his time and earlier, who praise highly the eating qualities of the grayling, and both he and they are right. When Izaak Walton remarked 'This dish of meat is too good for any but anglers, or very honest men', his mind had wandered from the pike confronting him to the grayling he had recently consumed, I am sure.

Carter Platts goes on to quote at some length a method of cooking the fish that he read about in a *Fishing Gazette* of the early 1930s by Egan Krall-Kralsberg of Vienna, a method apparently practised on the banks of Alpine grayling streams, the resultant delicacy being known in Bavaria as *steckerlfisch*. A stick is threaded through the prepared grayling and speared into the ground so that it is held over a pyramid of sticks in a hot fire, where, being turned from time to time, it is left until cooked. As you may guess, this is a very good way of dealing with the day's catch by those hardy fishermen who eat and sleep beneath the stars.

Those of us, however, whose grayling are more likely to have been caught during a day's or weekend's brief trip to the river, must do what we can in the kitchen, and in fact we can do very well with our silver lady. She has a firmer paler flesh than the trout, but eaten fresh, as all fish should be, she has a delicate flavour of her own. The grayling must be descaled. Set about this gently, using the blunt back of a knife, not the sharp edge of the blade, for you do not want to tear the skin or bruise the flesh. Work from tail to head. This accomplished, remove both tail and head, gut it, wash well and dry thoroughly.

To *fry or grill* is perhaps the best method of all of cooking the grayling. Season, lightly flour (or sprinkle with oatmeal to give crunchy crust) then using plenty of butter and a gentle heat, either pan-fry or grill the fish, turning it carefully when the first side is browned. Depending on the size, this will take anything from 5–10 minutes. When ready, lift gently on to a warmed plate. Squeeze juice from half a lemon into the tasty residues in the pan, reheat and pour over your grayling. You will now savour its full, delicious flavour.

If you prefer a *fat-free* recipe, try the following. Grate the rind from one lime and one lemon and reserve it. Squeeze the juices into a shallow dish and place strips of filleted grayling in them. Leave to marinate for at least 2 hours. Season with salt and pepper, cover with buttered foil or greaseproof paper, and bake in a moderate over 350–375°F, 180–190°C or Gas Mark 4/5, for 20–30 minutes. Serve with the juices and garnish with the peels.

You will surely enjoy a *pickled* grayling if you like soused herring. Arrange strips of filleted grayling in a dish. Sprinkle with a heaped table-spoon of finely choppd dill or fennel, a grated medium-sized onion and about a 3-inch segment of cucumber peeled and grated. Combine ¼ pint (150 ml) cider vinegar with 2 rounded teaspoons salt and the same of brown sugar. Thoroughly mix into it 3 tablespoons olive oil. Pour over the fish, turning it over several times to make sure the flesh is well coated, leave to marinate overnight or for at least 12 hours – 24 hours is better.

Stuffings add substance. Their ingredients are a matter of taste, ranging from traditional forcemeat to more adventurous and spicy kinds.

Herbs such as dill, fennel, parsley, tarragon, coriander, or whatever herb you will, all are flavour enhancers.

On both sides of the grayling make two or three 1-inch long slashes. Beat plenty of your chopped chosen herb into softened butter and fill the cavities with this. Leave for as long as you have time before cooking, or overnight, so that the flavour may permeate the flesh. Then fry, grill or bake, serving with lemon wedges and the buttery juices.

An alternative method to this is to brush the inside of the grayling with melted butter or oil, stuff it generously with plenty of herbs, 'sew' together the flaps of the opening with a couple of cocktail sticks and leave for the flavours to develop. Finally, brush with butter or oil, season, and grill, fry or bake as preferred. Serve after removing both the sticks and the cooked herbs, garnishing with fresh sprigs and lemon wedges.

Mushrooms. Chop some streaky bacon rashers and a small onion and fry gently over a very low heat in 1 oz (25 g) butter until the onion is transparent but not browned. Add chopped or halved small button mushrooms to this and continue cooking until they too are softened. Now add 1 tablespoon fresh breadcrumbs and 1 teaspoon chopped fennel or tarragon. Moisten if necessary with a little cream or crème fraîche.

There are obvious variations to this recipe, using whatever herb you choose, parsley being the favourite as it is most easily obtainable. Leave out the bacon/onion. Add a small amount of finely shredded horseradish (I think this is very good). Adapt as you think fit.

Cheese. Grated Cheddar cheese, oatmeal instead of breadcrumbs if preferred, mixed chopped chives and parsley, all added to the basic chopped onion melted in butter, with a dash of Worcester sauce, produces another tasty combination.

Nuts. Soften a chopped onion in butter. Add 2 oz (50 g) cooked rice, 1 oz (25 g) chopped nuts (dry-roast peanuts, walnuts, pecan), 1½ tablespoons chopped chives and parsley. Bind with the yolk of an egg. Season well, place in cavity, cook as usual.

More exotic. Sprinkle the cavity with chopped coriander or fennel. Combine with a 1-inch stick fresh grated ginger, half a crushed clove of garlic, 2 tablespoons fresh breadcrumbs, 1 oz (25 g) melted butter and a generous squeeze of lemon juice and stuff the cavity with this mixture. Brush fish with butter or oil and cook as desired.

Here is a pleasant accompaniment to grilled grayling. *Tomatoes.* 'Core' a large tomato. Stuff the cavity with a lump of butter into which plenty of chopped basil has been beaten, so that the 'plug' is really green. Brush both tomato and fish with melted butter or oil and grill both together till the grayling is nicely browned on both sides and the tomato thoroughly softened.

Some sauces that go well with grayling

Green mayonnaise

Finely chop 2 tablespoons parsley, 1 teaspoon lovage (for its celery-like flavour), thyme and chives, and 1 teaspoon of fennel and dill. Stir 2 tablespoons dill, fennel or tarragon vinegar into ½ pint (300 ml) mayonnaise. Now add the chopped herbs and the sieved yolk of a hard-boiled egg, and if liked, the white of the egg either also sieved or finely chopped. Mix all thoroughly together and leave for the flavours to develop.

This mayonnaise is delicious not only with grilled or fried grayling, but also with smoked grayling fillets.

White Sauces

With nuts

Soften a chopped medium-sized onion in 1 oz (25 g) of butter. Stir in 1 level tablespoon of flour over a low heat. Into ¼ pint (150 ml) of milk blend 2 tablespoons of dry-roasted peanuts or walnuts, 2 tablespoons of choppped coriander leaves, and 1 tablespoon of coriander seeds. Pour slowly into the flour mixture to make a thick sauce. Then still pouring slowly add ¼ pint (150 ml) cream to it, and stir continuously until the sauce is smooth and rich. Season well. I am told that the addition of turmeric or curry powder to this recipe adds bite, but too strong a flavour in the sauce destroys the delicate flavour of the fish.

With mushrooms

To a good white sauce add chopped or halved mushrooms that have been softened in butter, with a good squeeze of lemon juice to sharpen the taste, and a tablespoon of chopped parsley. Season well.

With cucumber

Grate a 3-inch piece of cucumber, sprinkle with salt and leave for 10–15 minutes, then drain and pat it dry. Make a rich white sauce, using ¼ pint (150 ml) milk and ¼ pint (150 ml) cream, ½ oz (15 g) butter and 1 level tablespoon flour, salt and pepper, stirring over a low heat till smooth and thickened. Stir in about 2 fl.oz (60 ml) dry white wine, a heaped teaspoon crushed dill or fennel seeds and 2 tablespoons finely chopped dill tops or fennel leaves. Finally add the grated cucumber and reheat for 2 or 3 minutes.

Smoked grayling

Home-smoking equipment has become a commonplace item among anglers today, whether for hot or cold smoking. And smoked grayling is a really appetizing delicacy.

Filleted or on the bone, served with lemon juice generously squeezed over it and eaten with buttered brown bread, it makes a delicious first course, or a satisfying lunch.

It is equally good served with lemon juice, black pepper and a helping of sour cream or crème fraîche. See also green mayonnaise.

Smoked grayling pâté

This is more or less the same recipe as I have always used for trout pâté. In a food processor put about 1 lb (500 g) smoked flesh, making sure all the skin and bones have been removed. Add 3 oz (90 g) butter, freshly ground black pepper, a good grating of nutmeg, 3 fl. oz (90 ml) cream and the juice of half a lemon. Finely grated horseradish is an optional extra. Blend well until smooth. Leave to get cold and firm.

My experience of grayling is limited to those caught in the Yorkshire Dales, the Ure, the Ribble and the Hodder, the Welsh Dee, the Derbyshire Derwent and Wye, and in the chalkstreams of the south where they were once so despised. Whether the taste and flavour of grayling from rivers outside England and Wales differ from those of our native streams, I do not know. But I am very sure that there are many anglers of many nationalities catching and cooking grayling in many ways that excel my modest attempts. Nevertheless, I hope that the few suggestions I have made may encourage those anglers who enjoy the excitement of the catch also to enjoy the cooking and eating of it.

Appendix I: Fishing and Accommodation Outside Britain

Austria

Michael Hofmaier advises that day tickets on many of the best beats may need detailed advance planning. A state licence, issued by the federal Province, is required as well as permission from the riparian owner.

Austrian National Tourist Office
14 Cork Street
London W1X 1PF
Tel: 020 7629 0461
Fax: 020 7499 6038
E-mail: infoetanto.co.uk
Website: www.austria-tourism.at/

There has been a serious attempt to help the travelling angler, and the Tourist Office now offers a booklet on angling, information on rivers and accommodation – unfortunately not translated into English.

Casting Club Gesäuse
Gasthof Gesäuse
A-8913 Gstatterboden

Apply here for fishing on the Enns in a breathtakingly beautiful gorge. The club will also pass on enquiries to the casting clubs in Steyr (Upper Austria), Klagenfurt and Spittal (both in Carinthia).

Forstverwaltung Traunstein
Klosterplatz 1
A-4810 Gmunden

This address is for the reaches of the Traun near Gmunden, though the river
– famous though it is – is a mere shadow of what it was ten years ago.

>Gemeindeamt Grünburg
>A-4594 Grünburg Nr. 63

Apply here for a magnificent beat on the Steyr.

>Österreichische Fischereigesellschaft
>Elisabethstrasse 22
>A-1010 Vienna

Founded in 1880, this is the oldest and best-known fishing association in
Austria. It administers one of the finest beats on the Steyr, near Pichlern, the
famous Salza beat at Gschöder and numerous smaller streams in the Alpine
foothills of Lower Austria.

Belgium and the Ardennes

>Commisariat Général du Tourisme, Région Wallonne, C.G.T.
>Place de Wallonnie 1, Bât. 111
>5100 Jambes (Namur)
>Tel: 00 32 81 333111; 00 32 81 334022

>Office de Promotion du Tourisme Wallonie-Bruxelles O.P.T.
>Grasmarkt 61
>1000 Brussels
>Tel: 00 32 2 5040390
>Fax: 00 32 2 5136950

Canada and Alaska

>Guide Outfitters Association of British Columbia
>PO Box 94675
>Richmond, BC
>Canada V6Y 4A4
>Tel: 001 604 278 2688

>Travel Arctic Government of the Northwest Territories
>PO Box 1320
>Yellowknife
>Northwest Territories X1A 2L9
>Canada

Travel Arctic will provide complete information for the Northwest Territories, the heartland of North American grayling.

Denmark

Danish Tourist Board
55 Sloane Street
London SW1X 9SY
Tel: 020 7259 5959
Fax: 020 7259 5955

The Danish Tourist Office in London gives detailed advice on fishing and accommodation, but it does not appear to have heard of grayling, a point which has been brought to its notice.

France

French Government Tourist Office
178 Piccadilly
London W1V OAL
Tel: 020 7493 6594

The Tourist Officer is extremely helpful and will give written information on the classification of waters, close seasons and the licences necessary. There are guides specifically for angling, printed in English, with fishery information and addresses of accommodation, both generally throughout France and for specific regions, such as Lorraine.

There are guides on self-catering Gîtes de Pêche setting out the rents of places within a 15-mile radius.

Small rural inns and the Hôtels Relais-Saint-Pierre will give advice on local fishing and cook your catch free of charge. Information on the latter may be obtained from:

Hôtels Relais-Saint-Pierre
Hotel du Département
25035 Besançon

Germany

Eifel Region

Ferdinand van der Assen advises that information on fishing and accommodation may be obtained from:

Touristik-Service Eifel (Südeifel)
Triererstrasse 1
54634 Bitburg
Tel: 00 49 6561 94340
Fax: 00 49 6561 94320

Touristinformation Hocheifel/Nürnburgring
Markt 11
53474 Bad Neuenahr-Ahrweiler
Tel: 00 49 2641 977350
Fax: 00 49 2641 977373
E-mail: TOUR-ARE@t.online.de

Robert Thomas makes the following suggestions for anglers visiting Germany. They are either hotels or towns which cater for anglers and offer access to good grayling fishing with the convenience of arranging the necessary licences.

Blau (Hotel Blautal, near Ulm)

This modern 90-room hotel just outside Ulm offers special arrangements for fly-fishing visitors. Fishing, on around 2 km of the River Blau, is for brown, rainbow and brook trout and grayling. Season from 1 April until 31 December. Fly (barbless hooks) only; no wading. Tackle as on the Pegnitz. Excellent mayfly hatches usually during the first two weeks of June.

Tickets cost DM 45.00 per day; the fishing is owned by the Angelgeräte Förg tackle shop in Ulm.

Hotel Blautal
Ulmerstrasse 4/1
89134 Blaustein
Tel: 00 49 7304 9590
Fax: 00 49 7304 959400

Angelgeräte Förg
Tel: 00 49 731 552743
Fax: 00 49 731 552542

Nagold (Bad Liebenzell)

The town of Bad Liebenzell, on the northern edge of the Black Forest, is an excellent base for exploring the region and offers a good variety of accommodation at reasonable prices, as well as two stretches of the River Nagold (one above and the other below the town) with a total length of around 5 km. Tickets (DM 35.00 per day) are available from the Tourist Office, which will also arrange accommodation and the necessary state visitor's licence. Tickets are limited, so advance booking is advised.

Season from 1 April (trout) to 30 Sept. Fly (barbless hooks) only. Mainly brown trout and grayling, some rainbow. The river here is between 10 and 18 metres wide; rods of around 8 ft, class 5/6, will be fine.

Tourist Office: Tel: 00 49 7052 4080
Fishery Manager (Hermann Rebmann) Tel: 00 49 7052 50162

Pegnitz (Velden)

In the Fränkische Schweiz, one of the most attractive areas of Germany, and within easy reach of Nuremberg, Velden offers excellent food and accommodation at very reasonable prices. The Pegnitz flows through the village, and enormous trout and grayling can be raised by dropping bread into the water from the main road bridge. The Tourist Office next to the bridge will issue all the necessary licences to guests who stay a minimum of three nights in the village.

The water, around 1.5 km long and 10 to 15 metres wide, is slow-flowing character apart from at the top end, where there is some faster water. Rods of around 7–8 ft, class 5, will be ample. Wading is neither allowed nor practical, as the water can be covered easily from the bank. Brown trout and grayling; fly (barbless hooks) only.

Tourist Office (Frau Regelein) Tel: 00 49 911 23360

Weisse Regen (Hotel 'Fischerstüberl' Höcherl, near Kötzing)

In the beautiful Bayerische Wald, halfway between Regensburg and the Czech border, the 'Fischerstüberl' Höcherl is a 24-room hotel specializing in catering for anglers. It owns fishing rights to around 6 km of the Weisse Regen, and the stretch is reserved for hotel residents. Tickets cost DM 30.00 per day (DM 65.00 for three days, DM 120.00 for a week); bed and breakfast costs DM 25.00 per night.

The season is from 15 April to 31 October. Fly (barbless hooks) only. Chest waders are recommended in places. The river is between 10 and 20 metres wide, and rods of 8–9 ft, class 5/6, are recommended.

You may catch brown, rainbow and brook trout, grayling and – if you are very lucky – huchen. The huchen, sometimes called Danube salmon in English, is the largest non-migratory European salmonid and can reach weights of up to 50 kg and a length of 150 cm. It is found only in rivers of the Danube system, where it tends to reside in deep holes in fast water, swallowing any fish that crosses its path. It is unlikely to take a fly; most huchen fishermen use heavy spinning tackle with a weighted 'Huchenzopf' (resembling a rubber squid), which is dragged through the bottom of known huchen holes.

Hotel 'Fischerstüberl' Höcherl
Pulling 12
93476 Blaibach
Tel: 00 49 9941 8161

Italy

A lot of useful information is in the annual 'Travellers' Handbook', available from:

The Italian State Tourist Board
Princess Street
London W1R 8AY
Tel: 09001 600280
Fax: 020 7493 6695

It is full of important non-fishing items, such as train and air travel information, various interesting festivals and advice on tipping (especially useful if you go to the cinema) and there is a small section on fresh-water fishing. Interestingly, the rod licence costs the same whether you use a reel for your line or not.

The best advice is to ask your travel agent or contact the Provincial Tourist Board of your chosen area for more detailed fishing information.

Mongolia

Frontiers
18 Albemarle Street
London W1X 3HA
Tel: 020 7493 0798
Fax: 020 7629 5569

Angling Travel
Orchard House
Gunton Hall
Hamworth
Norfolk NR1I 7HI
Tel/Fax: 01263 761602

Norway

Norwegian Tourist Board
5th Floor
Charles House
5 Lower Regent Street
London SW1Y 4LR
Tel: 020 7839 2650
Fax: 020 7839 6014

The Norwegian Tourist Office in London gives detailed advice on fishing and accommodation, but it does not appear to have heard of grayling, a point which has been brought to its notice.

Jan Kvil
Klara Camping
N-2420 Trysil

Russia

Roxton Bailey Robinson Worldwide
25 High Street
Hungerford
Berkshire RG17 ONF
Tel: 01488 689700
Fax: 01488 689730

Frontiers International
18 Albemarle Street
London W1X 3HA
Tel: 020 7493 0798

Michael Evans & Co
Little Saxby's Farm
Cowden
Kent TN8 7DX
Tel: 01342 850765
Fax: 01342 850926

Go Fishing
2 Oxford House
24 Oxford Road North
London W4 4DH
Tel: 020 8742 1556
Fax: 020 8742 4331

Northern Sweden and Lapland

Lars Olsson can be most helpful, and his two addresses are:

Sweden:

> Gimdalen 1426
> Bräcke 840 60
> Tel: 00 46 693 13056
> Fax: 00 46 693 13026
> E-mail: olsson@scandiwestflyfishing.com
> Website: www.scandiwestflyfishing.com

USA:

> PO Box 132
> Bozeman
> Montana 59771
> Tel: 00 1 406 587 5140
> Fax: 00 1 406 585 9625
> E-mail: olsson@scandiwestflyfishing.com
> Website: www.scandiwestflyfishing.com

Further information about grayling fishing in *Lapland* can be obtained from:
(for the southern county of Lapland):

> Västerbottens Länsturistnämnd
> Box 317
> S-901 07 Umea
> Sweden

(for the northern county of Lapland):

> Norrbottens Turistrad/Nordkalottresor
> Sandviksgat 53
> 951 32 Lulea
> Sweden

Appendix II: Biographies

Ferdinand von der Assen lives in Voorschoten near The Hague and works in the field of nature conservation for the Ministry of Agriculture, Nature Management and Fisheries. He is also the Dutch representative on the International Whaling Commission. He took up fly fishing thirty years ago, starting with dry-fly fishing for rudd in the canals near his home, which was soon followed by trips to Germany and Ireland in search of trout and grayling. He has also fished for large trout in Chile and New Zealand and for salmon in Canada and Russia, but loves to go back to the Eifel region in Germany to fish for the smaller grayling as often as he can.

R.B. Broughton, now retired from his single-handed medical practice in Salford, is a furniture-maker, wood-carver, painter with several exhibitions to his credit, and has been fascinated by life in water ever since discovering that a Dytiscus beetle and tadpoles do not live happily together in the same jam jar.

He was a founder member and first Chairman of the Grayling Society, and is now its President. He is on the executive committees of the Ribble, Lune & Wyre, and South and West Cumbria Fisheries Associations, and is a founder member and trustee of the Ribble Catchment Conservation Trust and the Cumbria Rivers Foundation and Chairman and founder member of the north-west branch of the Institute of Fisheries Management. He is Chairman of the Lancashire Fly Fishers Association and a member of several other fly-fishing clubs in northern England and Cornwall.

He is Chairman of the Lancashire Branch of the Salmon & Trout Association and is its Water Quality Officer.

He is a member of the Fly Dressers' Guild and contributes articles to the angling press, as well as occasional chapters and drawings of grayling in his friends' books.

E.M. Broughton a schoolteacher, has a flourishing family, and is an angler of considerable merit. With a strong and intelligent interest in the cooking of food and its presentation, she is not afraid to experiment with new dishes, her husband being the first to evaluate each new creation to his great pleasure.

Rod Calbrade has fished for 35 years and caught his first grayling at Addingham on the Wharfe in 1970. After a 25-year career in the advertising industry he retired in 1991 to learn photography, to travel and to have more time for fishing.

He has travelled extensively, catching many species of fish, both fresh- and salt-water, though latterly, as a member of Lancashire Fly Fishers and Prince Albert Fishing Clubs, he has concentrated on the native trout, salmon and grayling species at home. He has had several articles and photographs published in the game-fishing magazines, especially in *Trout and Salmon*, *Trout Fisherman* and *Flyfishing and Flytying*. He has recently become Editor of the *Grayling Society Journal*.

Stanislaw Cios was educated as an economist but became a diplomat by profession and is now serving in Helsinki. He is also a fly fisherman, hydro-biologist and aquatic entomologist and has a special interest in the feeding patterns of salmonids and in their external parasites (he discovered two new species of leach – *Ichthyobdella ciosi* and *Piscicola polonica*). Material from his detailed study of the stomachs of over 1,400 grayling from various European waters (Italy, Slovenia, Slovak Republic, Poland, Finland) has already been published or is in course of publication. He is also interested in the history of angling (in particular fly fishing), curious methods of fishing and the history of the fish hook, and is working on books on these issues). His *What Does the Trout Eat?* was published in 1992 (in Polish).

He is a fly-fishing instructor in Poland and has twice lectured at Roberto Pragliola's Italian School of Fly Fishing. Since 1996 he has been Polish Area Secretary of the Grayling Society of Great Britain. He contributes to the *Journal of the Grayling Society* and has also contributed to Italian angling journals, to *Truites, Ombres et Saumon* in France, and to a journal in Finland. He is Editor of the only Polish fly-fishing journal/newsletter, *Pstrig & Lipien* (*Trout & Grayling*) founded in 1993. Since 1982 he has taken part in many fly-fishing competitions in Poland, and was Polish team champion in 1993.

John S. Davison was born in Sheffield and studied Law at Sheffield University. He is currently Principal Crown Prosecutor with the Crown Prosecution Service in Wakefield. He has fished for 35 years, mainly in

Yorkshire and Derbyshire, but also in Alaska, New Zealand, Sweden, Japan and the Bahamas. A member of Myddleton, Huddersfield and Wakefield Metropolitan Angling Clubs and the Pickering Fishery Association, John is also a Salmon & Trout Association National Instructor. He was Editor of the *Grayling Society Journal* from 1989 to 1998.

Ross Gardiner is a fisheries scientist at the Freshwater Fisheries Laboratory at Pitlochry in the Scottish Highlands, where his work is mainly concerned with the biology of young salmon in rivers. A keen grayling angler, he is a founder member and the Scientific Officer of the Grayling Society.

Michael Hofmaier, who died in 1997, was born in Styria and studied Law at Graz and Vienna Universities. He became a Senior Civil Servant in Vienna. Until his last illness he loved to stay with his English wife Wendy in their cottage in Lower Austria, where he spent as much time as possible on the rivers. He was a regular contributor to the German angling journal *Der Fliegenfischer* and was a member of the Fly Fishers' Club in London.

Naïl Jones is now head of an extremely busy commercial consulate covering the north-west Pacific, which includes Alaska. Ironically, he is living near the best of salmon, trout and grayling waters in North America, but never has the time to pick up a fly rod. Fortunately, he was more relaxed when he was in Mongolia.

Hans van Klinken lives in Harskamp, a little village in the centre of Holland, and works for the Dutch Army, commanding a large simulation system. At the age of 6, he began bait fishing in a lowland brook. On holiday with his family in Norway seven years later, he caught his first salmon (9 kg) and in 1971 he began fishing for Atlantic salmon and Arctic char; by 16 he was travelling alone to fish in Scandinavia and spent most of his spare time in northern Norway, Sweden and Finland. His greatest outdoor experience was in 1975 when he spent almost 4 months in northern Lapland, learning how to survive in the forest and on the tundra, his teacher an old Lap. They communicated with their hands and feet. Hans began fly tying in 1976 and by the 1980s was creating his own designs, mostly parachutes, and later came to recognise the value of flies such as nymphs, streamers and emergers. His best-known patterns are given in this book; less well-known is his productive series of salmon patterns, many of them dry flies.

He has travelled in Ireland, the UK, Germany, Belgium, Luxembourg,

France, Switzerland, Canada and the USA, and he has given classes. In 1981 he and his wife moved to north Germany. He joined the editorial staff of the *Dutch Flyfishing* magazine, became the Dutch Area Secretary for the Grayling Society, and began lecturing and holding fly-tying demonstrations and workshops. He has written for several international and club magazines and contributed to several books, such as *The World's Best Trout Flies* by John Roberts, *Fly Tyers Masterclass* by Oliver Edwards and *Modern Atlantic Salmon Flies* by Paul Marriner.

Hugo Martel's fly fishing started on the River Bocq, where he fished for more than twenty years with his late father. He became a member of the Grayling Society in the 1980s, and Claire Pickover persuaded him to become the first European Area Secretary; he is now a lifetime Honorary Member. Hugo has fished in most European grayling rivers and has experience of fly fishing in Russia, Canada and the USA. He contributes regularly to fishing magazines, and his book *Vlagzalm & Vliegvissen* (*Grayling & Flyfishing*) was published in 1998.

Patrick Michiel lives with his wife and three children on a hobby farm in British Columbia's Peace River County, within sight of the northern Rockies. He began freelance writing in 1987 after a 10-year stint as a newspaper editor, but after twenty years as an outdoor writer retired and now works as Executive Director of a non-profit society working to assist handicapped people in community living. As a graduate biologist, he wrote mainly about natural history topics and issues. He and his family spend much of their leisure time watching moose, deer and bear in their front yard, and fishing, hunting, skiing and canoeing.

Robin Mulholland was born and brought up in County Durham, and learnt his grayling fishing on the Tees. As a Civil Servant with the Agricultural Development and Advisory Service, he was transferred to Skipton, from where he fished the Hodder, the Ribble, the Wharfe and the Ure. He has spent the last twenty years in the south of England, fishing the chalk streams of Hampshire and Wiltshire. He is an enthusiastic fly-dresser and bantam breeder and has been Chairman of the Grayling Society since 1995.

Louis Noble lives in Wrexham, North Wales, and is a factory manager in the clothing industry. Shropshire born and bred, he started coarse fishing at an early age on the Severn, but since then has for many years pursued trout and grayling with a fly rod. He has held local or national positions with the Grayling Society, the Fly Dressers' Guild and the Salmon & Trout Association and is also a member of the Association of Professional Game Angling Instructors.

Lars Olsson has fished for grayling, trout and arctic char for 41 years and taught fly fishing, fly casting and fly tying in Scandinavia for 30 years. He has written numerous articles about fly fishing for Swedish magazines; his first book *Ur Min Flugask* (*From my Fly-Book*) appeared in 1984, and his second, *Flugfiske i Fjallen* (*Fly Fishing in Lapland*) in 1989. He is currently working on his third book.

He learned nymph fishing from the legendary Frank Sawyer on the Wiltshire Avon during the 1970s and has fished in England for many years. Since 1976 he has been working on the restoration of the Gim River and has been a river keeper on the Idsjöströmmen below the village of Gimdalen in northern Sweden since 1989, when he leased the river and started the first catch-and-release water in Scandinavia. During June, July, August and September he guides and teaches fly fishing in Sweden, together with his American wife Jennifer, an author and former professional fishing guide in Montana and Yellowstone National Park. He also lectures and demonstrates fly casting in Sweden and the USA.

He ties and sells his Gim River flies, which he designed after 25 years of checking the stomach contents of grayling and trout and using a window trap on the Idsjöströmmen. He lives in Montana, USA, from October to May.

Raymond Rocher was born in Lyons but brought up in Haute-Loire and the Rhône valley, where there are many trout streams. After World War II he spent two years in London teaching French and completing his English studies at the French Institute. From 1953 until 1989 he was a high-school teacher in various regions of France, finally retiring near his beloved Lycée of Touron, the oldest in France, where he was a student during the war and later for many years an English teacher.

He has been a very keen fly fisher in France, Britain and Europe, numbering Frank Sawyer and Oliver Kite among his fishing friends, and is, as well, a prolific writer, with a number of fly-fishing books to his credit and various articles in French and English fishing magazines. He still fishes with fly regularly in France and Austria.

Antonio Sabbadini was born, and still lives, in Friuli, in the north-east corner of Italy, bordering Austria and Yugoslavia. He graduated in veterinary studies in 1954, having from childhood been interested in zoology, entomology and botany. He started fly fishing and fly tying in 1945 and since then has pursued these interests passionately at home and abroad, alongside his active engagement in research and study of freshwater biology and in promoting better fishery management. He has written a number of journal articles, technical or scientific reviews and reports. He is a member, among other bodies, of the Italian Entomological Society, the Italian Natural Sciences Society, the Institute of Fisheries Management, the American Fisheries Society, the Fisheries Society of the British Isles, the Thymallus Society and, from its beginning, of the Grayling Society.

Neil Sinclair is an operational officer in the Strathclyde Fire Brigade, and one of the original members of the Grayling Society. He has fished extensively for the species in Scotland and further afield (often in the company of the late Reg Righyni) and is a tackle fanatic and an enthusiastic amateur engineer. During the season he is a regular participant in competitive trout fishing, but in winter he is to be found in single-minded pursuit of the grayling, regularly employing the innovative 'pole' technique he describes in the book.

Robert Thomas learnt to fish for trout on the streams of his native South Wales after inheriting his father's old split-cane spinning rod. He has travelled widely in Australia, Africa, Israel and Europe. He has lived in Germany since 1977, and is the Grayling Society Area Secretary for Germany, as well as being a member of the British Embassy, Bonn, Fly Fishing Syndicate. He still fishes for trout and bass in Wales, where he has a cottage that he uses when he has a chance. He runs his own business supplying aviation repair materials to airlines and repair companies throughout the world.

Bibliography

Bainbridge, G.C. *The Fly Fisher's Guide*, 4th ed. (Longman, Rees Orme, Brown, Green and Longman, 1840).

Best, Thomas *A Concise Treatise on the Art of Angling* (C. Stalker & H. Turpin, 1787).

Bowlker, Charles *The Art of Angling* (Longman, Rees, 1833).

Carter Platts, W. *Grayling Fishing* (A. & C. Black, 1939).

Courtney Williams, A. *A Dictionary of Trout Flies* (A. & C. Black, 1950).

Cross, Tom *Jim Wynn's Recommended Flies for the River Wharfe* (Waltonian's Angling Club, 1992).

Edwards, Oliver *Oliver Edwards' Flytyers Masterclass* (Merlin Unwin, 1994).

Foster, D. *The Scientific Angler* (Bemrose, 1886).

Jackson, J. *The Practical Fly-Fisher* (John Stark, 1888).

Lawrie, W.H. *A Reference Book of English Trout Flies* (Pelham, 1967).

— *Modern Trout Flies* (Macdonald, 1972).

Leighton, Michael *Trout Flies of Shropshire and the Welsh Borderland* (Redvers, 1987).

Pritt, T.E. *Yorkshire Trout Flies* (Goodall & Suddick, 1885); 2nd ed.

— *North Country Flies* (Sampson Low, Marston, Searle & Rivington 1886).

— *The Book of the Grayling* (Goodall and Suddick, 1888).

Righyni, R.V. *Grayling* (Macdonald, 1968).

Roberts, G. *The Grayling Angler* (Witherby, 1982).

Ronalds, A. *The Fly-Fisher's Entomology* (Longman, Brown, Green and Longman, 1844).

Skues, E.M. *The Way of a Trout with a Fly* (A. & C. Black, 1955).

Rolt, H.A. *Grayling Fishing in South Country Streams* (Sampson, Low Marston, 1901).

Stewart, W.C. *The Practical Angler* (A. & C. Black, 1950).

Theakston, M. *British Angling Flies* (William Harrison, 1883).

Townsend, D.C. *Fly Tying with Harold Howarth* (A. & C. Black, 1980).

Walbran, F.M. *Walbran's British Angler* (Simpkin, Marshall, 1889).

Woolley, R. *Modern Trout Fly Dressing* (Fishing Gazette, 1932).

On Italy and the Balkan Peninsular:

Aelianus, Claudius Praenestinus, *On the Characteristics of Animals*, trans. A.F. Scholfield, 3 vols (London 1958–60).

Balzat H. and E. Van Hecke *Guide de la Pêche en Ardenne* (Nederlandsche Boekhandel, Kapellen, 1978).

Buxton, A. *Fisherman Naturalist* (Collins, 1946).

Caligiani, A. *Il temolo con la mosca artificiale* (Olimpia, Firenze, 1984).

Cios, S. 'Note sur l'alimentation des truites de l'Aoos (Grèce)', *Truites, Ombres et Saumons*, 178, Jan–Feb 1997, 19–20.

Clegg, J. *Freshwater Life* (Warne, 1974).

Claypoole, H.C.G. *Grayling: How to Catch Them* (Herbert Jenkins, 1957).

Colero, M.J. *Oeconomia, ruralis et domestica* (Maynss, 1645).

Collins, H.B. *Archeology of St Lawrence Island, Alaska*, Smithsonian Miscellaneous Collections 96(1) (Smithsonian Institution, 1937), p. 431.

De Boisset, L. *Écrit le soir* (Librairie des Champs Élysées, Paris, 1953).

— *L'ombre, poisson de sport* (Librairie des Champs Élysées, Paris, 1958).

Di Biase, N. *Temolo e mosche artificiali* (Olimpia, Firenze, 1991).

— 'Ambienti fluviali e temoli a mosca artificiale' (AmicoLibro-Quintano (CR) 1996).

Dziêdzielewicz, J. 'Wycieczki po wschodnich Karpatach. I. Rhys ogólny, podgórska dolina Prutu, Slobódka lésna, Kolomyja, Kniazdwór i Peczynizyn. Pamiêtnik Towarzystwa Tatrzanskiego, 2: 40-67. 1877.

Fabricius, E. and Gustafson, J. *Observations on the spawning behaviour of the Grayling, Thymallus thymallus* (Institute of Freshwater Research Report No. 36 (Drottingholm 1955, 75–103).

Frost, W.E. and M.E. Brown *The Trout* (Collins, 1967).

Gesner, C. 'De Piscium et Aquatilium Animantium Natura' in *Historiae Animalium*, vol.4 1558.

Grasse, P.P. (ed.) *Traite de Zoologie* tome IV, fasc.III, 1201-1222 (Masson, Paris, 1965).

Hills, J.W. *A History of fly fishing for trout* (1921; Barry Shurlock, 1973).

Huet, M. 'Biologie, profils en long et en travers des eaux courantes' *Bull. Fr.Pisc.* 175, 1954 41-53.

Jankovic, D. *Sistematika i Ekologija Lipljena Jugoslavije* (Belgrade, 1960). *Synopsis of Biological Data on European Grayling, Thymallus thymallus* L.1758 (FAO Fish Synop. (Rev.1), 1964).

Legrand, P.A. (ed.) *Guide du Pêcheur Belge* (c.1949).

Lusk, S. and L. Skácel, 'Lipen' (Vydala Príroda v Bratislav pre Slovensk˝ rybársky zväz v Ziline, 1978).

Magee, L. 'Yorkshire mayflies' *The Naturalist* 120(1012), 1995, 3-13.

Menzebach, F. *So fängt man Äschen* (Paul Parey, Hamburg and Berlin).

Nikolsky, G.V. *The Ecology of Fishes* (Academic Press, 1963).

Oppian of Cilicia *Cynegetica and Halieutica*, trans. by A.W. Mair (London 1958).

Pequegnot, J.-P. *Répertoire des mouches artificielles françaises* (Besançon, 1975); English ed. *French Fishing Flies* trans. Robert A. Ghino (Nick Lyons Books, 1987).

Persat, H. 'Photographic identification of individual grayling, *Thymallus thymallus*, based on the disposition of black dots and scales', *Freshw. Biol.*, 12 (1982), 97–101.

Pietruski, K.S. 'Odpowiedzi na pytania Zawierajace w sobie plan krótki do jednostajnego opisu ... Rozprawy c.k. galicyjskiego towarzystwa gospodarskiego, 2: 128-162 (fishing on pp. 145-7).

Radcliffe, W. *Fishing from the Earliest Times* (1921; 2nd ed. Murray, 1926).

Rozwadowski, J. (1st edn 1900, 2nd edn 1908) 'Poradnik dla milósnikow sportu wedkowego. Wroclaw, 1992.

Rzączyński, *Auctuarium historiae naturalis curiosae Regni Poloniae, Magni Ducatus Lithuaniae annexarumquae provinciarum* (1742).

Svetina, M. and F. Verce, 'Ribe in Ribolov v Slovenskih Vodah' (Zalozila Ribiska Zveza Slovenije, Ljubljana, 1969).

Thymallus (Society) 'Situazione del temolo nelle acque del nord italia' (Relazione annuale 1996. Pogliano Milanese.

— 'Situazione del temolo nelle acque del nord italia' (Relazione annuale 1997. Pogliano Milanese.

Tortonese, E. 'Osteichthyes-Pesci Ossei' 1p., vol.X (Calderini, Bologna, 1970).

Waldstein, C. and L. Shoobridge, *Herculaneum, Past, Present and Future* (Macmillan, 1908).

Witowski, A., M. Kowalewski, and B. Kokurewicz, *Lipien* (Panstwowe Wydawnictwo Rolnicze i Lesne, Warsaw, 1984).

On Outer Mongolia:

Bawden, C.R. *The Modern History of Mongolia* (Weidenfeld & Nicholson, 1968).

Bisch, Jorgen, *Mongolia, Unknown Land* (Allen & Unwin, 1963).

Jagchid, S. and P. Hyer, *Mongolia's Culture and Society* (Westview Press, 1979).

Murphy, George G.S. *Soviet Mongolia* (University of California Press, 1966).

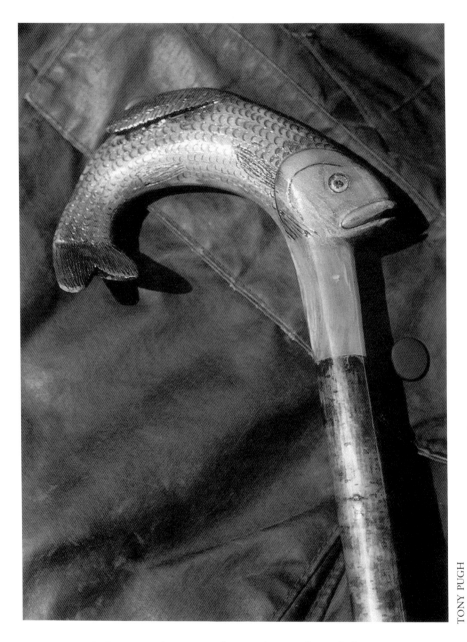

Ron Broughton's grayling wading-stick, made by
G.C.A. Sticks of Clay Cross

Index